TEACH
YOUR OWN

Books by John Holt

How Children Fail

How Children Learn

The Underachieving School

What Do I Do Monday?

Freedom and Beyond

Escape from Childhood

Instead of Education

Never Too Late

Teach Your Own

Learning All the Time

A Life Worth Living: Selected Letters

TEACH YOUR OWN

The John Holt
Book of Homeschooling

JOHN HOLT
PATRICK FARENGA

A Merloyd Lawrence Book
PERSEUS PUBLISHING
A Member of the Perseus Books Group

Copyright © 2003 by Holt Associates

Portions of this book appeared earlier in *Teach Your Own: A Hopeful Path for
Education*, copyright © 1981 by John Holt, and *The Beginner's Guide to
Homeschooling*, copyright © 2000 by Pat Farenga.

Library of Congress Control Number: 2003101364
ISBN 0–7382–0694–6

Perseus Publishing is a member of the Perseus Books Group.
Find us on the World Wide Web at http://www.perseuspublishing.com.
Perseus Publishing books are available at special discounts for bulk purchases
in the U.S. by corporations, institutions, and other organizations. For more
information, please contact the Special Markets Department at the Perseus
Books Group, 11 Cambridge Center, Cambridge, MA 02142, or call (800)
255–1514 or (617) 252–5298, or e-mail j.mccrary@perseusbooks.com.

Text design by Lisa Kreinbrink
Set in 11-point New Caledonia by the Perseus Books Group

First printing, March 2003

1 2 3 4 5 6 7 8 9 10—06 05 04 03

This book is dedicated to all those who have supported *Growing Without Schooling* and John Holt's work and ideas. This book could not have been written without your courage and determination in teaching your own children and then sharing your stories.

Contents

Acknowledgments

THOUGH THEY INITIALLY thought homeschooling was a crazy idea, my parents and in-laws have all come to appreciate and support home-schooling. They've watched their grandchildren grow and thrive, and have supported my family in ways that have allowed this book to be created. I'm very grateful to them.

I want to thank Phoebe Wells and Dick Westheimer for their encouragement to write my first book, *The Beginner's Guide to Home-schooling*, which is incorporated into parts of this book.

I could not have written *Teach Your Own* at all without the friendship and stimulating conversation of the following people: Larry and Susan Kaseman, Gene Burkart, and Aaron Falbel, who continue to challenge my ideas about education and its role in modern society; and Donna Richoux, Susannah Sheffer, and Meredith Collins, whose sharp editing and thinking made *GWS* such a great publication. I am particularly indebted to Susannah Sheffer for her spirit and intellect that helps me focus my thinking and writing.

A special thanks to all of my colleagues who worked at Holt Associates/ *Growing Without Schooling* and their families who helped it to continue after John Holt died in 1985. There are too many colleagues to mention here, but there are a few who always were there when I needed them most: Peggy Durkee, Mary and Mark Van Doren, Ginger Fitzsimmons, Mary and Tom Maher, Randi Kelly, Dawn Lease, Maureen Carey, Sophia Sayigh, Marion Webster, and Ron Rubbico.

I also owe many debts to the writers and thinkers who have encouraged me in my work, either in person or in their books, in particular: George Dennison, John Taylor Gatto, and Ivan Illich. I also want to thank Suzanne MacDonald, who cheered me on through all sorts of peaks and valleys over the last few years, and who helped me update the resource section of this book. I especially want to acknowledge Merloyd Lawrence, who for many years has helped me preserve and expand John Holt's literary legacy with supreme insight and grace.

Most of all, I want to thank my wife, Day, and my children, Lauren, Alison, and Audrey, for their love, work, and support both at home and in the Holt office over the years, but, most important, for turning unschooling theories into practice every day of the year for me.

—Pat Farenga

NOTE

Growing Without Schooling (GWS) magazine is mentioned frequently throughout this book. GWS was the first magazine about homeschooling, and was founded by John Holt in 1977. When John died in 1985, I became the magazine's publisher; my colleagues Donna Richoux, Susannah Sheffer, and Meredith Collins were subsequent editors of GWS after John's death, until GWS ceased publication in December 2001. Some original GWS back issues are still available (see FUN Books in Appendix E to order them).   —P. F.

Preface

Education Is What Goes
on in Schools—Or So I Thought!

PATRICK FARENGA

LIKE SO MANY ENGLISH MAJORS, I decided I would parlay my bachelor's degree toward becoming an English professor. Because so much of my youth had been spent in school sitting before teachers while I listened, I felt very comfortable with the idea of getting paid to stand in front of students while I talked. The social routines, schedules, and expectations of the workplace were all quite familiar to me; I like reading and writing, so I figured becoming an English professor would be my adult work. However, after receiving a master's degree in English, I decided I wasn't cut out for a doctorate. During this period I still wanted to be a teacher, but teachers weren't being hired in 1980—in fact, the glut of teachers was so bad that they were being laid off in Massachusetts, where I decided to settle to be near my future wife. To sustain myself financially I worked at various jobs and continued to seek out ways to stay in touch with teaching, and to develop contacts and skills. While working as assistant manager in a bookstore in downtown Boston, I volunteered at Holt Associates, an education consulting and publishing firm founded by John Holt; I did so primarily to learn how to use a word processor, and to do something to tide me over while waiting for a teaching position to open up. Yet the more I learned about the organization, the more I also learned about education, homeschooling, and, eventually, myself.

John had been publishing *Growing Without Schooling* magazine since 1977, as well as selling books and materials to people interested in homeschooling. And there were several opportunities for me to advance in this small, growing company. I went from being a volunteer to a paid employee, and have been with the company ever since.

I usually volunteered in the evening, a time when John Holt happened to be in his office—writing, reading, or waiting to go to a concert. Music was John's mistress and, in his spare time, if he wasn't listening to concert tapes, he was at a concert or playing his cello somewhere. One night John stepped out of his office to engage me in conversation. A bachelor then in his late fifties, he wore his glasses loosely on his nose. His white hair formed a wispy border around the bald spot on the center of his head; his pens and a little notepad were bulging out of his shirt's breast pocket. In a soft, deliberate voice, he asked, "So, where are you from, Pat?"

"New York. I moved up here to be with my girlfriend."

"I'm from New York too . . . " and before I knew it we were chatting away. He eventually asked me about work.

"I work in a bookstore. But I want to get out of there and do other things, which is why I'm learning word processing here."

"What do you really want to do?"

"I want to be a teacher."

"Really? Why?" John asked.

"Because I enjoy working with kids."

John swiftly pulled off his glasses and looked me squarely in the eyes. "Pat, you have it all wrong. If you become a teacher you won't be working *with* children, you'll be working *on* children."

I was dumbfounded. Who was he to say such a thing about this important profession?

"What do you mean?" I asked.

"Have you ever read any of my books?"

"No."

"Well, no problem if you haven't. But if you do, you'll see that this is a theme of mine. I've developed my ideas over many years, and don't want to go over old ground with you. After you've read one of my books, I'll be happy to discuss it with you if you like."

Thankfully for me, the conversation veered elsewhere. That night, as I walked out of the office and onto Boylston Street, I resolved to read one of John's books.

It was 1981, and the first printing of John's newest book, *Teach Your Own*, had recently arrived in our office; I thought that would be a good place to start. He promptly lost me. His points about how ordinary parents can help their children at home learn as well as, if not better than, in school struck me as an impractical option for most families. I couldn't step outside my core assumptions about the place of school in my life: School is how we all learn; an education is an expensive investment to make, which pays us big dividends like any good investment; you won't get a good job unless you go to college and get good grades. I couldn't finish reading *Teach Your Own* the first time I tried. When I presented my dilemma to Holt's office manager, Peg Durkee, she had the correct answer—as usual. Peg said, "My favorite is his first book, *How Children Fail*. Try that."

I immediately identified with John's descriptions in that book of what school is like, not only from a teacher's perspective, but most important, from a child's perspective. *How Children Fail* spoke to my own experiences and feelings as a student, and to my current situation as a would-be teacher. Without a pile of research citations and academic credentials, John clearly explains what he observed and how he worked with this information to help children learn; his experiences made deep sense to me. John almost always theorized from the specific to the general, whereas in my school experiences, particularly in higher education, I was taught to apply general theories to specific work. The details and processes of working with children became vivid and important to me through John's writing. Grand theories and institutional concerns are considered yet they don't cloud his sharp and original observations of the ways children learn. His writing about children and school surprised me in many ways, and he quickly disabused me of the notion, long fixed in my mind, that "schooling" is the same as "education."

Soon, I was engaged in conversation with John, often on a daily basis. In retrospect I realize how patient he truly was with many of my ill-formed objections and comments about his work. Although I didn't understand or agree with everything he wrote or said then, I nonetheless kept coming away from these conversations with a very unsettling feeling: that my years of schooling may not have been the best way to spend my youth. The more I learned what school teaching was really like from John and the various teachers and authors to whom he introduced me, the more naïve my goal of becoming a teacher who would help children learn in interesting ways began to seem. John's conviction—that most adults don't want school to be less coercive of children, but actually more so—at first struck me as being a bit cranky. But over time, I felt this feeling no longer applied, especially now in this new millennium of rigid standards, and high-stakes schooling and testing.

I especially looked forward to coming to the office when John was in, but because he was an active writer and lecturer, he would often be away for a week or more every month. Fortunately, I was able to enjoy conversations with my colleagues at the office who shared ideas about education similar to John's, as well as with homeschoolers and others who would visit Holt Associates. Eventually, I came to appreciate homeschooling as a sound educational choice. However, even after two years of working at Holt Associates, my wife, Day, and I were still uncertain if we were going to homeschool our future children.

It wasn't a single homeschooling encounter, book, or research paper that convinced my wife and I to try homeschooling—it was the increasing exposure to homeschoolers whose children were obviously thriving physically, mentally, and spiritually. Some parents' ideas about education—such as strict school schedules—were radically different from ours. Other families jettisoned school altogether. Yet there was a commonality that my wife and I noticed among all these families: The children were, on the whole, very comfortable in public with their parents and other adults. Indeed, many of the home-schooled children we knew were also fun to be with, good at conversation, and displayed wide-ranging interests and abilities. The education establishment's stereotype of homeschooled children as social misfits simply didn't ring true with our experience. Furthermore, as students of homeschooling, we reflected on our personal experiences, realizing that John's ideas held true: Much of what has stayed with us for use in our lives as adults has very little to do with our actual school work. Friends, including teachers, and extracurricular activities are far more lasting and important to us than long nights writing papers or cramming for math. Working at Holt Associates made me question education, and the value of my own schooling, in ways I never thought of before.

For instance, why do parents and educators insist that our children labor joylessly to learn things most adults never even use? The same pedagogical justifications that now I hear as answers are the same ones I heard when I posed the question as a smart-aleck prep school student: "To make you a well-rounded individual;" "learning calculus (algebra, trigonometry, Latin, chemistry, take your pick) will help you learn to think." Why is learning piano, football, painting, horseback riding, poetry, electronic instruments, dancing, drama, or reading less an activity that instills discipline and thinking than forcing children to attend classes and do homework for which they have little aptitude, purpose, or liking? I'm all for helping children, indeed, all people, learn to think; but why must learning be so joyless and so often useless in our daily lives? Don't useful and joyful things teach us to think?

In workshops I give about abandoning our notions of traditional curricula, I am usually challenged by someone who pronounces, "But you need to know trigonometry! You need to know this in order to be a literate person in today's complicated, technological society." Society is complicated and increasingly technological, but many of us will have to admit that learning trigonometry or calculus in school was not a prerequisite for learning how to use computers as adults. The vast majority of adults who learned to use computers in the eighties did so without attending classes of any sort. There are multiple ways to learn skills when we need to, and using courses with well-designed lessons is but one. Now, I run spreadsheets, word process, do page layout, re-touch photos, e-mail, use the Internet, and so on. And I learned to do all these tasks by directly using these applications, not through high school and college classes in algebra, graphics, and other disciplines.

Day and I took John's challenges to education seriously, raising questions to each other and to our friends, such as:

"Why force students to study things they're unlikely to use?"

"Are homeschoolers risking their children's futures—their ability to find good jobs, meet decent people, catch literary references at cock-tail parties—by not educating them as we were educated in private and public schools?"

"Must we act like schools and make our children learn as we did in school in order to find success as adults?"

Day and I discussed these sorts of questions intensely when we were in our twenties, sometimes causing family uproar over education topics raised during holiday meals (a mistake we try not to duplicate). No matter what concerns or objections we raised about compulsory education, including ones we all agreed upon, it often seemed that the final consensus was that forcing kids to learn is a necessary evil. "We must control a child's attention and action," goes this argument, "or else they will spend all their time playing games, watching TV, or get-ting into trouble. Furthermore, they won't be able to do what they want as adults, so the sooner they learn to buckle under authority and get with the program, the better for us all."

Certainly we might need to do things we don't like doing in order to achieve our goals. Before we were married, Day worked for an auto-cratic theatrical producer for a year in order to gain her ultimate goal of work experience in the theater. But in school one is often forced to do undesirable things just for their own sake: Is that really a good use of anybody's time? Though we both enjoyed good public- and private-school experiences throughout our youth, Day and I still remember the periods of waiting to be allowed to move on when we were done with our work, the periods that ended before we completed work, the frustration of being moved along according to a schedule we only vaguely, at best, understood. Perhaps, as Day and I began to think, these homeschoolers who let their kids study astronomy or play with dolls for hours on end do have a better way, or at least a more interesting way, of doing things than school. As we continued meeting home-schoolers, as well as thinking of how we'd prefer to raise our not-yet-born children, Day and I realized that there are many different ways to raise a family, and many different ways of teaching and learning besides the traditional "sit down, shut up, and do as I say" model.

Patient, observant people can help the young learn well, without resorting to the all-too-common instruction techniques of fear, humiliation, and force. John often shared books with his friends and sold them through his mail order catalog, *John Holt's Book and Music Store*, about schools and teachers and parents and children who learn in unconventional ways. These books serve not only as evidence that alternatives to conventional school do exist for our young, but also demonstrate that the values John treasured and found flourishing in homeschooling can also be found in, or transferred to, other people and places.

Our innate ability to learn by experience and example is so powerful that we are practically programmed to teach the way we were taught in school. We've all spent so much time in school that it's difficult for us to imagine that there actually are other ways to live and learn in our current society. Therefore, it's very easy to duplicate conventional schooling at home. After all, we know what school is like from our own experiences as students, perhaps even as teachers, and when we homeschool our own kids, that word "school" connects it all for us. In response to the prevailing definition of the word "school," John created the word "unschooling" to describe how we help children learn without duplicating ideas and practices that we learned in school.

For instance, you can unschool lessons in organized football, which I always thought had to be learned by emphasizing painful, fiercely competitive, win-at-all-costs sportsmanship. Then I read the following article about Minnesota's St. John's University head football coach John Gagliardi:

> [His] record, if accomplished using conventional football wisdom, would be one thing, but Gagliardi practically throws away the book. In

fact, he says St. John's doesn't have a playbook, only a single page listing assignments.

"The guys learn everything on the field," he says . . . . "To me, a lot of this [printed] stuff is like giving a kid a description of how to ride a bike. You can write it up, but the kid doesn't understand it. He's just got to get on the bike and try it a lot of times."

Gagliardi doesn't say "no" just to playbooks, but to a whole host of other standard procedures in football . . .

Some quotes from Gagliardi's "Winning with No's Philosophy:"

- No player cut.
- No one considered too small.
- No grading of game films.
- No signs in dressing rooms.
- No laps.
- No use of the words "hit, kill," etc.
- No practice on Sundays or Mondays.
- No statistics posted.
- No cheap shots tolerated.
- No practice in rain, mud, or excessive wind.
- No timing anyone in forty yards, mile, etc.[1]

That's one example of challenging assumptions and achieving great results by not following conventional practice. It also shows how counter to popular wisdom the elements of success can be. As of 2002, Gagliardi is the winningest active coach in collegiate football and the second all-time winningest in collegiate football history. He has achieved these by doing the opposite of what all other coaches in football do. By not following the standard procedures, best practices, and the typical motivation of players to "kill or be killed," Coach Gagliardi has provided us with new ways to work with young athletes that are far more interesting than the increasingly common "Little Napoleon" coaches that dominate sports for young people.

Monty Roberts, partly in reaction to violence done to animals, people, and himself as a young man, sought out new ways of training horses, working with the disabled, and raising children. He would base his practices on observation, patience, and communication rather than procedures, results, and coercion. His record of success, particularly with difficult horses, is impressive, and his technique—horse whispering—is safer, more humane, and quicker than conventional horse-breaking. Roberts has little to say about his formal school experiences ("my attendance record was slim"), but a nun, he claims, was his most influential teacher.

> What I will always remember about her is her statement that there is no such thing as teaching—only learning. She believed that no teacher could ever teach anyone anything. Her task as a teacher was to create an environment in which the student can learn. Knowledge . . . is not to be forced on anyone. The brain has to be receptive, malleable, and most important, hungry for that knowledge.
>
> That same philosophy I apply when training horses. To use the word "teach" implies an injection of knowledge. Like Sister Agnes Patricia, I came to agree that there is no such thing as teaching, only learning.[2]

What Roberts did with horses, Holt was doing in his fifth-grade classroom: facilitating learning rather than imposing instruction. Like Roberts, Holt's work was not greeted with enthusiasm by the authorities, but individual teachers and parents greeted his work with interest. Holt emphasized, time and again, that he never studied education in school, which he considered a benefit. He wasn't full of the assumptions and dictates of education theory, just full of hard thought about what was working and not working when he tried to teach children. Monty Roberts spent weeks in the desert following herds of wild horses and learning their physical language by closely observing their interactions and how they reacted to his presence when he made it known; likewise, John paid attention to children. This is not a matter of free and easy observation; as John wrote to the *Harvard Education Review* in 1969:

> I learned whatever I have learned about children by prolonged and careful observation, and even more importantly, as a result of continued failures to teach them, in more or less orthodox school fashions, the things people said they should learn. There seems to me a sugges-

tion—forgive me if I'm wrong about this—that in learning about the world, other people's books are more important than observation. With this view I most emphatically and strongly disagree. This is indeed part of what I am trying to tell teachers—that the things they learn or feel they are learning from their direct contact with and observation of children are more important and what is even more important more to be trusted than what the theoreticians may tell them. This is a heretical view, I know, but it is my own.[3]

John came to feel that parents can do as well as he did in the classroom, if not better, because, if they are careful in nurturing their relationships, children will show parents (or other patient, concerned adults) how they learn best. His support for people to try homeschooling, regardless of their social class or education background, is rooted in his own experience of trial and error, of seeing what worked and didn't work in his classrooms.

However, John Holt and other educators have received criticism, even by homeschoolers, that they don't know what it is like to be with children twenty-four hours a day as they may not have children of their own. "If he only spent a day with my kids he'd change his tune!" is how many parents react to John's admonitions to be gentle, patient, and understanding in the face of children's strong emotions and actions.

But John never wavered in his empathy for children and in his wish that parents give second, third, fourth, and more chances for children to learn, academically and emotionally. Nor did John feel that children should be allowed to treat parents as doormats! John didn't arrive at his advice about living and learning with children solely from his classroom experiences; he deliberately, indeed, eagerly, placed himself in situations where he could spend time being with, and observing, children of all ages. When I booked his speaking engagements, he had me seek out families he could stay with rather than stay in hotels. In his books he often mentions his sisters' children, the children of his friends, as well as the children in his and others' classrooms. He would discuss all sorts of issues about raising children with homeschoolers, both in the pages of GWS (and quoted in this book), and with parents directly. John became a wise old uncle to many people in the early years of homeschooling.

It's ironic that one of the common criticisms of homeschooling, that children won't be properly socialized, was actually, in John's mind, a major reason homeschooling makes sense. His observations led him to believe that children are, above all else, social creatures, and that socialization into one's family, one's extended family, one's community, and so on, helps children to learn and grow. A child's interest in learning to speak, for example, wouldn't be nurtured without a community of talkers, without people to listen, and to respond and talk with him. The fact that school too often denies children social opportunities—indeed creates negative social experiences in many cases—was never lost on John.

Educators seeking to dismiss Holt's ideas as impractical often dub him a "romantic child-worshipper" and put him in the same category as the famous liberal French philosopher Jean-Jacques Rousseau. John is most definitely *not* influenced by Rousseau, who felt that children learn best when they are kept away from the corrupting influences of adult society and, in particular, from their parents. Nor was John an advocate of tough love with children. In the chapter "Living with Children," John views adult relationships with children most clearly. He writes:

> Children do often seem to me like talented barbarians, who would really like to become civilized. Many free schools, and some kindly and well-meaning parents, have suffered from the notion that there was something wild and precious in children that had to be preserved against the attacks of the world for as long as possible. Once we get free of this idea we will find our lives with children much easier and the children themselves much happier. As I write this, I have spent much time recently with young babies, and my overwhelming impression is that basically they want to fit in, take part, and do right—that is, do as we do. If they can't always do it, it is because they lack experience, and because their emotions sweep them away.
>
> Oddly enough, the reactionary view and the romantic liberal view of children are like opposite sides of the same coin. The hard-nosed types

say that to fit children for the world we have to beat the badness out of them. The romantic child-worshippers say that in fitting children for the world we destroy most of the goodness in them. One group claims that children are undersized and defective adults; the other, that adults are oversized and defective children. Neither is true. There really are ways to help children, as they grow, to keep and build on all their best qualities.

John's calm reasoning helped many parents continue to home-school when their children were a strain on them. He helped parents understand the different learning schedules and styles that children exhibit once they start learning outside of school, and he urged parents to relax and enjoy their time with their children rather than encouraged parents to be academic task-masters. But when *Teach Your Own* was first published in 1981, he was also an important figure who dispensed political and legal advice. He knew that public and private schools had power and money on their side, but he also knew that families and children had more rights and options for schooling than they were aware of. John advised parents, whenever possible, to avoid trouble with school officials, even to the point of moving to a friendlier school district. When families worried about the authorities, John provided court cases, stories, and analyses for support and advice, much of it quoted in the original edition of *Teach Your Own*. Fortunately the political climate has changed considerably in the past twenty years in favor of homeschooling, and homeschooling is now legal in all of the fifty states, as well as in Canada, England, Ireland, Australia, France, Spain, Japan, Scandinavia, and many other regions and countries. Many of John's references in the book's original edition concerning school officials, legal decisions, and school politics are now dated, and most of these have been edited from this edition. However I've kept some of his commentary for the historic record as well as for his astute advice.

Homeschooling isn't just another instruction-delivery system; it shows us alternative ways to teach and learn, and to participate in family and community life; ways to find work or get into higher education without jumping through the standardized hoops of mass-market schooling; ways to use school rather than have school use you. Home-schooling also offers ways to think about "democracy" and "individu-ality," while, at the same time, avoiding the polarization that places people into lone-survivalists or drone-collectivists camps; and ways for children and adults to reunite living and learning that go far be-yond doing homework together. Read this book to find out how.

It is, in fact, nothing short of a miracle that the modern methods of instruction have not yet entirely strangled the holy curiosity of inquiry; for this delicate little plant, aside from stimulation, stands mainly in need of freedom; without this it goes to wrack and ruin without fail. It is a very grave mistake to think that the enjoyment of seeing and searching can be promoted by means of coercion and a sense of duty. To the contrary, I believe that it would be possible to rob even a healthy beast of prey of its voraciousness, if it were possible, with the aid of a whip, to force the beast to devour continuously, even when not hungry, especially if the food, handed out under such coercion, were to be selected accordingly.

⟨@ ALBERT EINSTEIN

Introduction

JOHN HOLT

THIS BOOK IS ABOUT WAYS WE CAN teach children, or rather, allow them to learn, outside of schools—at home, or in whatever other places and situations (and the more the better) we can make available to them. It is in part an argument in favor of doing it, in part a report of the people who are doing it, and in part a manual of action for people who want to do it.

Many events, some public, some personal, some in my own mind, led me to write this book. It began in the late 1950s. I was then teaching ten-year-olds in a prestige school. I was also spending a lot of time with the babies and very young children of my sisters, and of other friends. I was struck by the difference between the 10s (whom I liked very much) and the 1s and 2s. The children in the classroom, despite their rich backgrounds and high I.Q.'s, were with few exceptions frightened, timid, evasive, and self-protecting. The infants at home were bold adventurers.

It soon became clear to me that children are by nature and from birth very curious about the world around them, and very energetic, resourceful, and competent in exploring it, finding out about it, and mastering it. In short, much more eager to learn, and much better at learning, than most of us adults. Babies are not blobs, but true scientists. Why not then make schools into places in which children would be allowed, encouraged, and (if and when they asked) helped to explore and make sense of the world around them (in time and space) in the ways that most interested them?

I said this in my first two books, *How Children Fail* (1964) and *How Children Learn* (1966). They were soon widely read, and translated in many other countries. Along with others saying much the same thing, I found myself busy as a lecturer, TV talk show guest, etc. Many people, among educators, parents, and the general public, seemed to be very interested in and even enthusiastic about the idea of making schools into places in which children would be independent and self-directing learners. I was even asked to give a course on Student-Directed Learning at the Harvard Graduate School of Education. For a while it seemed to me and my allies that within a few years such changes might take place in many schools, and in time, even a majority.

When parents told me, as many did, that they were dissatisfied with their children's schools, I urged them to form committees, hold meetings, and organize public support for school reform, pressuring school boards and if need be electing new ones. In a few places, parents actually did this.

At first I did not question the compulsory nature of schooling. But by 1968 or so I had come to feel strongly that the kinds of changes I wanted to see in schools, above all in the ways teachers related to students, could not happen as long as schools were compulsory. I wrote about this in an article, "Not So Golden Rule Days," which appeared first in the *Center Magazine* of the Center for the Study of Democratic Institutions, and later in my third book, *The Underachieving School*. Since compulsory school attendance laws force teachers to do police work and so prevent them from doing real teaching, it would be in *their* best interests, as well as those of parents and children, to have those laws repealed, or at least greatly modified. In the article, I suggested some political steps or stages in which this might be done.

In such ways many of us worked, with great energy, enthusiasm, and confidence, for this kind of school reform. As people do who are working for change, we saw every sign of change, however small, as further proof that the change was coming. We had not yet learned that in today's world of mass media ideas go in and out of fashion as quickly as clothes. For a while, school reform was in fashion. There is no way we could have known that it was only fashion. One only finds out later what is fashion and what has lasting effect.

There were signs, even then. I had been one of a number of speakers invited to Minneapolis, a liberal city in a liberal state, to talk to a large conference of Minnesota teachers. At my meeting there were perhaps seven hundred. After my talk, during the questions, which had seemed friendly, a stout woman, thin pressed-together lips turned way down at the corners, said in a harsh angry voice, "What do you do with the children who are just plain lazy?" The entire audience burst into loud applause. I was startled and shocked. When the applause died down, I replied as best I could, and the meeting resumed its normal polite course. Later, I pushed aside the awkward memory of that little incident. I did not want to hear what it was plainly saying, that for a second the silent majority had spoken, and said, "Children are no damned good."

In my travels I was often invited to visit schools and classes by people who said, "We've read your books, we think they're wonderful, and we're doing all the things you talked about." Well, they usually were, but not in the way they meant—they were doing all the mistaken and harmful things that I described in the books and had once done myself. People also talked to me with great enthusiasm about innovative programs. But these were always paid for with federal money, and as time went on, it always turned out that when the federal money stopped, so did the program. People might feel badly about losing these wonderful programs. But pay for them with local money, their own money? It was never considered.

When I went to places to talk I was always met at the airport by two or three people. Usually, we were friends from the start. They had read my books, saw things much as I did. We always had a good time together, talking about the things we agreed on, sharing success stories, horror stories, hard luck stories. They always made me feel so at home that by lecture time, I assumed that with a few exceptions the people there must all be like my friends. Only slowly did I realize that the people who brought me in to speak were almost always a tiny minority in their own school or community, and that my task was to say out loud in public what people were sick of hearing *them* say, or even what they had been afraid to say at all. They hoped that if people heard me—famous author, guest on the *Today* show, etc.—they might pay attention.

From many such experiences I began to see, in the early '70s, slowly and reluctantly, but ever more surely, that the movement for school reform was mostly a fad and an illusion. Very few people, inside the schools or out, were willing to support or even tolerate giving more freedom, choice, and self-direction to children. Of the very few who were, most were doing so not because they believed that children really wanted and could be trusted to find out about the world, but because they thought that giving children some of the appearances of freedom (allowing them to wear old clothes, run around, shout, write on the wall, etc.) was a clever way of getting them to do what the school had wanted all along—to learn those school subjects, get into a good college, etc. Freedom was not a serious way of living and working, but only a trick, a "motivational device." When it did not quickly bring the wanted results, the educators gave it up without a thought and without regret.

At the same time I was seeing more and more evidence that most adults actively distrust and dislike most children, even their own, and quite often especially their own. Why this should be so, I talked about in my books, *Escape From Childhood* and *Instead of Education*. In a nutshell, people whose lives are hard, boring, painful, meaningless—people who suffer—tend to resent those who seem to suffer less than they do, and will make them suffer if they can. People who feel themselves in chains, with no hope of ever getting them off, want to put chains on everyone else.

In short, it was becoming clear to me that the great majority of boring, regimented schools were doing exactly what they had always done and what most people wanted them to do. Teach children about Reality. Teach them that Life Is No Picnic. Teach them to Shut Up And Do What You're Told. Please don't misunderstand me on this. People don't think this way out of pure meanness. A man writing, sympathetically, to a radical paper, about life in small towns in Iowa, where in order to pay their debts many full-time farmers have to do extra work in meat-packing plants—as he says, "shoveling lungs"—says, "The work ethic has been ground into these folks so thoroughly that they think anyone who doesn't hold down, continually, a full-time *painful* job is a bum." They don't want their kids to be bums. Back To The Basics, for most of them, is code for No More Fun and Games In School. Most of them don't care particularly about reading, as such. They read little themselves—like most Americans, they watch TV. What they want their child to learn is how to *work*. By that they don't mean to do good and skillful work they can be proud of. They don't have that kind of work themselves, and never expect to. They don't even *call* that "work." They want their children, when their time comes, to be able, and *willing*, to hold down full-time painful jobs of their own. The best way to get them ready to do this is to make school as much like a full-time painful job as possible.

Of course, they would be glad to see their children go to a "good" college, become lawyers, doctors, corporation executives, part of that world of wealth and power they see every day on TV. But this is like winning the lottery. You may hope for it—about the only hope you've got—but you don't plan on it. Anyway, most people know by the time their children finish second or third grade that they are not going to win the big prize. What's left is that full-time painful job. To get them ready for that is what most schools are for, always were for.

Just the other day, this truth was once again thrust in my face. Taking a cab to the airport, I fell into conversation with the driver, a cheerful, friendly man. He asked me where I was going and what I did. I said I wrote books about children, schools, and education, and also published a little magazine about people teaching their children at home. He said he didn't think that was a very good idea, and went on to talk about schools and what was wrong with them. As soon as I reached the airport, I wrote down all I could remember of his words. The fragments I quote here give a fair picture of the whole.

Early in our talk he said,

> Seems to me the students are directing the teachers these days, instead of the other way round. . . . When I was a kid, if I'd ever talked back to a teacher, I would have got a face full of knuckles. (Laughed.) Then I would have had to hope to God he didn't tell my father about it.

Print can't convey the approval, even the *pleasure*, with which he said this. I rarely meet people who have this faith in violence to solve problems. When I do, they scare me. I thought in the cab, "What have I got myself into now?" During the ride, I said little, tried once or twice without success to change the subject, and at the end said nothing at all. He did all the talking, getting angrier and angrier. Yet when we reached the airport he said good-bye and wished me a good trip, in the most friendly way. I looked at him as we parted. In the city I see many faces that look angry, brutal, and cruel. He did not look that way at all.

After saying the words quoted above, he said, "God help any of my children if they had ever talked back to a teacher," with such ferocity that it froze the tongue in my mouth. Yet I wonder now what he would have done if they had, and whether in fact he had actually ever done it. Suppose one of his children had claimed to be the victim of a teacher's injustice. My guess is that he would have told them to forget about justice, that the teacher was the boss, and that their job was to do whatever he said.

This thought recalled a scene in Frederick Wiseman's film *High School*, in which a student and a disciplinary vice-principal were arguing. The student, wearing glasses, good at using words, obviously not a poor kid, was stubbornly insisting that he hadn't done something he was accused of doing, and therefore, that he shouldn't be punished for it. The vice-principal, a big man, a former athlete and probably once a poor kid, was just as stubbornly trying to explain to the student that it didn't make any difference whether he had done what he was accused of or not; the people in charge had *decided* that he did do it, and there was nothing for him to do but take his punishment—"like a man," he said, implying that only crybabies and troublemakers whine about justice. Theories about what was true, or fair, were beside the point. In the real world, Authority had declared him guilty and he was going to be punished, and he might as well accept it.

Later in our conversation the driver spoke admiringly of Catholic schools, saying,

I know a guy who had a couple of high school kids who were kind of wild. He sent them to Saint—School. There, if a kid talked back to one of the priests, he'd deck him, right then and there, no questions asked. (He laughed approvingly.)

I know well and on the whole believe all the conventional arguments about the futility and destructiveness of violence. None of them would have made the slightest dent on this driver. For in our conversation he told me that all six of his children had gone to college, earned the money for it themselves, and made it through. One had finished at the top of her class of 170 at a school for dental technicians. Another was trying to get into medical school, but (so the driver said) had not yet been able to, because he was not black or Puerto Rican or Mexican. (He talked a long time, and very bitterly, about this.) But in any case, here he was, driving a cab, and here were his six children, all college graduates, on their way to higher levels of society. Here was all the proof he needed that his threats and toughness worked. Not for a moment would he ever have considered the possibility that his children might have done what he wanted not so much because they feared his fist as because they valued his good opinion.

We must be clear about this. It is not because he is cruel himself that this father, like many others, insists that the schools be harsh and cruel to his children. It is because he believes that this is how the world really works, that only by being tough on kids can we help them to live better than we do, working at good jobs instead of waiting on tables and driving crummy cabs. Nor is it only working-class people who take this harsh view of life. Let me tell again a story I told in an earlier book. A boy in one of my fifth-grade classes was the son of a middle executive in a large corporation, perhaps not extremely wealthy but certainly in the top 5 percent in income. In the two or three years before the boy came to my class he had done poorly in his studies and had been a behavior problem both at school and at home. Expert "help" had been called on, and had not helped. In my less rigid class the boy found many things to do that interested him, became the class chess champion, did much better in his studies, particularly math, which he had always hated, and became much better behaved, both at school and at home. His mother, a gentle and soft-spoken woman, came to see me one day after school. She said how pleased she and her husband were that their son was doing so much better in his school work, and was so much more pleasant and easy to live with. She told me how much he enjoyed my class, and how much he talked about all the interesting things that went on in it. Then she paused a while, frowning a little, and finally said, "But you know, his father and I worry a little about how much fun he is having in school. After all, he is going to have to spend the rest of his life doing things he doesn't like, and he may as well get used to it now."

As long as such parents are in the majority, *and in every social class they are*, the schools, even if they wanted to, and however much they might want to, will not be able to move very far in the directions I and many others have for years been urging them to go. These parents do not want their children in or anywhere near classes in which children learn what interests them most, for the satisfaction and joy of doing it. They want their children to believe what countless teachers and parents have told me: "If I wasn't *made* to do things, I wouldn't do anything." They don't want them to think that the best reason for working might be that the work itself was interesting, demanding, and worth doing. For the real world, as they see it, doesn't run that way and can't be made to run that way.

While the question "Can the schools be reformed?" kept turning up "No" for an answer, I found myself asking a much deeper question. Were schools, however organized, however run, necessary at all? Were they the best place for learning? Were they even a good place? Except for people learning a few specialized skills, I began to doubt that they were. Most of what I knew, I had not learned in school, or in any other such school-like "learning environments" or "learning experiences" as meetings, workshops, and seminars. I suspected this was true of most people.

As time went on I began to have more and more doubts even about the word "learning" itself. One morning in Boston, as I walked to work across the Public Garden, I found myself imagining a huge conference, in a hotel full of signs and posters and people wearing badges. But at this conference everyone seemed to be talking about *breathing.* "How are you breathing these days?" "Much better than I used to, but I still need to improve." "Have you seen Joe Smith yet—

he certainly breathes beautifully." And so on. All the meetings, books, discussions were about Better Breathing. And I thought, if we found ourselves at such a conference, would we not assume that everyone there was sick, or had just been sick? Why so much talk and worry about something that healthy people do naturally?

The same might be said of our endless concern with "learning." Was there ever a society so obsessed with it, so full of talk about how to learn more, or better, or sooner, or longer, or easier? Was not all this talk and worry one more sign that there was something seriously the matter with us? Do vigorous, healthy, active, creative, inventive societies—Periclean Greece, Elizabethan England, the United States after the Revolution—spend so much time *talking* about learning? No; people are too busy *doing* things, and learning from what they do.

These ideas led into my book *Instead of Education* where I tried to make clear the distinction between *doing*, "self-directed, purposeful, meaningful life and work" and *education*, "learning cut off from life and done under pressure of bribe or threat, greed and fear." Even as I wrote it I planned a sequel, to be called *Growing Up Smart—Without School*, about competent and useful adults who during their own childhood spent many years out of school, or about families who right now were keeping their children out.

During the late '60s and early '70s I knew a number of groups of people who were starting their own small, private, alternative schools. Most of them did not try to start their own school until after years of trying to get their local public schools to give them some kind of alternative. When they finally decided to make a school of their own, they had to persuade other parents to join them, reach some agreement on what the school would be like, find a place for it that the law would accept and that they could afford, get the okays of local fire, health, safety, etc., officials, get enough state approval so that their students would not be called truants, and find a teacher or teachers. Above all, they had to raise money.

One day I was talking to a young mother who was just starting down this long road. She and a friend had decided that they couldn't stand what the local schools were doing to children, and that the only thing to do was start their own. For many months they had been looking for parents, for space, for money, and had made almost no progress at all. Perhaps if I came up there and talked to a public meeting. . . .

As we talked about this, I suddenly thought, is all this really necessary? I said to her, "Look, do you really want to run a school? Or do you just want a decent situation for your own kids?" She answered without hesitation, "I want a decent situation for my own kids." "In that case," I said, "Why go through all this work and trouble—meetings, buildings, inspectors, money? Why not just take your kids out of school and teach them at home? It can't be any *harder* than what you are doing, and it might turn out to be a lot easier." And so it soon proved to be—a lot easier, a lot more fun.

In talking with young families like these, I found that what they most needed was support and ideas from other families who felt the same way. For this reason, I began publishing a small, bimonthly magazine called *Growing Without Schooling*, in which parents could write about their experiences teaching their children at home. Some of the material in this book first appeared in that magazine. Of this material, some is quoted from books, magazines, news stories, court decisions, etc. Some was written by me. Much of it comes from letters from parents. The letters quoted here are only a small part of the letters we have printed in the magazine, which in turn are only a very small part of those that people have sent us.

The ones quoted here are of course some of the best, but many others that we might have printed are just as good. I have had to break up many of these letters so as to fit the parts under different chapter headings. This may have caused a loss of some of the impact and flavor of the originals, which were often very long and covered many topics. Still, what we have quoted will give some idea how affectionate, perceptive, and eloquent most of these letters are. Reading the mail sent to *Growing Without Schooling* has been one of the great rewards of doing this work. I hope readers of this book will enjoy these letters as much as I have.

1

Why Take Them Out?

WHY DO PEOPLE TAKE or keep their children out of school? Mostly for three reasons: they think that raising their children is their business not the government's; they enjoy being with their children and watching and helping them learn, and don't want to give that up to others; they want to keep them from being hurt, mentally, physically, and spiritually.

First, before some unschoolers tell you in their own words why they took their children out of school, two questions: (1) How many such people are there? (2) What kind of people are they?

Good short answers to these questions would be (1) nobody knows and (2) all kinds.

The reason no one knows or can find out how many families are teaching their own children is that many of these people, fearing with good reason that if the local schools knew they were teaching their own children they would make trouble for them, are doing this in secret. Sometimes they simply hide their children from the local schools, don't even let them know they exist. Sometimes they tell the local schools, perhaps truthfully, perhaps not, that they have registered their children in some private school. Sometimes they have registered their own home as a school, which in many states is easy to do.

Sometimes they and a few other families register as a church-related school. There is simply no way to tell how many such people there are. Thus, there is no way to tell how many of the registered private schools in any state are schools as most people understand that word, i.e., special buildings with specialized hired teachers, and how many are disguised homes with the parents doing the teaching.

Who are these homeschooling families? Again, it is hard to tell. Only a minority of them read *Growing Without Schooling*, not all of those who read it write to us, and those who write talk mostly about their children, not about their background or work or income. Most of our subscriptions and letters come from rural or star routes, small towns, or low- to middle-income suburbs. I have traveled enough so that I know the names of the wealthy suburbs of many large American cities, and I know that we get almost no mail or subscriptions from these. We also get very little mail from the cities themselves.

What about income, education, race? The little evidence we have suggests that the average income of homeschooling families is close to the national average. We have had almost no correspondence with people who, judging by their addresses, writing paper, businesses, etc., were obviously rich. Many families who write us have incomes well below the national average; they have chosen to live in the country or in small towns on very modest incomes, supporting themselves by small-scale farming, crafts, small businesses, etc. Some home-schooling mothers are on welfare. As to educational background, my guess is that most of the families who read *GWS* have been to college. Some of our most successful homeschooling families, however, have not been beyond high school. I suspect that a somewhat higher percentage of the people now using church-based correspondence schools have not been to college. As to race, I have no way even of guessing. A few of our readers and subscribers have Hispanic surnames. Other than that I know nothing, except, as I say, that so far we have had little contact with people in cities.

In sum, we are so far talking about a group of Americans, probably mostly white, more rural than urban, otherwise quite average in everything except stubbornness, courage, independence, and trust in themselves and their children.

◄€ Twenty years after Holt wrote the preceding material, the U.S. Department of Education, National Center for Education Statistics released a study "to attempt to estimate the number of homeschoolers in the United States using a rigorous sample survey of households."[1] The Department of Education researchers reached almost exactly the same conclusions Holt did: Homeschoolers in the 1999 survey are quite average in terms of income, largely white (though the researchers note "growth in homeschooling may be reaching a broader range of American families and values"), more rural than urban, and homeschoolers tend to have more children in their families than nonhomeschoolers. Holt estimated that less than 30,000 children were being homeschooled in 1981 but that the numbers would grow rapidly. By 1999 there were 850,000 children, according to the statistics from the Department of Education. As I write this in 2002, probably more than 1 million children are being taught at home, about 2 percent of the total school-age population.

To Holt's three major reasons for taking children out of school, I now add two more: (1) the desire of some families to spend more time together, not just "quality time," and (2) the growing acceptance of Internet correspondence schools and other forms of distance learning in lieu of attending conventional school.

Families having more time together won't automatically solve any problems between parents and children, but if both parties are willing to work on their relationships and use their time together to develop better communication, then it will be time well spent. By having more time together the chances increase that not only relationships, but also academics, can flourish. A well-publicized study by Harvard University found that both children's literacy and school success could be linked to pleasant dinner table conversation about current events.[2] In addition, Blake Bowden, a researcher at Children's Hospital Medical Center of Cincinnati, "conducted a study to see what protects teenagers against maladjustive behaviors. The answer: sitting down to a meal with a parent at least five times a week."[3] It isn't necessary to take children out of school to eat meals together, but doing so can make it easier to achieve, since long breakfasts, picnic lunches, breaks for a snack together, and in-depth nonmealtime conversations can become options for homeschoolers who are too busy during dinnertime.

There is, of course, too much of a good thing, and homeschoolers need to pay special attention to the dynamics of togetherness as their children get older. My colleague, Susannah Sheffer, studied adolescent homeschooled girls, and the increased togetherness they have with their mothers. Sheffer writes:

> Several of the girls acknowledged their unusually good relationships with their mothers and said they hoped that the openness would continue. Others wished for the chance to talk and to be heard, which they didn't feel they currently had. But no one said, "I'd rather *not* be close to my mother." These girls remind me of what researcher Teri Apter has said about the traditional view of adolescence as a time of separation from one's parents. After interviewing pairs of mothers and daughters, Apter concluded that adolescent girls do indeed want to be recognized as separate individuals and want to be truly seen and understood by their mothers, but they want to maintain connections to their mothers at the same time. They use conflict with their mothers to grow, to understand themselves, and to demand understanding *of* themselves.[4]

Conflicts and resolutions with one's mother may not seem as important as school, but they are. All too often we are led to believe that success in school translates into success in life, and therefore time spent on school preparation and school subjects is time better spent than time eating, walking, or playing together with children. Yet, by viewing education as more than just the accumulation of credits and degrees, you are not only helping your child grow emotionally, but intellectually as well.

The growing acceptance of distance learning has been surprising due to the fact that distance-learning programs—primarily correspondence-study programs—have been part of homeschooling for as long as I can remember. Often viewed as the poor cousins of conventional schooling, correspondence-study programs were advertised on matchbook covers, not in the *Atlantic Monthly*, as they are now. Throughout the past twenty years, videotapes, computers, and the Internet have all made distance learning far more acceptable, even desirable, to the public. Furthermore, with major universities and big businesses promoting on-line learning, a new era of distance learning is beginning.

And it is a humble beginning. Most of the on-line course offerings are no better, and often far worse, than courses conducted by mail, contained in a book, or supervised by a teacher. If you like using your computer a lot, you may enjoy on-line learning (for suggestions see the Bibliography, subsection Homeschooling, listing for *Homeschool Your Child for Free: More Than 1,200 Smart, Effective, and Practical Resources for Home Education on the Internet and Beyond*), but I'm not a big fan of the computer as instructor. I appreciate and use a computer for its research, entertainment, and communication features. As technology changes, particularly with real-time, two-way video, and audio transmissions, distance-learning programs will most likely become better. But at this time, it's too early to say that homeschooling will explode in popularity, even though homeschooling has gained some legitimacy or cachet, due to the Internet, that it didn't have in the eighties. Homeschooling has grown for twenty years because of the efforts of real people in the real world, not chatroom personas operating in virtual reality. I hasten to add that among the earliest adapters of computers and the Internet that I know of are homeschoolers, who often used the first consumer-level computers to surf the electronic bulletin boards and chatrooms to seek support and advice, as well as for all sorts of political action. This legacy has expanded so much that any Internet search engine will give you thousands of references to your queries about "homeschooling" and "distance learning." But the promise of distance learning is still unrealized, and I urge you to consider the computer as you do a textbook, a pencil and paper, or a calculator; something that supports learning at home, not something *you need* in order to homeschool.

The federal education researchers, mentioned earlier, also studied the reasons parents homeschool—quality of education, religion, and poor learning environments in their respective schools are the top-three reasons cited. One interesting statistic in the 1999 Federal Department of Education study showed that 22 percent of homeschooled parents have graduate/professional-school degrees compared to 16 percent of non-homeschooled parents. Why are increasing numbers of people who have spent most of their youth in school and gone on to higher education, keeping their children out of school?

Perhaps it is for the same reason my wife and I decided to homeschool: We didn't want our children to waste their time in the same empty rituals of education that we did: passing tests only to forget the subject matter when the grades were given; spending years with passing grades in foreign-language instruction yet being unable to have even a rudimentary conversation in the language outside of the classroom; struggling to learn advanced math skills that were seldom used outside of class; doing lab experiments that were more rote exercises than scientific inquiries. Time and youth cannot be regained, so perhaps, ultimately, the real crisis in education may be one of disillusionment among graduates rather than poor performance among current students. ☙

THE INCOMPETENCE OF SCHOOLS

When I began work at the Colorado Rocky Mountain School, my first teaching task was to tutor an otherwise bright and capable seventeen-year-old whose school skills were at about second-grade level. High-priced specialists in his hometown had pronounced him "brain damaged." In spite of the label, he wanted to read, write, and figure like everyone else, wanted me to help him, and thought I could help him.

Not having studied "education," I had never heard of "brain damage." But it was clear to me that whatever those words might mean, it was my responsibility and duty to find out what was keeping this boy from learning and to figure out something to do about it. I soon learned that he had a very precise and logical mind, and had to understand one thing thoroughly before he could move on to the next. What had stopped his learning almost at the start of his schooling was that he had not been able to understand fully many of the things that teachers were telling him about reading, arithmetic, spelling, etc., and either could not ask the right questions to find out what he needed, or else could not get answers to the questions he asked. Some of his questions I could answer right away; others kept me thinking and wondering for many years. But even though I did not solve all his problems, my conviction that they *could* be solved may have been help enough. A few years later he wrote me from an army post, telling me what books he was reading—serious, adult books. He had clearly solved his problem himself.

What I had tried to be is what I would call now a *serious* teacher. I was not willing to accept fancy excuses as a substitute for doing what I had undertaken to do—help children learn things. When, as often happened, they did not learn what I was teaching, I could not and did not blame it on them, but had to keep trying new ways of teaching it until I found something that worked. As *How Children Fail* makes clear, this often took a long time, and I failed more than I succeeded. Another book about serious teaching is James Herndon's first book, *The Way It Spozed to Be*, a very funny, truthful, and in the end sad story about his first year's painful but successful struggles—for which he was then fired—to help students that the rest of his inner-city school had long since given up on.

One reason that so few schools are any good at their work is that they are not serious. "Good" schools and "bad," private and public, with only a few exceptions have always run under the rule that when learning happens, the school takes the credit, and when it doesn't, the students get the blame. Where in earlier times the schools might have said that some kids were bad, stupid, lazy, or crazy, now they say they have mysterious diseases like "minimal brain dysfunction" or "learning disabilities." Under whatever name, these remain what they always were—excuses for the schools and teachers not doing their job.

For further evidence of the incompetence of schools, we have this quote from the Chicago *Tribune* (1977):

> It has been ten years in the making, but Chicago school officials now believe they have in place a complete sweeping program to teach children to read—a program that may be the pacesetter for the nation. . . . For some years, a Board of Education reading expert, Bernard Gallegos, has been putting together a package of the reading skills children need to learn in elementary school. At one point, Gallegos' list topped 500 elements. It has since been reduced to 273 over grades 1 through 8.

This might be rather comic if it were not so horrifying. Five hundred skills! What in the world could they be? When I taught myself to read, I didn't learn 500 skills, or even 273; I looked at printed words, on signs, in books, wherever I might see them, and puzzled them out, because I wanted to know what they said. Each one I learned made it easier for me to figure out the next. I could read before I went to school, but insofar as that school taught reading, they did it by what we might call the Spell-and-Say method— "c, a, t, cat." Most people who read, above all those who read well, were never taught 273 separate skills. And by what process was that list of 500 cut down to 273?

It's worth noting that the first of these skills is to repeat two-and three-syllable words. In practice, this is probably going to mean that all children, including black, Hispanic, Asian, or from other non-WASP groups, are going to have to pronounce these words "correctly," i.e., the way the teacher pronounces them. Children who can't, don't, or won't talk like middle–class North American white people will almost certainly be branded as not being "ready" to move to the next of the 273 steps. We can expect the schools to spend years trying to teach many of these children to talk "right," so that they can then begin teaching them to read. This, in spite of the fact that the world is full of people who read English fluently, though they speak it in a dialect or with an accent that few Chicago teachers (or few Americans) could understand.

As I write, it is about three years since that story was printed. I don't know whether the Chicago schools ever put that scheme into practice, or if they did, whether they are still using it. One thing is sure—if Chicago children are learning to read better than children anywhere else, it has been a well-kept secret.

Some years ago I heard from a teacher in another large city who, being serious, had over the years *found* a way to help children who had never read before become good readers. She had just been fired, because when the school board adopted some new reading program and ordered all teachers in the city to use it, she sensibly and responsibly refused to scrap her reading program that worked. This no doubt happened in Chicago; the best reading teachers were probably asked to change their methods or be fired. The children must be so busy trying to learn how to pass 273 reading tests that they have no time to read, and what's worse will soon not even want to. Indeed, as in many other schools, quite a few children who *can* read are probably held back because they can't pass some of the 273 tests. Then, ten years or so from now, we will read in the papers about some great *new* plan.

A teacher who had been doing some substitute teaching in a private elementary school, wrote to *GWS*:

> I found myself . . . in third grade for four days. The two teachers team teach and so I had to team teach. Both are old-fashioned types who push math and reading workbooks. I almost went wild. I couldn't figure out the questions and answers (I refuse to use the teacher's answer book) and the kids were frustrated and in pain sitting still. By the second day I could see these kids never had time to think, let alone read as a pleasure—just word-grabbing, mind-reading workbooks. In their room were paperbacks, *Charlotte's Web* and many more goodies not yet touched, because apparently the kids "can't read well enough yet." I went to the . . . principal and said I couldn't continue unless the reading time while I was there became silent reading. She agreed to it but was not very happy about me, I could easily sense. I told the kids new rules, "If you don't know a word and are really bothered by it, signal and I'll come whisper in your ear. No sounding it out, no vowels, no syllables, no questions, just the word." Very few asked after the first few minutes. But they asked for silent reading twice a day.

James Herndon makes much the same kind of report in his book *How to Survive in Your Native Land*. When he and one or two other teachers stopped asking the children questions about their reading, stopped grading them, stopped tracking them, and *just let them read*, they very soon read much better, even those who had been very poor readers. But his school and fellow-teachers refused to learn anything from this experience.

Another familiar complaint is that students can't write. An article entitled "Pumping Polysyllabism" from the August 1977 issue of *Mother Jones*, suggests that the students may not always be the ones to blame:

> Two Chicago English professors have found that a good way to improve your grade on a term paper is to use what they call "verbose, bombastic" language.

Professors Joseph Williams and Rosemary Hake say they took a well-written paper and changed the language a bit. They kept the ideas and concepts the same, but wrote two different versions—one in simplified, straightforward language and another in verbose language, loaded with pedantic terms.

They then submitted the two papers to nine high school teachers; they were surprised to find that all nine gave the verbose papers nearly perfect scores but downgraded the straightforward essays as too simple and shallow.

The professors then submitted the same two papers to ninety more teachers and came up with similar results. Three out of four high school teachers and two out of three college professors gave higher marks to pompous writing.

THE CIVIL LIBERTIES OF CHILDREN

I don't want to and am not going to make this just a collection of bad stories about schools. The arguments against compulsory schools go much deeper. Some of them I expressed in a letter to the American Civil Liberties Union:

Though the courts have not yet agreed, compulsory school attendance laws, in and of themselves, seem to me a very serious infringement of the civil liberties of children and their parents, and would be so no matter what schools were like, how they were organized, or how they treated children, in other words, even if they were far more humane and effective than in fact they are.

Beyond that, there are a number of practices, by now very common in schools all over the country, which in and of themselves seriously violate the civil liberties of children, including:

1. Keeping permanent records of children's school performance. This would be inexcusable even if there were nothing in the records but academic grades. It is nobody's proper business that a certain child got a certain mark in a certain course when she or he was eight years old.

2. Keeping school records secret from children and/or their parents, a practice that continues in many places even where the law expressly forbids it.

3. Making these records available, without the permission of the children or their parents, to whoever may ask for them—employers, the police, the military, or other branches of government.

4. Filling these records, as experience has shown they are filled, with many kinds of malicious and derogatory information and misinformation. These may include not just unconfirmed teachers' reports of children's misbehavior, but also all kinds of pseudopsychological opinions, judgments, and diagnoses about the children and even their families. For examples, see *The Myth of the Hyperactive Child*, by Peter Schrag and Diane Divoky. (More recent books are in the Bibliography.)

5. Compulsory psychological testing of children, and including the results of these tests in children's records.

6. Labeling children as having such imaginary and supposedly incurable diseases as "minimal brain dysfunction," "hyperactivity," "specific learning disabilities," etc.

7. Compulsory dosing of children with very powerful and dangerous psychoactive drugs, such as Ritalin.

8. Using corporal punishment in school, which in practice often means the brutal beating of young children for very minor or imagined offenses.

9. Lowering students' academic grades, or even giving failing grades, solely for disciplinary and/or attendance reasons. Not only is this practice widespread, but school administrators openly boast of it, though what it amounts to in fact is the deliberate falsification of an official record, a kind of printed perjury.

10. In all of these matters, and indeed in almost any conflict between the child and the school, denying anything that could fairly be called "due process."

To return once more to compulsory school attendance in its barest form, you will surely agree that if the government told you that on one hundred and eighty days of the year, for six or more hours a day, you had to be at a particular place, and there do whatever people told you to do, you would feel that this was a gross violation of your civil liberties. The State, of course, justifies doing this to children as a matter of public policy, saying that only thus can it keep them from being ignorant and a burden on the State. But even if it were true that children were learning important things in schools and that they could not learn them anywhere else, neither of which I admit, I would still remind the ACLU that since in other and often more difficult cases, i.e., the Nazi rally in Skokie, Ill., it does not allow the needs of public policy to become an excuse for violating the basic liberties of citizens, it ought not to in this case.

Over the years the ACLU has tended to see as a civil liberties matter the right of children to go to school, but not their right not to go. I have been told that a committee of the ACLU is now discussing when and in what circumstances compulsory schooling may be an infringement of civil liberties. In some cases local branches of the ACLU, or ACLU attorneys, have given support to unschooling families. But it would surely be helpful if someday the national organization took a strong position on some of the issues I have mentioned.

◄◖ To date, the ACLU, as a national organization, has not taken a strong position on the issues Holt mentions. Indeed, many court decisions since Holt wrote this book have eroded the civil liberties of children both in and out of school, but the ACLU, and most other progressive institutions, continue to see the right of children to go to school as paramount over their right not to go.

The situation regarding corporal punishment in school is slowly changing; in 1998 the United Kingdom banned caning and other forms of corporal punishment in all schools, but it isn't clear that change will be as encompassing for the United States. In 2000 the American Academy of Pediatrics recommended "that corporal punishment in schools be abolished in all states by law and that alternative forms of student behavior management be used."[5] But America is slow to heed this recommendation. For instance, as of February 2002 the two school districts of Moorhead, Minnesota, and Nashville, Tennessee, passed policies that forbid teachers from hitting, spanking, or using physical force, that can cause emotional and physical harm to their students; although, also in February 2002, Wyoming's state legislature voted to continue to permit paddling children in school.[6] Hitting or shutting students in closets as punishment in school is not as common as it was in the fifties and sixties, but corporal punishment is still openly supported by some states and school districts in the United States. ৯

A NEW SENSE OF RESPONSIBILITY

Even though many and perhaps most adults today dislike and distrust children, there is at the same time a growing minority of people who like, understand, trust, respect, and value children in a way rarely known until now. Many of these people are *choosing* to have children as few people before ever did. They don't have children just because that is what married people are supposed to do, or because they don't know how not to have them. On the contrary, knowing well what it may mean in time, energy, money, thought, and worry, they undertake the heavy responsibility of having and bringing up children because they deeply want to spend a part of their life living with them. Having chosen to have children, they feel very strongly that it is *their* responsibility to help these children grow into good, smart, capable, loving, trustworthy, and responsible human beings. They do not think it right to turn that responsibility over to institutions, state or private, schools or otherwise, and would not do so even if they liked and trusted these institutions, which on the whole they do not.

We may think of these views as very old-fashioned or very modern. They are probably some of both.

৫ More and more people are homeschooling today than when Holt wrote this book and school officials are far more used to dealing with homeschooling requests than they were in the seventies and eighties. Few who wish to homeschool today find that in order to do so they must engage in pitched battles with their schools, hire lawyers, or move to a friendlier school district. Indeed, today, under the rubric "Independent Study Program" many schools are actually seeking out homeschooling families to join their programs, and some charter and for-profit schools are actively wooing homeschoolers with promises of free computers for home learning, ongoing professional support, and so on. More important, many more homeschoolers are benefiting from the growth of local, state, and national homeschooling support groups and businesses. Services and materials can be found through these homeschooling sources rather than conventional school institutions. Options abound for homeschooling in the twenty-first century.

Attitudes have also changed considerably in the past twenty years regarding homeschooling. All three of my homeschooled daughters have gone in and out of public and private schools, at their request and at different times of their lives, without any difficulties coming from the schools. For instance our youngest, Audrey, insisted on going to first grade because she didn't think we were "teaching her enough." Within a couple of days Audrey was in love with her first-grade teacher, a talented veteran teacher, but in despair over school.

"What's the matter?" I asked.

"I've been in school a week and they are still learning the alphabet! I know the alphabet already!" (Audrey often speaks with exclamation marks in her voice.)

"But there must be other things you are learning there. Can't you wait until the class finishes the alphabet and catches up with you?"

"Dad! It's so boring! And in math they are just learning to count up to twenty by twos now! I can count all the way up to one hundred by ones, twos, and fives!"

Day, my wife, went to the school a few days later to speak with Miss Reppucci, Audrey's first-grade teacher. Miss Reppucci understood exactly what Audrey was talking about and she complimented Day on the fine job of homeschooling she had done with Audrey. (We never thought of what we were doing with Audrey as some type of preschool "homeschooling" when she was so young—it was just what we did with all our girls: talk, listen, and explore the world together.) Then Miss Reppucci told Day, "I have so many children in my first-grade class that aren't anywhere near where Audrey is right now, though they should be. I need to spend extra time with each of them, and that's time I can't spend with Audrey. Why don't you consider homeschooling Audrey again?"

When Audrey heard that her beloved first-grade teacher thought homeschooling was going to be just fine for Audrey, she seemed relieved and, after eleven days of public school, Audrey willingly came home to learn—with the blessings of her schoolteacher.

Not all teachers are so sympathetic, of course, and not all homeschoolers want help from public school. Homeschoolers are an independent lot, and some of them feel that *any* connection to local, state, or federal government that doesn't mesh with their personal beliefs is an illegal burden to be fought. These people define their sense of personal responsibility in such a way that they are almost in conflict with nearly every conventional practice in school and law, as is their right to do, of course; most homeschoolers take a more flexible stand, trying to work with, around, and without schools while not getting needlessly entangled with the law. ☙

Judy McCahill, wife of a career officer in the U.S. Navy, explains her sense of personal responsibility:

Always, always must we parents and any others who undertake a revolutionary change which seriously affects the lives of others remind ourselves that we do so for selfish reasons. My husband and I began to get cold feet ("sounds like an epidemic," our daughter said) two or three days before school started this year; what urged me to continue with our plans was the thought that I would be very unhappy if I didn't give it a try. It was certainly not that we didn't consider what was best for the children; we believe (and still believe) they would be better off growing up at home than in a classroom. But keeping them home was mostly *my* decision, *my* experiment, *my* act of faith. What I hope is that the children not only will flower more truly in their home environment, but also will be enriched by growing up with parents who are attempting to live their beliefs. I hope that they will learn the true meaning of action, that a wrong seen is a wrong to be righted; a better way seen, one to be taken.

The mother of a Muslim family living in this country expresses similar reasons for keeping her youngest children at home:

. . . Like many other families who are schooling their children at home, our main reason for wanting to make this move was a religious one. In our case, however, the religion is Islam, not Christianity. We are a very committed Muslim family, and it is of the greatest importance to us that our children grow up in an atmosphere which is not destructive to their religious orientation and values. For this reason, we are obviously in total disagreement with many social and moral values (or "unvalues") which are being propagated in schools, as well as with the limited educational approaches. Moreover, in our faith religious and other learning is not to be approached as two separate matters since Islam does not acknowledge any schism between "sacred" and "secular" aspects of life.

Our three older children had grown up in public schools, with very serious consequences to their sense of self-worth and the rightness of their values, and above all on the integratedness of their personalities. They passed through the hands of a series of junior high and high school teachers and situations in which religion, and anyone who upholds high moral and ethical values, was viewed with contempt or at least stigmatized as being very, very strange and abnormal. When my son was in the first year of junior high, we had just come back from a year overseas and the boy was feeling very much at odds with the school atmosphere. I went to the principal and expressed my concern about him, saying that he was a very religious youngster with high values. Would it not be possible to form a club or association for youngsters of similar inclinations? The response of the principal was astonishing. He told me he would look into my son's record and behavior and talk with his counselor to see if he was really normal and fit in. Of course, you can imagine how I felt after this encounter, and the club idea naturally died of its own accord although I tried without success to interest other people in the community in it. I felt and still do feel that such an organization would be very important and meaningful to young people who care about religion and values but have no support and are even afraid to voice their opinions under prevailing conditions.

When the fourth child, Y, was old enough for kindergarten, we enrolled him in a Catholic school, hoping it would be in some significant way an improvement over public school. But it was a total disappointment, in no real way different in atmosphere or approach. Thus, toward the end of Y's kindergarten year, seeing that there was no workable solution except to teach the children at home, I went to discuss the matter with the local superintendent of instruction.

Although he made it clear that he is not in favor of homeschooling, he was helpful and cooperative. We must, he said, submit a letter to him by early summer, which he would submit to the local school board, who would in turn submit it to the state board of education. My husband and I wrote a very brief statement that "because the religion of our family, Islam, is a complete way of life which requires that religious education go hand-in-hand with secular education, the educational needs of our children cannot be met in a normal school situation." We also mentioned that we might be spending time outside the country and hence needed to have a method of schooling which could be continued wherever we might be residing. Permission for homeschooling was given under the understanding that I would be using the Calvert materials, would teach 176 days a year, and would be under the general supervision of the local school principal (i.e., would submit the Calvert tests and confer with her once a quarter, and the child would have to take standard achievement tests and end-of-the-year tests, if any, annually).

The experience of teaching my children has given me endless new insights concerning the role of parents (especially mothers), both what it is for most of us and what it could and should be, and the nature and meaning of education. I cannot express what a satisfaction it is to see my children growing up with stable, integrated, happy personalities, especially after the struggle of watching the harmful effects of school on the three older children. . . .

PROTECTING CHILDREN FROM HARM

Most people, however, take their children out of schools not so much for philosophical or political reasons as for the more direct and personal reason expressed by the Muslim mother: to prevent the schools from hurting their children, or hurting them any more than they already have. Many parents write to tell a story like this: Their child has taught himself to read, or somehow learned, before he went to school. He finds himself, perhaps in the pre-school, perhaps in one of the early elementary grades; reading from one to three years ahead of his class. Naturally he does not want to do the reading readiness exercises or other workbook tasks that the other children are doing, to "teach" them to do what he already knows how to do. He wants to read the kind of books he is able to read. But when he tries to do this, he gets in trouble. The teacher orders him to do the work the other children are doing, and when he naturally and sensibly says he doesn't want to, or simply doesn't, the teacher punishes him. She may bawl him out in front of other children, take his books away from him, stand him in a corner, shut him in a closet, strike him, give him a failing grade, call him "hyperactive." Quite often such teachers tell the parents of such children that unless the child does the work the other children are doing, he will fail and will have to *repeat the grade*, in spite of reading a year or more ahead of the grade level.

Naturally the amazed parents point out that since the child is reading far ahead of the class, it makes no sense to have him do the work the other children are doing or to fail him for not doing it. This seldom does any good. The teacher says stubbornly that the child has to do what the others are doing. If the parents then go to the principal, the principal usually backs up the teacher. This experience makes unschoolers out of many people who might otherwise have been content to send their children to school.

Other parents tell an opposite story. In these cases the children are not ahead of the grade, but a little behind it. Like the boy I tutored in Colorado, they are having trouble in reading or arithmetic, don't understand something in the workbooks, and so on. They can't do the homework, and are often punished, even beaten, for that. They tell their parents that they don't understand, and that when they ask the teacher for help, the teacher won't help them. The parents—many of whom, to judge from what they say or from the look of their letters, are poor—go to the teacher and ask her please to give their child a little extra help. The teacher then usually says, "I can't be giving special help to your child, I have all the rest of the children to look after." So the child falls further and further behind.

Of course, the parents themselves are in most cases perfectly capable of giving their children the help they need. But they have been told so often by the school not to interfere in the child's learning, not to try to teach the children anything, that they have come to feel as helpless as if they were facing some rare disease. The teacher won't help; the parents don't think they can. The children, who along with their other problems are probably being teased and laughed at by the other children for being behind, get more and more discouraged. Many of them drop out of school. Many of the parents tell me that when they were children the same thing happened to them.

Another mother writes:

> J has been set free! He is enrolled at the Santa Fe Community School but is actually learning at home. As soon as the decision was made he seemed to be released from some terrible burden, he immediately began taking charge of his own life and learning, and began to approach everything with the zest and enthusiasm formerly reserved for his own nature study, sports and building projects. For example, he always hated math, and the necessity of doing math homework caused the most unhappy and miserable hours in our household. Now he has set himself the task of getting math and is proceeding to do so with none of the emotional overtones formerly present.
>
> It's not an easy task for a poor working-class family to attempt this kind of thing—in fact it's a bit terrifying. Yet I feel strongly that working-class kids are most hurt by public schools and most in need of being set free.

A report from the Fort Lauderdale *News and Sun-Sentinel*, July 1, 1979, speaks of similar changes in a child:

> . . . It was the disappearance of a smile, a simple thing, that led Ms. O'Shea, a certified elementary school teacher, to question the value of public education.
>
> "When Kim was little, she was such a happy, laughy little person. When she went to school, that completely changed. She stopped smiling. She went for six months, and she was very unhappy. It was weird.

When I went to the school, the teacher kept apologizing for the noise, and I thought, 'There's not any noise. These kids are like little robots.' It wasn't that healthy. So when that day was over, I said to Kim, 'What's the story?' and I looked at her, and I could feel what she felt. And I said, 'Let's give it a try.'

"A lot of people, when we tell them what we are doing," says Ms. O'Shea, "say, 'Well, you're a teacher, so that's OK.' But they don't understand. Anyone can teach. We sell ourselves short; we don't believe in ourselves enough. We think school can do something for us that we can't do ourselves."

She admits her own training in education has not helped that much, because the girls often want to learn things she doesn't know herself. "But I think whenever you want to learn something, you're going to find a way to learn it. If you have the need, the answer is always there, too."

The answers may be unorthodox, but they are available. The girls have gone to adult education classes to learn watercolor painting and nature studies; they recently learned typing and practiced making change while helping in a friend's key shop for a few days; they have taken lessons in diving, judo, and music; their mother teaches them arts and crafts at home, and they use workbooks, magazines, and library books for math, reading, and spelling.

In school, Ms. O'Shea contends, much of their time would be spent in quiet busywork. "Here, if Layne can do two or three division problems, she can do division. I don't sit there and make her do 70. If feel people should be free to explore life. And they can't do that with people telling them what to do all the time. And who decides what they are supposed to learn? That's what I want to know. Putting children into a fixed or six-hour program at school is just squashing them. All the spirit and spunk they have when they are little is just wiped out."

◖◗ The harm Holt wrote about was often intellectual and emotional in nature, but the harm children face today is even more virulent and physical than Holt could ever have imagined. Violence in schools is nothing new—think of the well-known movie of the fifties, *The Blackboard Jungle*, or the high school principal Joe Clark, who, during the eighties, often wielded a baseball bat in the school to keep discipline and who was praised by many, including President Ronald Reagan, for doing so. Clark's story also became a movie, *Lean On Me*. Think of Columbine and its tragic spawn today. Movies will, no doubt, be forthcoming about these horrors, too. But what is new is having parents remove their children from school because of the level of such violence. In the past parents would transfer their children to a private school if one was affordable, or they'd just tell the kid "Buck up. The world is cruel, and school is preparing you for the real world." Now that our children can lose far more than their self-esteem in a fight at school this attitude strikes me as even more mean-spirited than I thought previously. Simply telling our kids to "toughen up" and accept bullying, metal detectors, body and property searches, high degrees of surveillance, random drug tests, and other "facts" of school life today strikes me as a self-fulfilling prophecy about the sort of world we want our children to inherit. Homeschooling isn't the right answer for all children facing violence in school, but it is an option for everybody to explore.

The pressures our children face today are much worse than what we faced as children in school, because we've made schooling so much more a part of their lives, while at the same time school has become a more difficult environment for children in which to grow and learn. Some researchers have noted the loss of spontaneous neighborhood and family play among our young because, in addition to more homework than we had as kids, they are being taken to more enrichment classes, organized sports run by adult professionals, and extracurricular activities. Parents do this believing that children need to do these things in order to get good jobs as adults, or scholarships, or just entrance to colleges. Such pressures are not unique to American society, but they are unique to conventional schooling, which is the same around the world. The London *Times* published an article recently about research done by Dr. Jacqui Cousins, an adviser on early education to the United Nations, that shows four-year-olds in nursery school even feel upset and anxious about expectations for them to succeed at school.[7] Some four-year-olds spoke seriously about not getting a job if they didn't work hard enough. One girl said that she had to work hard and not play so she could "get ready to pass my Key Stage One tests" (the tests given to five- to seven-year-olds in Great Britain).

In Japan, the pressure to do well in school has resulted in some well-publicized suicides by children, to the point that some children are refusing to go to school. At present, there are more than 65,000 children in Japan who simply refuse to go to school, and their families are then stigmatized by such an attitude. Because homeschooling is still a rare act of independence for a Japanese family, and school choice is not wide in Japan, it is not uncommon for "school refusers," typically middle-school-age children, to be sent to a mental institution for their "illness." The *Kyodo News* on the Web reported that in 2001 there was a record number of prolonged absences from school in all grades:

> Eizaburo Yamashita, a social caseworker and organizer of free space for absentee students, said schools are not attractive to children.
>
> "By the middle of the 1990s there were excessive expectations in education from parents that studying hard in schools would guarantee a stable life later," Yamashita said.
>
> "That's why children felt pressure and stress, and it led to absenteeism," Yamashita explained.
>
> He said life goals became fuzzy when Japan's "bubble" economy collapsed. He said children still refused to attend school because it was not attractive to them.
>
> Yamashita said Japan should give students choices in education such as homeschooling, which has been adopted in the United States.[8]

Though America has more educational choices than Japan has, the pressure to do better than others in school is taking a toll on our youth as well. Doriane Lambelet Coleman, a professor at Duke Law School, notes

> The nation's child suicide rate increased 400 percent from 1950 to 1990. And even this extraordinary number was most recently reported to have doubled since 1990 . . .
>
> According to the World Bank, which has cataloged the total number of suicides committed by children in the 25 most industrialized nations, approximately 50 percent of the total is the result of suicides among U.S. children.[9]

The gross incivility schools can have toward their students has been remarked upon for years by liberal critics such as Theodore Sizer (*The Children Are Watching*), and by conservative critics such as Charles Silberman (*Crisis in the Classroom*), yet little has been done to make school society more civil. Pitting children against one another for the reward of grades and individual class standing, and showing how much we value these prizes by continually funding it over other less "educational" areas such as athletics, art, drama, extracurricular activities, volunteerism, community activism, or clubs, sends a clear message to our children about what is really important to adults and our conception of "the social good." The typical pressures reported by the media on high school students, for instance, are sex and drugs; however a poll conducted in 1999 by the Shell Oil Company of more than 1,000 high school students with questions formulated in collaboration with the U.S. Department of Education found the "top two [pressures] are the pressure to get good grades (44%) and the pressure to get into college (33%), followed by the pressure to fit in socially (29%) . . . the pressure to get good grades is felt similarly by students who receive high grades (48%) and those who receive lower grades (46%)."[10] Pressure to use drugs or alcohol came in at 19 percent and pressure to be sexually active was 13 percent. Schooling, in general, has become much more intense for our children than it was for us in school, and nearly all our current school reforms keep ratcheting up this pressure to get high grades and get into college as if there were nothing but good consequences for doing this to our children. The Shell poll did find those teens that they surveyed to be happy and resilient in the face of these pressures, but learning to cope with them is not negotiated well by all children, as the suicide rates noted above attest.

This problem is not just one of large urban school systems, like New York's, London's, or Tokyo's. A friend of mine, Tom Maher, has been a public school teacher in Massachusetts for over twenty years, and he sent me this report from his local newspaper about a high school survey conducted in his home town, Wakefield, Massachusetts, in 2000:

> The Wakefield Youth Risk Behavior survey . . . showed that one out of 10 Wakefield students from grades 9–12 have physically tried to commit suicide.[11]

The flip side to all this is that being a teacher to children under such conditions is equally stressful. The National Education Association, the nation's largest teachers' union, has decided to offer homicide insurance to teachers; the Associated Press reported that the union will "offer a $150,000 benefit for families of members slain on the job at school."[12]

There is so much talk and action in education today regarding test scores as a true measure of accountability for school funding that we've forgotten that we're still very much accountable for the physical and emotional welfare of our children. Trying to balance the academic and emotional lives of our children is not as easy as helping our children with their homework. This is where homeschoolers, in particular, have much to teach schools about, such as feeling good about ourselves and what we can do; respecting people who are different from us; working with people from different social classes and educational backgrounds; and becoming good citizens. How is school supposed to accomplish these things by pitting student against student, school against school, district against district, in a race for higher test scores? It's striking that in our day and age, where you went to school classifies you rather than equalizes you.

Integrating different people into a social whole is achieved best through group activities, teamwork, cooperative efforts and projects, games, conversation, and sharing common goals, not by separating out the economic winners and losers of society based on tests taken in their youth and where their parents can afford to live. Homeschooling shows that many parents support and create group activities, such as play groups, prayer and meditation groups, Ultimate Frisbee, film and drama clubs (to name just a few that occur in my neighborhood), as an integral part of their children's school day, not as extracurricular activities. Often, as many classroom teachers as well as homeschoolers have written, the needs of children have little to do with the needs of the school curriculum. ☙

2

Common Objections to Homeschooling

PEOPLE, ESPECIALLY EDUCATORS, who hear me talk about home-schooling, raise certain objections so often that it is worth answering them here.

Since our countries are so large and our people are from so many different kinds of backgrounds (this was said most recently to me by a Canadian), don't we need some kind of social glue to make us stick together, to give us a sense of unity in spite of all our differences, and aren't compulsory public schools the easiest and best places to make this glue?

About needing the glue, he's absolutely right. We do need such a glue, certainly in big diverse countries like the U.S. and Canada, but also in much smaller and more tightly-knit countries, many of whom are also breaking apart under the stresses of modern life. Right now, the main social glue we seem to have here in the U.S. is hatred of "enemy" countries. Except when briefly united in such hatred, far too many of us see our fellow-citizens, even those of our own color, religion, etc., only as our natural enemies and rightful prey, to do in if we can. Indeed, we insist that this way of looking at other people is actually a virtue, which we name "competition." This outlook may have worked fairly well when our country was young, nearly empty, and rich in natural resources but not anymore. For our very survival, let alone health and happiness, we need a much stronger and better social glue than this.

Some kinds of community gathering places and activities might help us form this social glue. But not schools—not as long as they also have the job of sorting out the young into winners and losers, and preparing the losers for a lifetime of losing. These two jobs can't be done in the same place at the same time.

People are best able, and perhaps only able, to cross the many barriers of race, class, custom, and belief that divide them when they are able to share experiences *that make them feel good.* Only from these do they get a stronger sense of their own, and therefore other people's, uniqueness, dignity, and worth. But as long as schools have their present social tasks, they will not be able to give such experiences to most children. In fact, most of what happens in school makes children feel the exact opposite— stupid, incompetent, ashamed. Distrusting and despising them- selves, they then try to make themselves feel a little better by finding others whom they can look down on *even more*—poorer children, children from other races, children who do less well in school.

Even if children do learn in school to despise, fear, and even hate children from other social groups, might they not hate them even more if they did not meet them in school? At least in school they see these other groups as real people. Without school, they would know them only as abstractions, bogeymen. This might sometimes be true, but only of those few children for whom the world outside of school was as dull, painful, humiliating, and threatening as school. Most children who learn without school, or who go only when they want to, grow up with a much stronger sense of their own dignity and worth, and therefore, with much less need to despise and hate others.

The important question, how can people learn to feel a stronger sense of kinship or common humanity with others who are different is for me best answered by a story about John L. Sullivan, once the heavyweight prizefighting champion of the world. Late one afternoon he and a friend were riding standing up in a crowded New York City streetcar. At one stop a burly young man got on who had had too much to drink. He swaggered down the center of the car, pushing people out of his way, and as he passed John L. gave him a heavy shove with his shoulder. John L. clutched a strap to keep from falling, but said nothing. As the young man went to the back of the car, John L.'s friend said to him, "Are you going to let him get away with that?" John L. shrugged and said, "Oh, I don't see why not." His friend became very indignant. "You're the heavyweight champion of the world," he said furiously. "You don't have to be so damned polite." To which John L. replied, "The heavyweight champion of the world can *afford* to be polite."

What we need to pull our countries more together are more people who can afford to be polite, and much more—kind, patient, generous, forgiving, and tolerant, able and willing, not just to stand people different from themselves, but to make an effort to understand them, to see the world through their eyes. These social virtues are not the kind that can be talked or preached or discussed or bribed or threatened into people. They are a kind of surplus, an overflowing, in people who have enough love and respect for themselves and therefore have some left over for others.

Children in public schools are able to meet, and get to know, many children very different from themselves. If they didn't go to public school, how would this happen?

The first part of the answer to this question has to be that it very rarely happens *in* public schools. Except in very small schools, of which there are few, and which tend to be one-class schools anyway, children in public schools, other than a few top athletes, have very little contact with others different from themselves, and less and less as they rise through the grades. In most large schools the children are tracked, i.e., the college track, the business track, the vocational track. Even within each major track there may be subgroupings. Large schools may often have a half-dozen or more tracks. Students in one track go to one group of classes, students in another track go to others. Very rarely will students from different tracks find themselves in the same class. But—and here is the main point—study after study has shown that these tracks correlate perfectly with family income and social status, the richest or most socially prominent kids in the top track, the next richest in the next, and so on down to the poorest kids in the bottom track.

In theory, children are assigned to these tracks according to their school abilities. In practice, children are put in tracks almost as soon as they enter school, long before they have had time to show what abilities they may have. Once put in a track, few children ever escape from it. A Chicago second-grade teacher once told me that in her bottom-track class of poor nonwhite children were two or three who were exceptionally good at schoolwork. Since they learned, quickly and well, everything she was supposed to be teaching them, she gave them A's. Soon after she had submitted her first grades the principal called her in, and asked why she had given A's to some of her students. She explained that these children were very bright and had done all the work. He ordered her to lower their grades, saying that if they had been capable of getting A's they wouldn't have been put in the lowest track. But, as she found upon checking, they had been put into this lowest track almost as soon as they had entered school.

Enough has been written about class and racial conflict in schools, above all in high schools, so that I don't want to add much to it here. Where different races are integrated in schools, even after many years, this usually begins to break down around third grade, if not even sooner. From fifth grade on, in their social lives, children are almost completely separated into racial groups, which become more and more hostile as the children grow older. Even in one-race schools, white or nonwhite, there is class separation, class contempt, and class conflict. Few friendships are made across such lines, and the increasing violence in our high schools arises almost entirely from conflicts between such groups.

So the idea that schools mix together in happy groups children from widely differing backgrounds is for the most part simply not true. The question remains, how would children meet other children from different backgrounds if they did *not* go to school? I don't know. While the numbers of such children remain small, this will be difficult. But as the numbers of such children grow, there will be more places for them to go and more things for them to do that are not based in school. We can certainly hope, and may to some extent be able to arrange, that in these places children from different backgrounds may be more mixed together. Also, people who teach their children at home already tend to think of themselves as something of an extended family, and through networking, write each other letters, visit each other when they can, have local meetings, and so on. I hope this will remain true as more working-class and nonwhite families begin to unschool their children, and it well may; people who feel this kind of affection and trust in their own children tend to feel a strong bond with others who feel the same.

How are we going to prevent parents with narrow and bigoted ideas from passing these on to their children?

The first question we have to answer is, do we have a right to try to prevent it? And even if we think we do, can we?

One of the main differences between a free country and a police state, I always thought, was that in a free country, as long as you obeyed the law, you could believe whatever you liked. Your beliefs were none of the government's business. Far less was it any of the government's business to say that one set of ideas was good and another set bad, or that schools should promote the good and stamp out the bad. Have we given up these principles? And if we haven't, do we really want to? Suppose we decided to give the government the power, through compulsory schools, to promote good ideas and put down bad. To whom would we then give the power to decide *which* ideas were good and which bad? To legislatures? To state boards of education? To local school boards?

Anyone who thinks seriously about these questions will surely agree that no one in government should have such power. From this it must follow that people have the right not only to believe what they want, but to try to pass their beliefs along to their children. We can't say that some people have this right while others do not. Some will say, but what about people who are prejudiced, bigoted, superstitious? We're surely not going to let people try to make their children believe that some races are superior or that the earth is flat? To which I say, what is the alternative? If we say, as many would like to, that people can tell their children anything they want, *as long as it is true*, we come back to our first question—who decides what is true? If we agree, as I think and hope we do, that there is no one in government or anywhere else whom we would trust to decide that, then it follows that we can't give schools the right to tell all children that some ideas are true and others are not. Since any school, whether by what it says or what it does, must promote *some* ideas, it follows that while people who approve of the ideas being taught or promoted in government schools may be glad to send their children there, people who don't approve of those ideas should have some other choice. This is essentially what the U.S. Supreme Court said in *Pierce v. Society of Sisters* (see Chapter 11).

One of the reasons why growing numbers of people are so passionately opposed to the public schools is that these schools are in fact acting as if someone *had* explicitly and legally given them the power to promote one set of ideas and to put down others. A fairly small group of people, educational bureaucrats at the state and federal level, who largely control what schools say and do, are more and more using the schools to promote whatever ideas they happen to think will be good for the children, or the country. But we have never formally decided, through any political process, to give the schools such power, far less agreed on what ideas we would like the schools to promote. On the contrary, there is every reason to believe that large majorities of the people strongly dislike many or most of the ideas that most schools promote today.

Even if we all agreed that the schools should try to stamp out narrow and bigoted ideas, we would still have to ask ourselves, does this work? Clearly it doesn't. After all, except for a few rich kids almost all children in the country have been going to public schools now for several generations. If the schools were as good as they claim at stamping out prejudice, there ought not to be any left. A quick glance at any day's news will show that there is plenty left. In fact, there may well be less support today than ever before for the tolerance and open-mindedness that the schools supposedly promote.

If you don't send your children to school, how are they going to learn to fit into a mass society?

If you don't send children to school, how are they going to be exposed to any values other than the commercial values of a mass society?

Educators often ask me these two questions in the same meeting, often within a few minutes of each other. Obviously, they cancel each other out. The schools may in fact be able to prepare children to fit into the mass society, which means, among other things, believing what most people believe and liking what most people like. Or they may be able to help children find a set of values with which they could resist and reject at least many of the values of the mass society. But they certainly can't do *both*.

It seems to be one of the articles of faith of educators that they, and they alone, hold out to the young a vision of higher things. At meetings they often talk as if they spent much of their time and energy defending children from the corrupt values of the mass media and the television set. Where, but from us, they say, are children going to hear about good books, Shakespeare, culture? We are the only ones who are thinking about what is good for them; everyone else is just trying to exploit them. The fact is, however, that most schools are far more concerned to have children accept the values of mass society than to help them resist them. When school people hear about people teaching their children at home, they almost always say, "But aren't you afraid that your children are going to grow up to be different, outsiders, misfits, unable to adjust to society?" They take it for granted that in order to live reasonably happily, usefully, and successfully in the world you have to be mostly like most other people.

In any case, the schools' efforts to sell children the higher culture seldom work, since they obviously value it so little themselves. In my introduction to Roland Betts's *Acting Out*, a frightening account of life in New York City's public schools, I wrote:

> . . . Our big city schools are largely populated, and will be increasingly populated, by the children of the nonwhite poor, the youngest members and victims of a sick subculture of a sick society, obsessed by violence and the media-inspired worship of dominance, luxury, and power. This culture, or more accurately, anticulture, has done more harm to its members and victims, has fragmented, degraded, and corrupted them more than centuries of slavery and the most brutal repression were able to do. Every day this anticulture, in the person of the children, invades the schools. If the schools had a true and humane culture of their own, which they really understood, believed in, cared about, and lived by, as did the First Street School some years ago, they might put up a stiff resistance, might even win some of the children over. But since the culture of the school is only a pale and some-

what more timid and genteel version of the culture of the street outside . . . nothing changes. Far from being able to woo the children away from greed, envy, and violence, the schools cannot even protect them against each other.

A friend of mine, in his early thirties, is a journalist, generally liberal, sympathetic to the young. Not long ago he visited a number of high schools in the affluent suburbs of Los Angeles where he grew up, talking to the students, trying to find out what they seemed most interested in and cared most about. I asked eagerly what he had found. After a silence, he said, "They seem to be mostly interested in money, sex, and drugs." He was clearly as unhappy to say it as I was to hear it. We would both like to have found out that these favored young people wanted to do something to make a better world, as many did fifteen years ago. But we should not be surprised that young people should be most interested in the things that most interest their elders.

Nor is it fair to blame the schools, as many people do, for the interest of the young in these things. Attacked from all sides, the schools say plaintively, "But we didn't invent these values." Quite right; they didn't. What we can and must say is that to whatever extent the schools have tried to combat these values, they have almost totally failed. In any case, to return once more to my first point, they can hardly claim that they are at one and the same time teaching children to accept and also to resist these dominant values of our commercial culture.

If children are taught at home, won't they miss the valuable social life of the school?

If there were no other reason for wanting to keep kids out of school, the social life would be reason enough. In all but a very few of the schools I have taught in, visited, or know anything about, the social life of the children is mean-spirited, competitive, exclusive, status-seeking, snobbish, full of talk about who

went to whose birthday party and who got what Christmas presents and who got how many Valentine cards and who is talking to
so-and-so and who is not. Even in the first grade, classes soon divide up into leaders (energetic and—often deservedly—popular
kids), their bands of followers, and other outsiders who are
pointedly excluded from these groups.

I remember my sister saying of one of her children, then five,
that she never knew her to do anything really mean or silly until
she went away to school—a nice school, by the way, in a nice
small town.

Jud Jerome, writer, poet, former professor at Antioch, wrote
about his son, Topher, meeting this so-called "social life" in a
free school run by a commune:

> . . . Though we were glad he was happy and enjoying himself (in
> school), we were also sad as we watched him deteriorate from a
> person into a kid under peer influence in school. It was much like
> what we saw happening when he was in kindergarten. There are
> certain kinds of childishness which it seems most people accept
> as being natural, something children have to go through, some-
> thing which it is, indeed a shame to deny them. Silliness, self-
> indulgence, random rebelliousness, secretiveness, cruelty to
> other children, clubbishness, addiction to toys, possessions, junk,
> spending money, purchased entertainment, exploitation of adults
> to pay attention, take them places, amuse them, do things with
> them—all these things seem to me quite unnecessary, not "nor-
> mal" at all (note: except in the sense of being common), and just
> as disgusting in children as they are in adults. And while they de-
> velop as a result of peer influence, I believe this is only and
> specifically because children are thrown together in school and
> develop these means, as prisoners develop means of passing dull
> time and tormenting authorities to cope with an oppressive situa-
> tion. The richer the families the children come from, the worse
> these traits seem to be. Two years of school and Topher would
> probably have regressed two years in emotional development. I

am not sure of that, of course, and it was not because of that fear that we pulled him out, but we saw enough of what happened to him in a school situation not to regret pulling him out. . . .

One of our readers gave us a vivid description of what must be a very typical school experience:

My mother tells me that after the first day in kindergarten I told her that I didn't need to go to school anymore because I knew everything already. Great arrogance? Not really. I knew how to be quiet, how to listen to children's stories, and how to sing. I wanted to learn about the adult world but was restricted to a world which adults believed children wanted. My great pre-school enthusiasm died an early death. . . .

Shame was one of the first lessons that I learned. In the first grade I was told to color a picture of a mother and daughter working in a kitchen. It struck me that if I were to color the entire picture yellow, then it would be different from all the other pictures. When I handed it in to the teacher I expected her to be pleased, if not genuinely excited. She, instead, glared at me for what seemed to be a long time and caused me to feel the deepest shame and self-contempt. . . . I was six years old.

Since spontaneity was dangerous—it conflicted with the teacher's view of how children should act—lying was a valuable survival technique. . . . In first grade, the class was sent to the kindergarten room to do some work without supervision. I used this opportunity to take a plastic doll and stick the head into a plastic toilet in one of the furnished doll houses in the room. No one was sure who did it, but everyone thought it was amusing— except the teacher. She was red with anger (she was a nun, and working-class Catholic schools in the early 1960s were not the most humane institutions) and I feared a severe beating. Suspicion was eventually focused on me and I lied with complete success, at least for me; another boy was blamed for the incident. I wish that I had said, "Yes, I did it, so what." But I was afraid. This teacher, the principal, was a textbook authoritarian. Every violation of her largely unwritten rules would lead her to deliver the same angry statement: "Don't challenge me." She saw challenges in virtually everything even though we would never have challenged her. I'll just give two of her biggest challenges.

Challenge number one involved misbehavior which the teacher present did not see, but the principal looking into the room did. The fifth, sixth, seventh, and eighth grades (it was a small school) were in this room to practice singing. She was furious, talked about challenges, and scolded the student vehemently.

Challenge number two involved the same boy. This time he urinated, or defecated, or both, in his pants. Perhaps he was ill or maybe he had a mental problem. [Author's note: Or perhaps he had merely been denied permission to go to the bathroom, which happens quite often in school.] He didn't do this regularly. He was about twelve years old. Naturally this called for punishment. He was forced to stand in front of each class in the school while the teacher explained to the class his crime. When he came to our classroom the principal named him the school's stinker and told us why. But what I remember most clearly is the pained smile on his face.

There were many incidents of fear and humiliation. Even though there were not many savage beatings, the point is that we lived in an environment where this could happen anytime. And we knew that. I had no clear idea that there was anything wrong with the school; I only had a vague feeling that things didn't have to be the way they were. I wasn't a noble child resisting tyrannical teachers. No, I loved the game of fear and humiliation and played like the masters.

"We can hardly wait to make someone pay for our humiliation, yield to us as we were once made to yield" (*Freedom and Beyond*, p. 114).

I'm not sure when it started, but in the eighth grade a number of us would terrorize some of the timid boys in the school. We would push the victim around, ridicule him, pull his shirt out, spin him around, dust the chalk erasers on his clothes, mess up his hair, and chase him on the playground. It was easy to be friends with these boys when I was alone with them. But when there was a group of us the teasing would begin. *Since we were always in groups* [Author's emphasis], the teasing of these boys, two in particular, was nearly unending. On the playground they had to avoid being seen. One of the boys would go home for lunch and not return until the last minute of recess. We did it without thought and it seemed to be only boyish pranks. It was sadism and I found it to be almost irresistible.

We then started to turn on the group members and practice our arts on the selected victim. I remember coming home with sore sides from laughing so hard at another's humiliation, but I felt empty and actually unhappy. The next day I would do it again. This only stopped when I became the victim. It was pure hell. Everyone you knew devoted all his time to your being humiliated. Any one act was insignificant: slapping an unaware student in the back of the head was popular. But it happened all day long in a multitude of ways. Christmas vacation came and one of my prime torturers transferred to another school. Things cooled off for me, but not for the timid boys or the younger children in the school. We almost had serious violence with the male students several years younger than us.

I don't remember the beginning or the end of this sadistic behavior. I know that I didn't act this way before my last two years in grade school or since then.

This reader's experience is surely not unusual. When I was nine, I was in a public elementary school, in a class in which almost all the boys were bigger and older than I was, most of them from working-class Italian or Polish families. One by one, the toughest ones first, then the others, more or less in order of toughness, they beat me up at recess, punched me until they knocked me down and/or made me cry. Once a boy had beaten me up, he rarely bothered to do it again. There didn't seem to me to be much malice in it; it was as if this had to be done in order to find my proper place in the class. Finally everyone had beat me except a boy named Henry. One day the bigger boys hemmed us in and told us that we had to fight to find who was the biggest sissy in the sixth grade. Henry and I said we didn't want to fight. They said if we didn't, they would beat up both of us. So for a while Henry and I circled around, swinging wildly at each other, the bigger boys laughing and urging us on. Nothing happened for some time, until one of my wild swings hit Henry's nose. It began to bleed, Henry began to cry, and so did I. But the bigger boys were satisfied; they declared that Henry was now the official biggest sissy in the class.

A teacher writes:

> On Friday I was reading GWS and intrigued with it as usual. I'm especially interested in the "social life" aspect of schools and the damage it causes. This morning I asked my third graders, "Do you feel that in our school kids are nice, kind to each other?"
>
> Out of 22 kids, only two felt that they saw kindness, and the rest felt most kids are mean, call names, hurt feelings, etc. Frankly I was amazed. I have always felt our school is a uniquely friendly place. . . .

When I point out to people that the social life of most schools and classrooms is mean-spirited, status-oriented, competitive, and snobbish, I am always astonished by their response. Not *one* person of the hundreds with whom I've discussed this has yet said to me that the social life at school is kindly, generous, supporting, democratic, friendly, loving, or good for children. No, without exception, when I condemn the social life of school, people say, "But that's what the children are going to meet in Real Life."

The "peer groups" into which we force children have many other powerful and harmful effects. Every now and then, in the subway or some public place, I see young people, perhaps twelve or thirteen years old, sometimes even as young as ten, smoking cigarettes. It is a comic and pitiful sight. It is also an ordeal. The smoke tastes awful. Children have sensitive taste buds, and that smoke must taste even worse to them than to most nonsmoking adults, which is saying a lot. They have to struggle not to choke, not to cough, maybe even not to get sick. Why do they do it? Because "all the other kids" are doing it, or soon will be, and they have to stay ahead of them, or at least not fall behind. In short, wanting to smoke, or feeling one has to smoke whether one wants to or not, is one of the many fringe benefits of that great "social life" at school that people talk about.

I feel sorry for all the children who think they have to smoke, and even sorrier for any nonsmoking parents who may desperately wish they could persuade them not to. If the children have lived in the peer group long enough to become enslaved to it, addicted to it—we might call them "peer group junkies"—then they are going to smoke, and do anything and everything else the peer group does. If Mom and Pop make a fuss, then they will lie about it and do it behind their backs. The evidence on this is clear. In some age groups, fewer people are smoking. But more children are smoking every year, especially girls, and they start earlier.

The same is true of drinking. We hear more and more about drinking, drunkenness, and alcoholism among the young. Some states have tried in recent years to deal with the problem by raising the minimum drinking age. It doesn't seem to have helped; if anything, the problem only gets worse. One news story sticks in my mind. One night last summer in a town near Boston four high school girls, all about sixteen or seventeen, were killed and another seriously injured in an auto accident. Earlier in the evening they had loaded up their small car with beer and several kinds of liquor and had gone out for an evening of driving and drinking. By the time of the accident, all were drunk. The one survivor was later quoted by the papers as saying, from her bed in the hospital, "I didn't think there was anything wrong with what we were doing; all the kids around here do it."

Of course, children who spend almost all their time in groups of other people their own age, shut out of society's serious work and concerns, with almost no contact with any adults except child-watchers, are going to feel that what "all the other kids" are doing is the right, the best, the only thing to do.

*How are we going to prevent children being taught by "unquali-
fied" teachers?*

First of all, to know what is meant by "qualified," we have to
know what is meant by quality. We could hardly agree on who
was or was not a good painter if we did not to a large extent agree
on what was or was not a good painting. The question asked
above assumes that since educators agree on and understand
correctly what is meant by good teaching, they are able to make
sound judgments about who is or is not a good teacher. But the
fact is that educators do not understand or agree about what
makes good teaching. The dismal record of the schools is proof
enough of this. Still further proof is that, when charged in court
with negligence (see the section "A Doubtful Claim" in Chapter
11), educators defend themselves by saying (with the approval of
the courts) that they cannot be judged guilty of not having done
what should have been done, because *no one knows what should
have been done*. This may be so. But it clearly follows that people
who don't know what should be done can hardly judge who is or
is not competent to do it.

In practice, educators who worry about "unqualified" people
teaching their own children almost always define "qualified" to
mean teachers trained in schools of education and holding teaching
certificates. They assume that to teach children involves a host of
mysterious skills that can be learned only in schools of education
and that are in fact taught there; that people who have this training
teach much better than those who do not; and indeed that people
who have not had this training are not competent to teach at all.

None of these assumptions are true.

Human beings have been sharing information and skills, and
passing along to their children whatever they knew, for about a
million years now. Along the way they have built some very complicated and highly skilled societies. During all those years there
were very few teachers in the sense of people whose *only* work
was teaching others what they knew. And until very recently
there were no people at all who were trained in teaching, *as*

such. People always understood, sensibly enough, that before you could teach something you had to know it yourself. But only very recently did human beings get the extraordinary notion that in order to be able to teach what you knew you had to spend years being taught how to teach.

To the extent that teaching involves and requires some real skills, these have long been well understood. They are no mystery. Teaching skills are among the many commonsense things about dealing with other people that, unless we are mistaught, we learn just by living. In any community people have always known that if you wanted to find out how to get somewhere or do something, some people were much better to ask than others. For a long, long time, people who were good at sharing what they knew have realized certain things: (1) to help people learn something, you must first understand what they already know; (2) showing people how to do something is better than telling them, and letting them do it themselves is best of all; (3) you mustn't tell or show too much at once, since people digest new ideas slowly and must feel secure with new skills or knowledge before they are ready for more; (4) you must give people as much time as they want and need to absorb what you have shown or told them; (5) instead of testing their understanding with questions you must let them show how much or little they understand by the questions they ask you; (6) you must not get impatient or angry when people don't understand; (7) scaring people only blocks learning, and so on. These are clearly not things that one has to spend three years talking about.

And in fact these are not what schools of education talk about. They give very little thought to the act of teaching itself—helping another person find something out, or answering that person's questions. What they spend most of their time doing is preparing their students to work in the strange world of schools—which, in all fairness, is what the students want to find out: how to get a teaching job and keep it. This means learning how to speak the school's language (teeny little ideas blown up into great big words), how to do all the things schools want teachers to do, how to fill out its endless forms and papers, and how to make the endless judgments it likes to make about students. Above all else, education students are taught to think that what they know is extremely important and that they are the only ones who know it.

As for the idea that certified teachers teach better than uncertified, or that uncertified teachers cannot teach at all, there is not a shred of evidence to support it, and a great deal of evidence against it. One indication is that our most selective, demanding, and successful private schools have among their teachers hardly any, if indeed any at all, who went to teacher training schools and got their degrees in education. Few such schools would even consider hiring a teacher who had only such training and such a degree. How does it happen that the richest and most powerful people in the country, the ones most able to choose what they want for their children, so regularly choose *not* to have them taught by trained and certified teachers? One might almost count it among the major benefits of being rich that you are able to *avoid* having your children taught by such teachers.

In this connection, the following story from the *Philadelphia Inquirer*, November 18, 1979, may be of interest:

> ... Rev. Peder Bloom, assistant headmaster of Doane Academy/St. Mary's Hall, an independent Episcopalian school founded in 1837, sees not only a larger, but a more varied clientele applying.
>
> "Any number" of parents are both working to pay tuition bills, he says, and presently *the biggest single occupational parent group is public school administrators* [Author's emphasis], according to private school administrators. It used to be doctors; now they are second. ...

When a district court in Kentucky challenged the state board of education to show evidence that certified teachers were better than uncertified, the board was unable to produce (in the court's words) "a scintilla of evidence" to that effect. The same thing happened more recently in a Michigan court. It is very unlikely that any other state boards would be able to do so.

In the state of Alaska, hundreds or perhaps thousands of home-steading families live many miles from the nearest town, or even road. The only way they can get in and out of their homes is by plane. Since the state cannot provide schools for these families, or transport their children to and from existing schools, it very sensibly has a correspondence school of its own which mails school materials to these families, who then teach their children at home. Nobody seems to worry very much about whether these families are "qualified," and no one has yet brought forth any evidence that home-taught children in Alaska do less well in their studies than school-taught children, there or in other states.

Perhaps the leading correspondence school for school-aged children is the Calvert Institute of Baltimore, Maryland. It has been in business for a long time, and for all that time most school districts (I know of no exceptions) have been willing to accept a year of study under Calvert as equal to a year of study in school. Indeed, this assurance that Calvert-taught children would not fall behind has been part of what Calvert offered and sold its customers and clients. These have been, for the most part, American families living overseas: missionaries, military or diplomatic people, people working in foreign offices of American firms, etc. But very few of these parents can have been certified teachers.

Years ago I read that one or more inner-city schools had tried the experiment of letting fifth graders teach first graders to read. They found, first, that the first graders learned faster than similar first graders taught by trained teachers, and secondly, that the fifth graders who were teaching them, many or most of whom had not been good readers themselves, also improved a great deal in their reading. These schools apparently did these experiments in desperation. It is easy to see why they have not been widely repeated. Even in those schools that are willing to allow "paraprofessional" adults, i.e., people without teachers' certificates, in their classrooms, the regular teachers almost always insist that these paraprofessionals *not* be allowed to do any teaching. But poor countries have found in mass literacy programs that almost anyone who can read can teach anyone else who wants to learn.

I found in my own classes, as in others I have since observed where children are allowed to talk to each other and to help each other with schoolwork, that many children were very good at teaching each other. There were many reasons for this. Even though I did my best to convince them that ignorance was no shame, they felt much freer to confess ignorance was no confusion to each other than to me, since they knew they knew little and wrongly thought that I knew almost everything. Also, they did not have to fear that their friends might give them a bad grade. I had told them that I did not believe in grades, and I think they believed me. But they understood, as I did, that this had little to do with reality; both the school and their parents demanded grades, and I had to give them. Some of them, who really liked me, may have feared that after struggling to teach them something I would be disappointed if they didn't learn it. Indeed this was true, and though I tried not to be disappointed or at least not to show that I was, I never really succeeded. They wanted to please me, and knew when they hadn't.

Learning from each other, they didn't have to worry about this. A child teaching another is not disappointed if the other does not understand or learn, since teaching is not his main work and he is not worried about whether he is or is not a good teacher. He may be exasperated, may even say, "Come on, dummy, pay attention, what's the matter with you?" Since children tend to be direct and blunt with each other anyway, this probably won't bother the learner. If it does, he can say so. Either the other will be more tactful, since he rightly values their friendship more than the effectiveness of his teaching, or the learner will find another helper. And this is another and important reason why children are good at teaching each other. Both child-teacher and child-learner know that this teacher-learner relationship is temporary, much less important than their friendship, in which they meet as equals. This temporary relationship will go on only as long as they are both satisfied with it. The child-teacher doesn't *have* to teach the other, and the child-learner doesn't *have* to learn from the other. Since they both come to the relationship freely and by their own choice, they are truly equal partners in it.

I want to stress very strongly that the fact that their continuing relationship as friends is more important than their temporary relationship as learner and teacher is above all else what makes this temporary relationship work. There is an old rule in medicine (not always obeyed): "First, do no harm." In other words, in treating patients, make sure you do not injure them. The rule is just as true for teaching. Above all else, be sure that in your eagerness to make them learn, you do not frighten, offend, insult, or humiliate those you are teaching. Teachers of animals, whether dogs, dolphins, circus animals, or whatever, understand that very well—it is the first rule in their book. It is only among teachers of human beings that many do not understand and even hotly deny this rule.

It is because they understand this rule, if not in words at least in their hearts, that the kind of parents who teach their own children are likely to do it better than anyone else. Such people do not knowingly hurt their children. When they see that something they are doing is hurting their child, *they stop*, no matter how good may have been their reasons for doing it. They take seriously any signals of pain and distress that their children give them. Of course, the distress signals that children make when we try too hard to teach them something are quite different from the signals they make when something hurts them. Instead of saying "Ow!" they say, "I don't get it," or "This is crazy." It took me years, teaching in classrooms, to learn what those signals were, and still longer to understand how I was causing the distress. But parents teaching at home are in a much better position to learn these distress signals than a classroom teacher. They are not distracted by the problems of managing a class, they know the children better, and their spoken and unspoken languages, and they care about them more. Also, as I have said elsewhere, they can try things out to see what works, and drop whatever does not. Since they control their experience, they can learn more from it.

This is not to say that all families who try to teach their own children will learn to do it well. Some may not. But such families are likely to find homeschooling so unpleasant that they will be glad to give it up, the children most of all. A homeschooling mother wrote me that when, simply out of fear of the schools, she began to give her children a lot of conventional schoolwork, they said, "Look, Mom, if we're going to have to spend all our time doing this school junk, we'd rather do it in school." Quite right. If you are going to have to spend your days doing busywork to relieve adult anxieties, better do it in school, where you only have one-thirtieth of the teacher's anxieties, rather than at home, where you have all of your parent's.

We can sum up very quickly what people need to teach their own children. First of all, they have to *like* them, enjoy their company, their physical presence, their energy, foolishness, and passion. They have to enjoy all their talk and questions, and enjoy equally trying to answer those questions. They have to think of their children as friends, indeed very close friends, have to feel happier when they are near and miss them when they are away. They have to trust them as people, respect their fragile dignity, treat them with courtesy, take them seriously. They have to feel in their own hearts some of their children's wonder, curiosity, and excitement about the world. And they have to have enough confidence in themselves, skepticism about experts, and willingness to be different from most people, to take on themselves the responsibility for their children's learning. But that is about all that parents need. Perhaps only a minority of parents have these qualities. Certainly some have more than others. Many will gain more as they know their children better; most of the people who have been teaching their children at home say that it has made them like them more, not less. In any case, these are not qualities that can be taught or learned in a school, or measured with a test, or certified with a piece of paper.

Are there then *no* requirements of schooling or learning? Isn't there some minimum that people ought to know? Could people teach their children who had never been to school themselves? Even if they didn't know how to read and write? I think even then they probably could. A woman told me not long ago, after a meeting, that though she had a degree from Radcliffe and a Ph.D. from Harvard, the most helpful, influential, and important of all the teachers she had ever had was her mother, who had come to this country as an immigrant and who was illiterate not only here but in the country of her birth. And while a consultant to a program to teach adult illiterates to read, I heard about one of the students, a middle-aged woman who had for years concealed her illiteracy from her college graduate husband and her children, whom she used to regularly help with their schoolwork. For many years I told her story to show how cleverly people can bluff and fake. Only recently did I realize that this woman's children would not have come to her year after year for help on their schoolwork *unless her help had been helpful.* She was in short not just a clever bluffer, but a very good teacher.

I don't expect many illiterate parents to ask me how they can take their children out of school and teach them at home. But if any do, I will say, "I don't think that just because you have not yet learned to read and write means that you can't do a better job of helping your children learn about the world than the schools. But one of the things you are going to have to do in order to help them is *learn* to read and write. It is easy, if you really want to do it, and once you get out of your head the idea that you *can't* do it. If any of your children can read and write, they can help you learn. If none of them can read and write, you can learn together. But it is important that you learn. In the first place, if you don't, and the schools find out, there is no way in the world that they or the courts are going to allow you to teach your children at home. In the second place, if you don't know how to read and write, your children are likely to feel that reading and writing are not useful and interesting, or else that they are very difficult, neither of which is true. So learning to read and write will have to be one of your first tasks."

How am I going to teach my child six hours a day?

Who's teaching him six hours a day right now?

As a child, I went to the "best" schools, some public, most private. I was a good student, the kind that teachers *like* to talk to. And it was a rare day indeed in my schooling when I got fifteen minutes of teaching, that is, of concerned and thoughtful adult talk about something that *I* found interesting, puzzling, or important. Over the whole of my schooling, the average was probably closer to fifteen minutes a week. For most children in most schools, it is much less than that. Many poor, nonwhite, or unusual kids never get any real teaching at all in their entire schooling. When teachers speak to them, it is only to command, correct, warn, threaten, or blame.

Anyway, children don't need, don't want, and *couldn't stand* six hours of teaching a day, even if parents wanted to do that much. To help them find out about the world doesn't take that much adult input. Most of what they need, parents have been giving them since they were born. As I have said, they need access. They need a chance, sometimes, for honest, serious, unhurried talk; or sometimes, for joking, play, and foolishness; or sometimes, for tenderness, sympathy, and comfort. They need, much of the time, to share your life, or at least, not to feel shut out of it, in short, to go some of the places you go, see and do some of the things that interest you, get to know some of your friends, find out what you did when you were little and before they were born. They need to have their questions answered, or at least heard and attended to—if you don't know, say "I don't know." They need to know more and more adults whose main work in life is not taking care of kids. They need *some* friends their own age, but not dozens of them; two or three, at most half a dozen, is as many real friends as any child can have at one time. Perhaps above all, they need a lot of privacy, solitude, calm, times when there's nothing to do.

Schools rarely provide any of these, and even if radically changed, never could provide most of them. But the average parent, family, circle of friends, neighborhood, and community can and do provide all of these things, perhaps not as well as they once did or might again, but well enough. People do not need a

Ph.D. or some kind of certificate to help their children find their way into the world.

How are children going to learn what they need to know?

About this, a parent wrote:

> . . . During his early years, my wife and I and a couple of friends taught him all he wanted to know, and if we didn't know it, which usually was the case, it was even better for we all learned together. Example: at 7, he saw the periodic table of elements, wanted to learn atoms and chemistry and physics. I had forgotten how to balance an equation, but went out and bought a college textbook on the subject, a history of discovery of the elements, and some model atoms, and in the next month we went off into a tangent of learning in which somehow we both learned college-level science. He has never returned to the subject, but to this day *retains every bit of it because it came at a moment in development and fantasy that was meaningful to him* [Author's emphasis].

Of course, a child may not know what he may need to know in ten years (who does?), but he knows, and much better than anyone else, *what he wants and needs to know right now*, what his mind is ready and hungry for. If we help him, or just allow him, to learn that, he will remember it, use it, build on it. If we try to make him learn something else, that *we* think is more important, the chances are that he won't learn it, or will learn very little of it, that he will soon forget most of what he learned, and what is worst of all, will before long lose most of his appetite for learning anything.

Other parents have asked me similar questions and to one I wrote:

> . . . With respect to your question, about how a parent could teach something like chemistry, there seem to be a number of possibilities, all of which people have actually done in one place or an-

other. (1) The parent finds a textbook(s), materials, etc., and parent and child learn the stuff together. (2) The parent gets the above for the child, and the child learns it alone. (3) The parent or the child finds someone else who knows this material, perhaps a friend or neighbor, perhaps a teacher in some school or even college, and learns from them.

As for equipment, you say that your high school had a very extensive chem lab, but I'll bet that very few of the students ever used more than a small part of the materials in the lab. I have known kids who were interested in chemistry and did it in their own basements, who were able to do a great deal of work with, at today's prices, less than $200 or maybe $100 worth of equipment. The catalog of the Edmund Scientific Corp. (and many other companies) is full of such equipment. The same thing is true of physics. As for biology, except perhaps in the heart of the city, it is not difficult to find plants and animals for observation and classification, if that is what children want to do.

I won't say these are not problems, but people who want to solve them can solve them.

You ask "Would you expect a parent to purchase test tubes, chemicals, instruments, etc., that would perhaps only be used for one or two years, only to have the child become an artist or musician?" Well, why not? People purchase bicycles, sports equipment, musical instruments, without knowing that their children will ever become professional athletes, musicians, etc. None of this equipment (unless broken) loses any of its value—it could probably be sold later for at least a significant part of the purchase price. And, as time goes on, and more people are teaching their children at home, it will be easier to get these materials from other parents who have used them, or to arrange for swaps, etc.

I see no real need for "institutional" education at *any* age. There is in Michigan a man named Ovshinsky who stood solid-state physics on its ear by inventing a theory by which noncrystalline substances could be used to do things which, according to orthodox theory, only crystalline materials could do. For a number of years orthodox physicists dismissed Ovshinsky's ideas. But he was able to demonstrate them so clearly in laboratory experiments that they were finally obliged to admit that he was right. *Ovshinsky never finished high school.* There are probably more cases like this than we know, and there would be a great many more except for compulsory schooling laws. It is a kind of Catch-22 situation to say, first, that all children have to spend all that time in schools, and then to say that all kinds of things can *only* be learned in schools. How do we know? Where have we given people a chance to learn them somewhere else?

A very important function of institutions of so-called higher learning is not so much to teach people things as to *limit* access to certain kinds of learning and work. The function of law schools is much less to train lawyers than to keep down the supply of lawyers. Practically everything that is now only done by people with Ph.D.'s was, not so very long ago, done by people with no graduate training or in some cases even undergraduate training.

I hope you will not doubt your competence to help your children learn anything they want to learn, or indeed their competence to learn many things without your help.

One mother wrote me some particularly challenging questions, to which I gave these answers:

Q. My greatest concern is that I don't want to slant my children's view of life all through "mother-colored" glasses. . . .

A. If you mean, *determine* your children's view of life, you couldn't do it even if you wanted to. You are an influence on your children, and an important one, but by no means the only one, or even the only important one. How they later see the world is going to be determined by a great many things, many of them probably not to your liking, and most of them out of your control. On the other hand, it would be impossible, even if you wanted to, not to have *some* influence on your children's view of life.

Q. I also wonder if I can have the thoroughness, the follow-through demanded, the patience, and the continuing enthusiasm for a diversity of interests they will undoubtedly have.

A. Well, who in any school would have more, or even as much? I was a good student in the "best" schools, and very few adults there were even slightly concerned with my interests. Beyond that, you may expect too much of yourself. Your children's learning is not all going to come from you, but from *them*, and their interaction with the world around them, which of course includes you. You do not have to know everything they want to know, or be interested in everything they are interested in. As for patience, maybe you won't have enough at first; like many home-teaching parents, you may start by trying to do too much, know too much, control too much. But like the rest, you will learn from experience—mostly, to trust your children.

Q. Most unschoolers seem to live on farms growing their own vegetables (which I'd like) or have unique life-styles in urban areas, and heavy father participation in children's education. What about suburbanites with modern-convenienced homes and fathers who work for a company 10 to 12 hours a day away from home? What differences will this make? Will unschooling work as well?

A. Well enough. You and your children will have to find out as you go along what differences they make, and deal with them as best you can. Once, people said that the suburbs were the best of all possible worlds in which to bring up children; now it is the fashion to say they are the worst. Both views are exaggerated. In city, country, or suburb, there is more than enough to give young people an interesting world to grow up in, plenty of food for thought and action. You don't have to have every resource for your children, and if you did, they wouldn't have enough time to make use of all of them. As for the father's involvement, it can certainly be helpful, but it is not crucial. Some of the most successful unschoolers we know of are single mothers.

Q. What if the children want to go to school?

A. This is a hard question. There is more than one good answer to it, and these often conflict. Parents could argue, and some do, that since they believe that school can and probably will do their children deep and lasting harm, they have as much right to keep them out, even if they want to go, as they would to tell them they could not play on a pile of radioactive wastes. This argument seems more weighty in the case of younger children, who could not be expected to understand how school might hurt them. If somewhat older children said determinedly and often, and for good reasons, that they really wanted to go to school, I would tend to say, let them go. How much older? What are good reasons? I don't know. A bad reason might be, "The other kids tell me that at school lunch you can have chocolate milk."

Q. I'm concerned that someone might be eager to take us to court and take away our children.

A. The schools have in a number of cases tried—shamefully—to take children away from unschooling parents. I think there are legal counters to this, strategies which would make it highly unlikely that a court would take such action. And if worse came to worst, and a court said, "Put your children back in school or we'll take them away," you can always put them back in while you plan what to do next—which might simply be to move to another state or even school or judicial district.

Q. I don't want to feel I'm sheltering my children or running away from adversity.

A. Why not? It is your right, and your proper business, as parents, to shelter your children and protect them from adversity, at least as much as you can. Many of the world's children are starved or malnourished, but you would not starve your children so that they would know what this was like. You would not let your children play in the middle of a street full of high-speed traffic. Your business is, as far as you can, to help them realize their human potential, and to that end you put as much as you can of good into their lives, and keep out as much as you can of bad. If you think—as you do—that school is bad, then it is clear what you should do.

Q. I value their learning how to handle challenges or problems. . . .

A. There will be plenty of these. Growing up was probably never easy, and it is particularly hard in a world as anxious, confused, and fear-ridden as ours. To learn to know oneself, and to find a life worth living and work worth doing, is problem and challenge enough, without having to waste time on the fake and unworthy challenges of school—pleasing the teacher, staying out of trouble, fitting in with the gang, being popular, doing what everyone else does.

Q. Will they have the opportunity to overcome or do things that they think they don't want to do?

A. I'm not sure what this question means. If it means, will unschooled children know what it is to have to do difficult and demanding things in order to reach goals they have set for themselves, I would say, yes, life is full of such requirements. But this is not at all the same thing as doing something, and in the

case of school usually something stupid and boring, simply because someone else tells you you'll be punished if you don't.
Whether children resist such demands or yield to them, it is bad
for them. Struggling with the inherent difficulties of a chosen or
inescapable task builds character; merely submitting to superior
force destroys it.

❧ To these important questions one might add an important issue
in today's economic climate.

Can two-income families homeschool?

My wife and I both work, and through the years we've found that
we can arrange our schedules to accommodate homeschooling. Until
recently, I would work at the office or work from home, usually from
9 A.M. to 5 P.M., and Day worked afternoons or evenings; this suited
Day's theatrical lighting career with my daily business hours. Now
Day works during the days teaching in public school while I work
from home and do more of the driving and helping with the girls.

When our children were very young, and Day and I worked together at Holt Associates, they spent quite a bit of time in the office
with us, particularly when there were other children around for
them to play with. Our oldest daughter, Lauren, now sixteen, loved
the office as a toddler. After "mom" and "dad," the next word she
learned was "mail," which wasn't surprising as we spent so much
time talking about "the mail" at work! Now, our daughters are involved in all sorts of activities of their own, and between those activities and the time they spend with friends, neighbors, relatives,
and paid babysitters, they aren't with us at work as much.

One of the first things we noticed as our children got older was
that they became increasingly involved in their own activities.
There was less of a need to think of having someone "watch" them
all the time and more of a need to think about scheduling. For instance, when Lauren went to gymnastics classes or when the
homeschool drama club holds a rehearsal, it doesn't mean my wife

and I need to be there, too. We're not the only ones involved in our children's homeschooling, and that has benefits for us as parents, as well as for our children. We don't let our kids do gym or drama in order to give us childcare while we work, but rather because this type of varied life is what homeschooling is for us. Parents can gently encourage a child's growth from dependence on their care to independence as young adults; when kids are older they are often more able to get around on their own, to be by themselves at home or the library, to work with other adults. Try not to think of homeschooling in terms of your kids being home all day or needing parental supervision every minute, because homeschooling naturally encompasses many different activities, as I've described.

Some two-income families deliberately work split shifts (one works days, the other nights), work only during evenings and weekends, or have one partner work at home. The book *The Four-thirds Solution: Solving the Childcare Crisis in America Today* by Stanley Greenspan shows how two working parents can each work two-thirds of the time to free up time that they can spend with their children. The creativity and resourcefulness of people who want to homeschool is amazing—mothers on welfare as well as wealthy celebrities homeschool: If you want to, you can find a way.

To get a firsthand overview of what homeschooling can be like, read some of the recommended books in the back of this book. But to get a true feel for what homeschooling can be like for your family I strongly urge you to attend a homeschooling conference or support group meeting in your area; you may need to try several sources before you find one that suits your specific needs of homeschooling, but it will be well worth your effort. Not only will you get the latest information about homeschooling issues and events in your local area, you may also find kindred spirits as well as potential friends for your children.

Another question that I'm often asked is:

Can families with children who have special needs homeschool?

Not only can such families homeschool, they have also found that their special-needs children can flourish in home school. Homeschooling provides lots of one-on-one attention; lots of time to accomplish tasks that other children can finish more quickly; and lots of opportunities to try various therapies or medications if the one the child is currently using fail. Some schools make a big deal about the lack of specialized training a parent may have for taking care of a special-needs child, sometimes unreasonably so. One parent I helped to get her special-needs child out of a well-regarded school program was a certified special-education teacher herself, and she was being told she couldn't provide her daughter with all the care she needed! This mom not only succeeded in homeschooling her special-needs daughter, but she feels their lives are better now that they are working so closely together.

This is a common reason that special-needs families decide to homeschool: They become worn out from their repeated attempts to get the services and attention their child needed and decide while they're waiting for the typical, unsatisfactory responses they could be working with their child themselves. Wendy Renish, who homeschools a child with autism and pervasive development disorder, wrote to *Growing Without Schooling*:

> With all the problems we were having getting her the right services in school, and spending time helping her to get ready for school, helping her with homework, and helping her with social issues, we had no time for the one-on-one work she really needed.

Derrick Simpson, a single parent in Illinois who adopted a special-needs child from Ethiopia, writes:

> I fought with the system for several years to give him speech therapy. They refused to do it. They thought he had no speech issues . . .
>
> My son was feeling like the school wouldn't teach him. He wanted to go to school very much, because in Ethiopia, going to school is a privilege, and that was how he saw it . . . . He was really hating the situation, and while I could probably get him the right

services if I continued to fight, my feeling was that I had fought for three and a half years and I wasn't going to wait any longer . . .

One night when Fasika and I were working on his homework I realized: he spends all day in school, and he's got to line up, wait, then wait in the classroom, wait for others to get ready, then line up again. And meanwhile we were spending several hours each night together doing homework, so I said to myself, "I'm teaching him anyway."

When parents hit these breaking points with the school system, homeschooling can be liberating as well as frightening. Parents may be choosing to homeschool not as a well-considered option but as a desperate measure made under enormous pressure in order to find a better situation for their child. Fortunately, support for these families is growing, as well as understanding by some medical professionals that parents can be much more involved with special-needs children than is commonly accepted. Wendy Renish writes:

We had met Dr. Stanley Greenspan, a psychiatrist from Bethesda, Maryland, and author of *The Challenging Child*. He's one of the leading child development specialists in the world, and he believes that through work, a child's autistic behavior can be changed. He has a program, similar to the mirroring we had done, called "floor time." He believes that parents play the major role in helping special-needs children; yes, you do need medical professionals for some things— Rosie needs help with allergies, a hearing impairment, and occupational therapy. When it comes to behavior, these intensive one-on-one programs take so much time that most of the work has to be done by the parents.

. . . In so many ways, not sending her to school has been liberation. We don't have to worry about things like combing her hair or getting her shoes on in the morning, and we now have a protective environment in which to work with her, concentrating on her real areas of need. This is a child who, up to the age of 10, didn't know who she was when she looked at herself in the mirror. She could recognize parts of the body, but she had no sense of herself as a person.

There are so many things that she missed, growing up, so many experiences that she participated in physically but not emotionally. So we can go to her level and fill in the gaps.

. . . Academically, Rosie is also improving at home. Her speech has improved, because she can talk more slowly, think more slowly . . . . We are using techniques for helping with her auditory and visual processing difficulties, and she is learning how to visualize what happens in each chapter [when reading books]. We play-act the sentences, or we incorporate them into art lessons. She is doing so much better.

Homeschooling is, of course, harder for us than it is for many other families . . . . It would help me to have other adults around and to have access to libraries and dance lessons and other activities that Rosie could benefit from and that would give me a respite. We plan to move closer to a city for that reason. The best schooling for Rosie would be homeschooling in the morning, where she gets the intensive one-on-one time she needs. In the afternoon we are looking to find group activities for the peer interactions she also needs.

Several books and groups about homeschooling and special needs are listed in the resource section at the end of this book, particularly *Homeschooling the Child with ADD (or Other Special Needs)*. ⌾

3

Politics of Unschooling

❧ IN A LETTER TO IVAN ILLICH written in 1972, John Holt wrote:

> . . . In working for the kind of changes we want, for a convivial society
> and a nonsuicidal technology, you and I may have slightly different func-
> tions. You may be somewhat more of a prophet and I somewhat more of a
> tactician . . .

Holt spent the remaining years of his life figuring out ways to create
these changes. Ivan Illich wrote in *Deschooling Society* that to disestab-
lish schools we must prevent government funds from supporting them
and, just as we disestablished church from the state, we should amend the
Constitution to prohibit the establishment of education because, to paraphrase Illich: In modern America we are no longer *born* equal, but must
be *made* equal by Alma Mater. While believing Illich was correct, Holt
felt the majority of people would never agree to stop funding government
schools, and he sought other ways to move toward the goal of empower-
ing people to grow without schooling. In 1977 Holt founded the magazine
Growing Without Schooling, thereby cementing his position as the primary tactician for showing people how to get from schooling to "un-

schooling," a neologism he created in place of the word "deschooling," which he felt "creates more confusion than understanding." "Unschooling" has not proven to be a much clearer word, but as I mentioned earlier it is a good attempt to describe the sort of education Holt encouraged: learning and teaching which does not in any way resemble school and which does not necessarily have to take place in one's home. By the early 1980s the term "homeschooling" had taken root, and even Holt started using it interchangeably with the word "unschooling" (as he does throughout this book). However, most homeschoolers, as well as the general public, feel that children won't learn something unless it is specially taught to them. The general public has no qualms about the need for education; educational methods and content, and private or public funding, are what concerns them. Here is where the important shade of difference between "unschooling" and "homeschooling" comes in.

By "education," I'm using it here as defined by Holt in his book *Instead of Education*:

> . . . something that some people do to others for their own good, molding and shaping them, and trying to make them learn what they think they ought to know.

Now in describing how families live and learn without education provided in compulsory schools I am not trying to demonstrate that schools should be eradicated: Neither was Illich when he wrote *Deschooling Society*. Homeschoolers can use classes, traditional teaching methods, even textbooks and canned curricula—in some states homeschoolers are even able to take public school classes—but they do so on their own terms. Homeschoolers have determined what, when, why, how, and from whom they want to learn, and are therefore in an entirely different relationship with their schooling than students who are in class simply because of their age. Many things can make school-like arrangements for learning desirable, and certainly interesting teachers will attract willing students no matter where or how they teach. It is the idea that education must be applied to everyone in mandated doses that I challenge. And this challenge is especially important today as we are creating laws and policies that expand the years of compulsory schooling, that determine future employment based directly on school tests and credentials, and that standardize our culture with lists of learning. Unschooling and homeschooling are deeply connected as practices, but the *concept* of unschooling is used in a political and highly specific way by Holt throughout this chapter. ⊙⟩⟩

In this chapter I want to look at what might be called some political objections to unschooling: (1) unschooling is something that can be done only by rich and/or otherwise privileged people; (2) people who unschool only make things harder for poor children who remain in school; (3) schools are by definition and philosophy in favor of equality, and in practice are or soon might become, or be made, very helpful to poor children; (4) people unschooling their own children ignore or don't care about the need for large-scale social and/or educational change, or are too selfish to do anything about it.

UNSCHOOLING AND SOCIAL CHANGE

When we began to advise people to take their children out of school, and began to publish *Growing Without Schooling*, we put into practice a nickel-and-dime theory about social change, which is that important and lasting social change always comes slowly, and only when people change their lives, not just their political beliefs or parties or forms of government. Real social change is a process that takes place over time, usually quite a long time. At a given moment in history, 99 percent of a society may think and act one way on a certain matter, and only 1 percent think and act very differently. In time, that 1 percent may become 2 percent, then 5 percent, then 10, 20, 30 percent, until finally it becomes the dominant majority, and social change has taken place. When did this social change take place? When did it begin? There is no clear answer, except perhaps that any given social change begins the first time any one person thinks of it.

We who believe that children want to learn about the world, are good at it, and can be trusted to do it with very little adult coercion or interference, are probably no more than 1 percent of the population, if that.[1] And we are not likely to become the majority in my lifetime.

This doesn't trouble me much anymore, as long as this minority keeps on growing. My work is to help it grow. If we think of the majority of our society (or world), with respect to children and schooling, as moving in direction X, and our small minority as moving in direction Y, what I want to do is to find ways to help those who *want* to move in direction Y to *move* that way. There's no point in shouting endlessly at the great X-bound majority, "Hey, you guys, stop, turn around, you're going the wrong way!" People don't change their ideas, much less their lives, because someone comes along with a clever argument to show that they're wrong. As a way of making real and deep changes in society, this shouting and arguing is mostly a waste of time.

It certainly has been so in education. As I said earlier, I and many others have for many years now been arguing about education with the X-bound majority, both among educators and the general public. In any large sense, this arguing has had no result whatever. Only a very few schools ever changed in the ways we proposed, few changed for long, and most are worse now than ever. What our talk does seem to have done is to help a small number of people to make truly radical changes in their work and their lives, to desert the X-bound army and strike off in directions of their own.

But are these kinds of small-scale personal changes political, that is, do they or could they help to bring about change in society as a whole? It depends. Are the things these people are doing things that many others, not rich nor powerful nor otherwise unusual, *could* do if they wanted, without undue risk or sacrifice? And are these people, as they change their lives, telling others about what they are doing and how they might also do it? Private action, however radical and satisfying, only becomes political when it is made known.

In other words, private or small-group actions are political if they have the power to *multiply*. When I used to urge people who did not like their local schools to start schools of their own, this seemed a political act, because it then looked as if almost anyone who wanted to could do the same. But we now know that if by "school" we mean a special learning place, not used for anything else, with full-time paid teachers, to run even a very small school takes far more money than most people have or can raise. As I write, one of the best small alternative schools in this area, after more than ten years of good work, has just closed its doors because it can no longer find the money to keep alive. Such schools have little power to multiply, while homeschooling does. No doubt to teach one's own children also takes special qualities. But these are qualities that many more people have, or with a little help, can get.

These qualities themselves can multiply. Though many unschoolers may not think of themselves this way, they are in the truest sense leaders. Leaders are not what many people think—people with huge crowds following them. Leaders are people who go their own way without caring, or even looking to see whether *anyone* is following them. "Leadership qualities" are not the qualities that enable people to attract followers, but those that enable them to do without them. They include, at the very least, courage, endurance, patience, humor, flexibility, resourcefulness, determination, a keen sense of reality, and the ability to keep a cool and clear head even when things are going badly.

This is the opposite of the "charisma" that we hear so much about. Charismatic leaders make us think, "Oh, if only I could do that, be like that." True leaders make us think, "If they can do that, then by golly I can too." They do not make people into followers, but into new leaders. The homeschooling movement is full of such people, "ordinary" people doing things that they never would have thought they could do—learning the law, questioning the experts, holding their ground against arrogant and threatening authorities, defending themselves and their convictions in the press, on TV, even in court. Seeing them, other ordinary people think they can do the same, and soon they do.

This is why it may be a little misleading to speak of the homeschooling "movement." Most people think of a movement as something like an army, a few generals and a great many buck privates. In the movement for homeschooling, everyone is a general.

AN IRONY

Just the other day someone sent us a news story about a working-class father in Philadelphia who found through his own investigation that on an average day more than half the students at his son's public junior high school were truant, a rate much higher than the official figure. Feeling that in many ways this must be lowering the quality of his son's school, the father demanded that the school authorities do something to cut down this truancy. The authorities, naturally, led him a dance through all the corridors of the school bureaucracy. For a year or more he tried to get someone in the school system to go after these truants, or even to confirm his estimate about how much truancy there really was. He got absolutely nowhere. Finally in desperation he took the story to the papers. Whether he ever got satisfaction, I don't know.

My point here is that in a year of hard work this father had not been able to get the schools to do anything about the serious truancy in his son's school. But suppose he had finally said in disgust, "I'm tired of begging you to put your schools in shape; I'm going to take my kid out and teach him at home." The schools would have had the police on his doorstep in a matter of days.

✊ The overall truancy rate has gone down in some cities in recent years, according to school officials, but in other cities truancy has become even worse. Yet the irony persists. For example, one homeschooling family was reported to a state department of social services for nutritional and educational neglect because the informant noted that the family was vegetarian and homeschooling; the family was found innocent after an investigation by the social service department.

Fortunately, such cases are not common, but they do occur. One wonders why the questions of "Why weren't these kids in school?" and "What food do you eat?" are asked so quickly of a homeschooling family when truancy and hunger continue to plague far more children in public school. The most visible effort being made by the government regarding truancy is to further regulate family life through the threat of punishment: In some states, parents are being held responsible, fined, and punished for their children's truancy.

The U.S. Justice Department wrote, in September 2001, that schools are using juvenile courts to handle a much greater number of truancy cases than ever before: "In 1998 truancy accounted for 26 percent of all formally handled status of offense cases, representing an 85-percent increase in truancy cases in juvenile court since 1989 (from 22,200 in 1989 to

41,000 cases in 1998)." To mitigate this increase, the Department of Justice reported how Arizona created an amendment to the state constitution that "strengthened the enforcement of the existing compulsory school attendance statutes by creating criminal fines and penalties for parents."[2]

The move to prosecute truancy can net homeschooled families, too, and a few instances of this has occurred over the past decade, usually when the authorities have decided to crack down on truants and find unchaperoned, homeschooled youngsters outside the home. As a result, in a few districts across the United States, homeschoolers need special ID cards to permit them to be in public during school hours, or they must be in the company of a parent. The infringement on personal liberties that ID cards and public questioning by police can cause are easily justified by school officials and politicians as an unforeseen consequence of their fight against truancy. However, if you encounter a motion in your town or city to create a daytime curfew to deal with truancy problems, don't take this bland justification lying down. Some homeschoolers have successfully fought these regulations when they've been proposed.

Prosecution and curfews may seem like reasonable responses to truancy by school authorities, and such responses are likely to proliferate given the enthusiasm of public support for them. But such a sledgehammer policy is only destined to injure innocent parties in many ways, mostly unintended but nonetheless injurious, as noted with homeschooling. We know how to wield the stick in education but seem to have forgotten what carrots even look like. For instance, the Juvenile Justice Department explicitly refers to school as "the carrot" when discussing their conception of the "carrot and stick approach to truancy." This reasoning makes it impossible for alternatives to school to be considered, let alone inform, decisions about truancy and public education. The social and personal reasons that school may not be viewed as a carrot by many children and their families are not addressed by lawyers simply declaring school the "carrot."

Furthermore, like the father in Philadelphia, I discovered that finding hard numbers about truancy is more difficult than you think. For instance, there is no national truancy data, and schools are slow to report accurate figures. However, news accounts from local and state sources about truancy can give us an idea about how large this issue is. According to the *Detroit Free Press* (2/4/2000):

Reducing Detroit's truancy rate is the "cornerstone" of the city's school reform efforts . . . . City officials are using established truancy laws that have never been tested before. Students with the worst records as truants and their families are being hauled to court in an attempt to reduce the high rate of truancy that plagues the city—nearly 40% of the district's 167,400 students.

The *parentingteens.com* Web site posts these numbers collated from reputable national education agencies and the Crime and Disorder Act:

In Pittsburgh, each day approximately 3,500 students or 12 percent of the pupil population is absent and about 70 percent of these absences are unexcused . . .

In Philadelphia, approximately 2,500 students a day are absent without an excuse . . .

In Milwaukee, on any given school day, there are approximately 4,000 unexcused absences . . .

In addition, conventional school reform programs such as the year-round school movement and the increase in dual-enrollment programs, wherein high school students can attend community college classes, are further blurring the line of when a person under the age of sixteen is truant when they appear in public during school hours. Unfortunately, rather than seek to win back truants, schools seek to compel them back and publicly shame their families at the same time. If we could spend money and focus on providing more alternatives to school rather than on penalizing people for not being in a school, we might learn what sorts of opportunities and needs these children and their families really have and want addressed.

Homeshooling gives us some clues about what these places can be like right now. One story that stays with me from *GWS* was published in 1994. In it Kathryn Miller Ridiman of Kentucky writes:

At home I was battered and demeaned—or at best ignored . . . . At school, I was an outsider, having a heavy Appalachian accent and a rural focus on life . . . . My real life, where I was competent, nurtured, and accepted, took place far from my school and family.

Kathryn Ridiman then describes how, at fifteen, she was able to become a manager at a suburban riding stable. In response, *GWS* editor Susannah Sheffer wrote:

> Of course kids who have a difficult home life need some kind of haven, some kind of place where they feel "competent, nurtured, and accepted." Many of them never get this, but I would certainly wish it for them. I can believe that for some kids school is a haven, or at least a place that is preferable to being at home. I can't believe that schools see themselves primarily as havens, however. If you were designing a haven for troubled kids, a place where they were more likely to feel competent and accepted than they were at home, would you design it as schools are now designed, with tests, grades, and very little chance to do real work, etc.? If we understand what Kathryn got out of working at the stable, we can see how few of the elements that were present there were present in school.
>
> But again, even if schools are indeed havens for some kids, for many other kids they are another place to feel humiliated, unappreciated, stupid, incompetent, and cut off from their real concerns. The question that seems crucial to me is, how can we give kids access to many different kinds of places, besides either school or home, so that when home is miserable and school presents its own set of frustrations, there is an alternative?[3]

Forcing kids back to the same situation they were fleeing is self-defeating to the school and the child; can't we help them find what they aren't getting in school instead? Doing so is surely a difficult and costly task, but so is putting every school-age child in America under increased surveillance. ☙

WHOM DO SCHOOLS HELP?

School people believe sincerely and even passionately that schools were invented to give, and do give, poor children a better chance to rise in society. We need to understand why this is rarely so, or likely ever to be so.

When we have in a country a few rich and powerful people, and many poor and weak, the rich naturally want to make sure, or as sure as they can, that their children will not be among the poor. To be able to do this is one of the most important benefits of being rich. One way to do it is to make knowledge, and so, access to power, privilege, and possessions, scarce, expensive, and hard to get. This is part of what schools do, and they do it in every country in the world, no matter what may be their political ideas and labels.

Today, in the U.S., many people in the fast-growing field of solar energy do not have college degrees in it. Much of the work and much of the most important work, is being done by small businesses, backyard inventors, hobbyists, amateurs. Anyone can find out what is known and can join in the work. The colleges and universities are only just beginning to give degrees in solar energy. Ten years from now many (but still not all) of the people in the field will have these degrees. When there are enough of them, they, and the colleges and universities which gave them their degrees, will begin to try to get laws passed and arrangements made saying that you can't do important work in solar energy *unless* you have a degree. They will, in short, try to turn one more field of human invention and action into a "profession," a legal monopoly, which only those can do who have had a lot of expensive schooling.

This has already happened in the law, as in many other fields. Abraham Lincoln, and many others, did not learn law by going to law school, but by reading law books. Until recently people used to speak, not of "studying" law, but of "*reading* the law." (In England, studying law is still called "reading law.") It was always possible for poor boys (more rarely girls) to become lawyers by reading the law, and then working in law offices, doing lowly jobs at first, but learning more and being given more responsibility as they learned, and perhaps in the long run setting up their own law offices. No doubt even then the sons of the rich had a big advantage. But the poor at least had a way in. Not anymore. In many or most states, you can't practice law or even take the bar exams unless you have been to law school—and there are many more people trying to get into law school than there are places for them.

Beyond this, the "good" jobs in law go, almost without exception, to the graduates of "good" law schools, most of them graduates of "good," i.e., expensive colleges. A few poor kids may make it through this obstacle race, just enough to fool people into thinking that it is a fair race. The vast majority are shut out. In fact, most poor people feel that, because they can't afford the schooling, their children are shut out of even such less prestigious careers as nursing. Yet almost everything that people now can't do without a degree, often an advanced degree, was not so long ago done by people without such degrees. How and where did they learn what they knew? They learned, like Lincoln, by reading books, by using their eyes and ears, by asking questions, by working with or for people who knew more.

Schools like to say they create and spread knowledge. It would be closer to the truth to say that they collect and hoard knowledge, corner the market on it if they can, so that they can sell it at the highest possible price. That's why they want everyone to believe that only what is learned in school is worth anything. But this idea, as much as any other, freezes the class structure of society and locks the poor into poverty.

One of the many fringe benefits of being rich and powerful, in any society, is that you are able to say that some kinds of knowledge, i.e., the kind of things *you* know, are much more important than others, and therefore, that the people who know these things, i.e., you and your friends, are much more important and deserving than people who know other things. It is easy to see why in any society the most powerful people, whether the rich or simply high government officials, should want to say that the kind of knowledge that most people pick up from everyday life and work is worth less than the kind that can only be picked up in special places, particularly when they control the access to those places.

A LIFE-TAUGHT MAN

In his book *Travels Around America* Harrison Salisbury described his efforts to trace the Westward path of some of his ancestors. He describes one of them thus:

He [Hiram Salisbury] was a man of this time [1815]. . . . I scan the journal for clues and reconstruct the post-Revolutionary American. I list his skills, one sheet of scratch paper after another. He knew every farm chore. He milked cows and attended the calves in birth. He physicked his horse. He plowed, he planted, he cultivated, hayed, picked apples, grafted fruit trees, cut wheat with a scythe, cradled oats, threshed grain with a flail on a clay floor. He chopped the corn and put down his vegetables for winter. He made cider and built cider mills. He made cheese and fashioned cheese tongs. He butchered the hogs and sheared the sheep. He churned butter and salted it. He made soap and candles, thatched barns and built smokehouses. He butchered oxen and constructed ox sledges. He fought forest fires and marked out the land. He repaired the crane at Smith's mill and forged a crane for his own fireplace to hang the kettle on. He collected iron in the countryside and smelted it. He tapped (mended) his children's shoes and his own. He built trundle beds, ox-carts, sleighs, wagons, wagon wheels and wheel spokes. He turned logs into boards and cut locust wood for picket fences. He made house frames, beams, mortised and pegged. With six men's help he raised the frames and built the houses. He made a neat cherry stand with a drawer for a cousin, fixed clocks and went fishing. He carved his own board measures (yardsticks) and sold them for a dollar apiece. He fitted window cases, mended locks, and fixed compasses. He hewed timber, surveyed the forest, wrote deeds and shaved shingles. He inspected the town records and audited the books of the Friendship Lodge, the oldest freshwater Masonic lodge in the country (still running). He chipped plows, constructed carding machines, carved gunstocks and built looms. He set gravestones and fashioned wagon hubs. He ran a bookstore and could make a fine coffin in half a day. He was a member of the state's General Assembly, overseer of the poor, appraiser of property and fellow of the town council. He made hoops by the thousand and also pewter faucets. For many years he collected the town taxes. . . .

I have not listed all of Hiram's skills but enough. I do not think he was an unusual man. Put me in Hiram's world and I would not last long. Put Hiram down in our world, he might have a little trouble with a computer, but he'd get the hang of it faster than I could cradle a bushel of oats.

I tend to agree with Harrison Salisbury that Hiram, though perhaps not an unusual man in his time, would be a most unusual one in ours, far more knowing, skillful, intelligent, resourceful, adaptive, inventive, and competent than most people we would find today, in either city or country, and no matter how schooled.

But the real question I want to raise and answer is how Hiram learned all those skills. To be sure, he did not learn them in school, nor in workshops or any other school-like activity. Almost certainly, he learned how to do all those kinds of work, many of them highly skilled, by being around when other people were doing them. But these people were not doing the work in order to teach Hiram something. Nobody raised a barn just so that Hiram could see how barns were raised. They raised it because they needed the barn. Nor did they say to him, "Hiram, as long as I have to raise this barn, you may as well come around and learn how it is done." They said, "Hiram, I'm raising a barn and *I need your help.*" He was there to help, not to learn—but as he helped, he learned.

Almost a century later John Dewey was to talk about "learning by doing." The way for young people to learn (for example) how pottery is made is not to read about it but to make pots. No argument about that. But making pots in school just to learn how it is done is still nowhere near as good as making pots (and learning from it) because *someone needs the pots.* The best incentive to learn how to do good work, and to do it, is to know that the work has to be done, that it is going to be of real use to someone.

In his essay, "Intellect," Emerson spoke eloquently about the worth of the knowledge of ordinary people:

> Each mind has its own method. A true man never acquires after college rules. What you have aggregated in a natural manner surprises and delights when it is produced. For we cannot oversee each other's secret. And hence the differences between men in natural endowment are insignificant in comparison with their common wealth. Do you think the porter and the cook have no anecdotes, no experiences, no wonders for you? Everybody knows as much as the savant. The walls of rude minds are scrawled all over with facts, with thoughts. They shall one day bring a lantern and read the inscriptions.

UNSCHOOLING AND THE WORKING CLASS

On the matter of who can unschool, a mother and teacher wrote me a very interesting letter. Here are some of her remarks, and my comments:

> The only people who can hope to get their kids out of the schools safely are upper- or middle-class whites.

This is not necessarily so, and not even so in fact. Some of the people who right now have their children out of school are not middle class at all. A number are mothers on welfare. Only a week or so ago I talked with a woman who some years ago ran a paid tutoring service in San Francisco for parents whose families were not in school. She told me that about *70 percent* of her clients had been working-class families. I don't know whether these people had taken their children out of school with the school's consent, or whether they had simply hidden their children from the schools. I remember her saying that it seemed as if every bus driver in the city had his kids out of school. I asked her why they had taken their children out. She said that in almost every case the schools were not helping these children learn and were saying that they were incapable of learning. Some families simply refused to accept this and began teaching or having their children taught at home.

> Working-class, and especially black, parents who take their children out of school are likely to be hounded by the authorities to the fullest possible extent.

First, the fact is that quite a few white, middle-class, and professional families have already been hounded by the authorities to the fullest possible extent. If the schools are in a hounding mood, they'll hound anybody. Indeed, they may be more worried about losing middle-class children than poor children, since they need the support of middle-class people, much more than poor, in order to get more and more money. When I talk to school people about unschooling, one of the nightmares they bring up is that they might have only poor children in their schools.

In any case, the authorities won't make trouble if they don't know the children are out of school. This seems to be easier to manage in large cities than anywhere else. As we know, in all big cities large percentages of the children are truant every day. If it is that easy for kids just to hang out in the streets, it ought to be even easier for them to be at home (or somewhere) doing something interesting and worthwhile.

I don't deny that if and when parents get into an open dispute with the authorities, poor people, especially nonwhites, will have a harder time of it than middle-class whites. No argument about that at all. But much of the time it may be possible to avoid such open disputes.

> Poor kids need a high school diploma more than middle-class kids do— they have a much harder time getting a job without it.

I don't know how much a high school diploma helps really poor kids; they have a very rough time whether they have one or not. But let's agree for the sake of argument that poor kids badly need high school diplomas. The point is that people can get high school diplomas without actually being in a high school, by taking high school correspondence courses, or by passing an equivalency exam. Also, people who stay out of schools for a number of years can always go back in if they feel they need some kind of school ticket. Experience has shown that when they go back in, they are usually well ahead of those who stayed in.

> Working-class parents have less confidence in being able to teach their own kids (because if you're so smart why ain't you rich), and therefore in fact *are* less able to teach their kids.

It may be true, but in this matter the difference between middle-class and working-class families is not very great. Parents with graduate degrees have often said to me that they didn't know enough to teach their own young children. In any social class, there will be few people who think that they are capable of teaching their children and doing a better job than the schools. We have to begin with these, whatever class they may be in, and hope that others will follow their example.

✒ Since John wrote the above there have been some pretty amazing stories about poor or lower-income families successfully homeschooling. In a study conducted about homeschoolers in the state of Washington that published in 1992 were answers to questions about homeschooling's effect on the parents. One lady responded with this story about how she and her children learned together:

> To begin with, my math skills (or lack of skills) were an embarrassment to me. When I would shop for groceries I would pray the checkout clerk wouldn't cheat me because I wasn't sure if I would know. Playing card games was a challenge of how to act blasé as I let someone else add my score. I worried about my ability to teach my children and how to go about getting help when I couldn't keep up. My girls are fourth and fifth grade and I have done well. My own skills have grown in leaps and bounds. Having started at the beginning, I have an understanding of how and why [math works] that I missed as a child. I love math! I can figure out my change to be returned before the cashier rings it up. And I can even, on occasion, show them their mistake. So homeschooling has been a blessing to me.

Beth V., one of the mothers who wrote to *GWS* and had been home-schooling three children for five years, had an early life that is hardly the norm for a homeschooling mother. Beth grew up without her mother, was sexually abused from the age of five until she was fourteen, and became addicted to drugs by the age of thirteen. Her husband came from an abusive, impoverished, alcoholic family. He dropped out of school when he was sixteen and became a junkie a few years later. Somehow, Beth managed to graduate from high school, and she met her future husband at a drug den.

Fighting addiction was a terrible struggle for them both, particularly for the husband, but they both managed to give up drugs and create a family for themselves. Both are now sober, and have been for several years. However, her oldest son, Vinnie, was having difficulties in school, while both parents were struggling to put their lives in order. Beth writes:

A dear friend of mine had homeschooled through the Learning Community, a satellite program in Maryland, and I began to educate myself about this intriguing topic. During this same time, when I was beginning to learn about homeschooling, my husband and I were beginning to make the major changes in our lives that I have described. I knew that Vinnie's previous environment had much to do with his perfectionism and low self-esteem. I called Manfred Smith of the Learning Community and talked with him about the possibility of homeschooling Vinnie. My main concern was my husband's drug use, our messed up lives, and how Vinnie could possibly benefit from being home with screwed up parents. Manfred's reply was that a child who had suffered this type of lifestyle would often be better off outside of the school environment, which often compounds the already existing problems. Of course, I had explained to Manfred our goals of being a decent family and being open to learning new skills so that we could become better parents. This was very important, and if I hadn't made this clear, I can imagine that Manfred might not have been so encouraging of the idea of our homeschooling.

Homeschooling forced me to become the kind of parent I needed to be for homeschooling to work. When my kids were in school, I could do whatever I wanted, including taking drugs. That's how it felt to me. But now I knew that if I were making a commitment to homeschooling, my children's health and safety were the most important things, so I had to change my whole life . . .

Homeschooling was what prompted me to change, and now it's what helps me stay on track and be the kind of parent I want to be.

In 1975, in his book *Freedom and Beyond*, John Holt wrote that poverty "is not caused by poor people not having enough schooling and cannot be reduced or done away with by giving them much more schooling." Holt later points out that, "Raising the income of a poor man, whether by getting him a job or by guaranteeing him an income, will not improve his material standards of life unless something is also done to make available the things he needs, and at prices he can afford. There is ample evidence that the profit or market economy cannot do this . . . "

Twenty-seven years later these words still hold much truth. For instance, in public and private education there has been a steady increase in the amount of money spent and degrees earned since 1975, yet our rate of poverty slowly increases. Further, our inner-city schools, which often serve the poor in particular, continue to decline as the cost of schooling escalates. A study done in 2001 by the Lumina Foundation for Education found that "only five states have four-year public colleges that low-income students can afford without financial aid."[4]

Plenty of evidence, statistical and historical, reveals that school degrees do not necessarily translate into social mobility and economic parity. African Americans and women with bachelor's, master's, doctoral, and other professional degrees are still fighting to be recognized as equals in pay and prestige to their educated peers, even at our highly esteemed universities. The *New England Journal of Medicine* reported that babies born to college-educated blacks die at twice the rate of similarly educated whites; thus, being better educated does not mean that one's social and health conditions are better. Some difficult choices about how we spend our taxes will have to be made in the near future, and it would be wise for us not to be blinded by education's promoters to other, more direct, solutions.

Much more is involved in getting out of poverty and finding work than just doing well in school, though you wouldn't think that from all the advertising we're bombarded with about the economic value of staying in school. Humanistic or personal development themes rarely occur in "stay-in-school" ads. Educationists emphasize making more money or getting a better job as the main reason to stay in school, though this argument is becoming more difficult to maintain as time advances and as more and more people graduate with college degrees. Now, as I write in early 2002, we are in the midst of a recession that is striking college graduates far more than high school graduates; in Massachusetts unemployment rose 114 percent for college graduates during 2001 compared to a 51-percent increase in unemployment for high school graduates.[5] Increasingly, schooling is not a vaccine against poverty, nor does an expensive four-year degree give you a guarantee of good work for the years to come.

UNSCHOOLING AND THE SINGLE PARENT

When Holt originally wrote the above chapter, he quoted two letters from single moms, and included a long reply to a self-described "feminist single mother" who wanted ideas about how she could homeschool her six-year-old daughter while she was also studying and teaching law. John's reply was full of useful ideas, including preparing the child for more independence and enlisting an older child to help. Rather than reprint Holt's somewhat conjectural reply, I thought having recent single-parent homeschoolers describe their arrangements would be more appropriate today. (Resources for single parents interested in homeschooling are also provided in the back of this book.)

Typically, single parents who homeschool find jobs in which their children are able to accompany them to the work site, or they're able to work at home. For example, Derrick Simpson decided to adopt his son Fasika as a single parent and homeschool him. Mr. Simpson had to make some deliberate choices to accommodate this arrangement:

> I design computer systems for the health-care industry . . . I work from my home. I designed my life this way because I knew that as a single parent, I was not going to adopt a child and then put him in day care. So I work with clients over the phone or via e-mail. When I have to go into the hospital once a week to meet with someone directly, Fasika goes with me, and he has made friends with some of the children in the hospital. He enjoys helping them, working with them on computers, and it's a good feeling for him to be helping.

Single parents often rely on older children, sitters, relatives, or close friends to watch their young children when they need to be away for work. Many parents find they can help their children to be independent and self-reliant as young as eight to ten years of age so that they can be left alone for a few hours at a time, if necessary. Teenage homeschoolers are able to be even more self-reliant, and are often involved in outside activities, such as volunteer work, music lessons, or clubs, that don't need as much parental involvement.

But to a single parent, homeschooling is more than just arranging childcare and learning opportunities. Diane McNeill of Wisconsin writes:

> An issue for me is being isolated. It's been a struggle for me to take time away from my kids and spend it on myself. Single parents have to carry

that burden of guilt about wanting to meet the needs of the kids all the time. We don't have anybody to hand it off to. But if you don't take care of yourself, you won't be able to take care of the kids as well. I've learned to say to the kids, "I've got to do this for myself." I joined a choir, and sometimes I will say, "I can't do that tonight, I've got rehearsal." They don't argue with me about this, and I can tell by their response that they're happy I'm going out to do things for myself. They don't like to see their parent dragging around saying, "I give you everything but I don't get anything for myself." It's really hard on them to have a parent feeling that way, so it's better for all of us if I have a couple of things that I do for myself.

Christine Willard, whose husband died when their daughter was three, wrote about the isolation and financial stress she feels as a single mom, and how she is successfully working through these issues:

As a mother and a daughter, we are the absolute minimum family group, and sometimes it is rather claustrophobic. We are always with each other. On the other hand, we have simply had to learn to get along with each other. Issues can't go unresolved, because all we have is each other and we just have to be able to find common ground . . .

As my daughter grows up, she is branching out to other adults for relationships. She has always loved horses. After we moved, we were able to find a ranch where she could take lessons. She often wanted to spend time just hanging around the ranch, and we gradually got to know everyone who keeps a horse or takes lessons there. She became friendly with the ranch manager and helped him feed all the horses. Then one day, a rather neglected old mare needed a home, and since we needed a pony, we found each other.

Having a horse has been a wonderful experience for us. It gives us a focus other than each other, and we have made many friends who share this interest. ☙

4

Living with Children

CHILDREN, THEIR NATURE AND NEEDS

MANY PEOPLE WHO QUITE like and enjoy children still seem to be in the grip of the old idea that in civilizing them we have to give up or destroy some important part of them. To me that idea seems mistaken and harmful. It simply is not true that every virtue is some kind of suppressed vice, or that civilized human beings are nothing but cowed savages. As Abraham Maslow used to say, this explains human virtues only by "explaining them away." Such explanations do not fit everyday experience. A famous child psychiatrist has long been quoted as saying that the infant is a psychopath. I take the side of a mother I know well, who after raising seven babies said, "Babies are nice people."

Paul Goodman once wrote of "the wild babytribe," an affectionate and accurate expression. Children do often seem to me like talented barbarians, who would really like to become civilized. Many free schools, and some kindly and well-meaning parents, have suffered from the notion that there was something wild and precious in children that had to be preserved against the attacks of the world for as long as possible. Once we get free of this idea we will find our lives with children much easier and the children themselves much happier. As I write this,

I have spent much time recently with young babies, and my over-whelming impression is that basically they want to fit in, take part, and do right—that is, do as we do. If they can't always do it, it is because they lack experience, and because their emotions sweep them away.

Oddly enough, the reactionary view and the romantic liberal view of children are like opposite sides of the same coin. The hard-nosed types say that to fit children for the world we have to beat the badness out of them. The romantic child-worshippers say that in fitting children for the world we destroy most of the goodness in them. One group claims that children are undersized and defective adults; the other, that adults are oversized and defective children. Neither is true. There really are ways to help children, as they grow, to keep and build on all their best qualities. How we may do this is the subject of this chapter.

We can learn much from *The Continuum Concept*, by Jean Liedloff, as important a book as any I have ever read. Liedloff (along with a number of others—Leboyer, Montagu, Bowlby, etc.) says and *shows* that babies grow best in health, happiness, intelligence, inde-pendence, self-reliance, courage, and cooperativeness when they are born and reared in the "continuum" of the human biological experi-ence, i.e., as "primitive" mothers bear and rear their babies, and prob-ably always have through all the millions of years of human existence. What babies have always enjoyed, needed, and thrived on, for the first year or so of their lives, until they reach the crawling and exploring stage, is constant *physical* contact with their mothers (or someone equally well known and trusted).

Babies have always had this, at least up until the last thousand years or so, and each newborn baby, knowing nothing of history but every-thing of his own animal nature, expects it, wants it, needs it, and suf-fers terribly if he does not get it.

Here, in only one of many passages of extraordinary vividness and sensitivity, is Liedloff's description of the early life of a baby among the Yequana Indians of the Amazon basin, with whom she lived for some time:

From birth, continuum infants are taken everywhere. Before the um-bilicus comes off, the infant's life is already full of action. He is asleep most of the time, but even as he sleeps he is becoming accustomed to the voices of his people, to the sounds of their activities, to the bumpings, jostlings, and moves without warning, to stops without warning, to lifts and pressures on various parts of his body as his caretaker shifts him about to accommodate her work or her comfort, and to the rhythms of day and night, the changes of texture and temperature on his skin, and the safe, right feel of being held next to a living body.

The result of this kind of treatment is not, as most modern people might expect, a timid, clinging, whiny, dependent infant, but the exact opposite. Liedloff writes:

When all the shelter and stimulus of his experience in arms have been given in full measure, the baby can look forward, outward, to the world beyond his mother. . . . The need for constant contact tapers off quickly when its experience quota has been filled, and a baby, tot, or child will require reinforcement of the strength it gave him only in moments of stress with which his current powers cannot cope. These moments become increasingly rare and self-reliance grows with a speed, depth, and breadth that would seem prodigious to anyone who has known only civilized children deprived of the complete in-arms experience.

As Liedloff shows, children so reared very quickly notice what people are doing around them, and want to join in and take part as soon and as far as their powers permit. No one has to *do* anything in order to "socialize" the children, or *make* them take part in the life of the group. They are born social, it is their nature. One of the most peculiar destructive ideas that "civilized" people have ever invented is that children are born bad and must be threatened and punished into doing what everyone around them does. No continuum culture expects children to be bad as a matter of course, to misbehave, to make trouble, to refuse to help, to destroy things, and cause pain to others, and in cultures with long traditions of child-rearing these common (to us) forms of child behavior are virtually unknown.

Some years ago a group of American child experts went to China to study Chinese children, child-rearing, and schools. To their Chinese counterparts they eagerly asked what *they* did when their children had tantrums, fought, teased, whined, broke things, hurt people, etc. The Chinese looked at them with baffled faces. The Americans might as well have asked, "What do you do when your children jump three hundred feet straight up in the air?" The Chinese could only say over and over, "Children don't do those things." The American visitors went away equally baffled. It never occurred to them to suppose that one reason Chinese children are not bad in the way so many of ours seem to be is that nobody expects them to be. Being small, ignorant, inexperienced, and passionate, they may now and then stray off the path of good behavior. But correcting them is only a matter of patiently pointing out that they *have* strayed, that here we don't do things like that. No one assumes that their deep intent is to do wrong, and that only a long hard struggle will break them of that intent and force them to do right.

In short, the problem children of the affluent Western world are as much a product of our culture as our automobiles. What we call psychology, our supposed knowledge of "human nature," is and can only be the study of the peculiar ways of severely deprived people, so far from the norms of long-term human biological experience that it would not be stretching matters to call them (us) freaks. Liedloff's description of "modern," "medical," "scientific" childbirth, and the ensuing days and months as a baby must experience them, is enough to make one weep, or have nightmares, or both. It's a wonder we're no worse off than we are.

But I wish that Ms. Liedloff had said early in the book what she finally says at the end, that some or many of the most harmful effects of severe early deprivation (of closeness and contact) can be largely made up for or cured if a human being is richly supplied with these necessities, in ways she suggests, later in life. This is important. Many sensitive and loving mothers and fathers who bore and raised children in the modern "civilized" way, upon reading this book and realizing what they had unknowingly denied their children, might be almost overwhelmed by guilt and grief. With enough kindness, tenderness, patience, and courtesy, one can make up for much of this early loss.

It is impossible for me to say how important I think this book is. For most of the past twenty-five years it has become clearer to me all the time that our worldwide scientific and industrial civilization, for all its apparent wealth and power, was in fact moving every day closer to its total destruction. What is wrong? What can we do? Many people have pointed toward some useful answers. But only in the last year or two has it become clear to me that one of the most deep-rooted of the causes of our problems is the way we treat children, and above all babies. I am equally convinced that no program of social and political change that does not include and begin with changes in the ways in which we bear and rear children has any chance of making things better.

I hope that many people will read *The Continuum Concept*, the more the better, and above all mothers and fathers of young children and babies, parents-to-be, people who have no children but think someday they might, young marrieds or marrieds-to-be, teen-agers, baby-sitters, older brothers and sisters of babies, and also doctors, nurses, psychologists, etc. In short, anyone who may have any contact with, or anything to do with, babies or little children. The human race, after all, changes with every new generation, and only a generation or two of healthy and happy babies might be enough to turn us around.

BORN KIND

From a letter to an old friend of mine, an elementary school teacher:

> Loved being with your kindergarten class. I don't remember when I have ever struck up so strong a friendship with a child so quickly as I did with Molly. Our conversation was very serious, the kind of talk you might expect to have with someone much older. Above all, I was so touched with her concern about me. At one point—I didn't tell you this—I was squatting down beside a table at which some of the children were working. After a long time I stood up, and as is always the case, I was a little stiff, and took a few seconds to get the kinks in my knees and back straightened out. Molly and a couple of the others asked me what I was doing, and I explained that when people my age squat down for a long time they tend

to get a little stiff. It must have been at least an hour later, when I was again squatting down beside some children, that Molly said to me, "Don't squat down too long." Surprised, I said, "Why not?" She said, "You'll get stiff." I had forgotten all about the earlier time. Then, as I said to you, when she saw where I had bumped and scratched the top of my head a week or so earlier in Maine, she was very concerned, wanted to know how I had done it, and did it hurt. This is much more empathy than I would have expected from such a little person, much as I like them.

◖ All of John Holt's books contain ideas and advice for adults to live and learn with children, but often in subtle and unconventional ways. For instance, the observation that children are "born kind" is not the same as they're being born without need of any moral upbringing as they are innately good. In our office I heard John talk angrily about people who he felt belonged in jail, who were just "bad cats" (John's phrase for such people), and children who were willfully bad in some pretty awful ways. He didn't view all people as innately good; he didn't view all people as innately bad, either. He simply wanted us to recognize that there is a tendency toward kindness present in children to which they respond, and that working with that tendency, rather than ignoring it, quashing it, or distorting it, can make living and learning with children easier for us all. The chances that good behavior, character, and morals will take root in an atmosphere of kindness are much better than if we assume the worst in children and use kindness only as a reward for good behavior, rather than the norm for our relationships. ◗

ON SAYING "NO"

Since few of us raise children in continuum ways, most of us still have the task of teaching them to live by our rules. We tend to make this task much more difficult than it needs to be, not least of all by the way in which we use the word "No."

Not long ago I visited a friend who had a beautiful, lively, affectionate year-old Husky pup. He had only one fault. He loved to be petted, and if you had been petting him, and stopped, or if he had just come up to you, he would put his paw up on your leg, let it fall, put it up again, and so over and over until you did *something*. This dirtied clothes, scratched skin, and hurt. His owner had tried now and then to break him of this habit, by scolding him, pushing him away, or whatever, but it hadn't done much good. He was too busy with his work to spend much time on it. One day I thought that as long as I was visiting, had some time, and loved the pup, I would see if I could break him of this habit.

So every time he came up to me I would pat him for a while and then stop and wait, my hand poised to block his paw when it came up. When he raised it, I would catch it a few inches off the floor and lower it gently to the ground, saying at the same time just as gently, "No, no, keep the paw on the floor." Then I would pat him, say what a nice dog he was, and after a while stop again. Soon the paw would come up once more, and I would catch it and go over the whole thing once again. Sometimes I would do this with him sitting, sometimes with him standing. After a few repeats I would back away from him; then, as he came toward me, I would say in a gentle but warning voice, "Now, keep those paws down," or "Now remember, four on the floor." I would have my hand ready to catch the paw when it rose, which at first it always did. But before long he began to get the idea, and quite often the tone of my voice, the sound of my words, and perhaps the position of my body and hand, would be enough to remind him, and he would keep the paw down. I was only there for a few days, and can't claim that I broke him of the habit altogether. But he was certainly much better about it, and usually only one warning and paw-catch would be enough to remind him.

The point is that even a young dog is smart enough to know that "No" does not have to be just a *signal*, an explosion of angry noise. It can be a word, conveying an idea. It does not have to say, "You're a bad dog, but we're going to beat the badness out of you." It can say instead, "You're a good dog, but this thing that you're doing isn't what we do around here, so please don't do it anymore." Even a young dog can understand that, and act on it.

And if a dog, why not a child? Except in rare times of great stress or danger, there is no reason why we cannot say "No" to children in just as kind and gentle a tone as we say "Yes." Both are *words*. Both convey ideas which even tiny children are smart enough to grasp. One says, "We don't do it that way," the other says, "That's the way we do it." Most of the time, that is what children want to find out. Except when overcome by fatigue, or curiosity, or excitement, or passion, they want to do right, do as we do, fit in, take part.

Soon after my visit with friend and dog, I visited two other friends, and their delightful fifteen-month-old boy. Around dinner time, in the little kitchen-dining room, I took out my cello and began to play. The baby was fascinated, as I hoped he would be. He stopped what he was doing and came crawling across the floor toward the cello at top speed. His parents looked a bit nervous, but I said, "Don't worry, I'll defend the cello, I won't let him hurt it." He came to the cello, pulled himself up to a standing position, and began to touch and pluck at the strings, below the bridge. At the same time, keeping the bow (which he might have been able to damage) out of his reach, I plucked the cello strings above the bridge, which made nice sounds. Now and then I could see that he was being overcome with a wave of excitement, and that he wanted to bang on the cello, as little babies like to bang on things. But when his hands began to make these impulsive gestures, I would catch them, like the paw of the pup, and slow them down, saying softly, "Gently, gently, easy, easy, be nice to the cello." When his motions grew smaller and calmer I would take my hands away. For a while he would caress the wood and pluck at the strings. Then he would begin to get excited again. But as soon as he did I would catch and slow down his hands again, saying as before, "Gently, gently, nice and easy." After a while he would crawl away, while I talked with his parents. Then I would play some more, and he would come crawling over for more looking and touching. I might have to say, "Gently, gently," once or twice, but hardly more than that. Most of the time this tiny boy, still just a baby, was as gentle and careful with the cello as I was. And all this in only one evening, the first time he had ever seen such a strange and fascinating object.

Louise Andrieshyn, a parent in Manitoba, says about this:

You've made an excellent point about the difference between "No" the angry signal and "No" the meaningful word. . . . There is a third kind of

"No," perhaps the most common of all, neither an angry explosion nor a meaningful word—the no, no, no that goes on all day with some parents. This constant hassling is simply a running, ineffective banter. The parents don't even *mean* it; there's no anger or even much reprimand in their voices . . . our cultural expectation is that kids are bad, always getting into trouble, and parents must be dictators controlling their kids (in the name of "protection").

How to cope with these 3 kinds of "No" is much more difficult, though, than you make it sound.

You're saying, if we can become aware of how we use "No" we can change our use of it. . . .

As parents, we can simply SHUT UP! If we can sit back and listen to ourselves, we can hear how much negative harassment we throw at our kids. If a parent would seriously and objectively listen to what he says (through his child's ears), he would be appalled and could probably with some effort change that kind of "No."

I think here of Lisey (then 3) who was pouring herself a glass of milk yesterday. She had gotten it from the fridge, opened it, poured from a fat 2-quart carton a very small juice-glass of milk, had drunk it, then had gotten a paper towel and was wiping up the milk spilt on the table. There was more milk spilt than the towel could absorb so as she wiped now, the milk was being pushed off the table onto the floor.

I walked in at this point and started with the running "No, No" commentary in a whiny voice: "Ooooh no, Lisey, you should have asked someone to pour you a glass of milk—no, don't wipe it up, it's going on the floor, now stop, don't do it, I'll do it, it's bad enough on the table—look, now you've got it on the floor—you're making more work for me."

Happily at this point I was struck by a rare beam of sanity and it said to me, "Oh, quit being such a bitch, Lisey has just poured her first glass of milk all by herself and you're ruining the whole thing for her."

And suddenly I looked and saw a very little girl trying very hard to grow up—trying to wipe up herself the mess she had made getting herself a drink of milk. And I said, "Lisey, I think Sparkle (dog) would like this extra milk."

Lisey stopped and looked at me. I had finally said something of meaning. All the negative harassment up till then she had been trying to ignore.

I said, "If you get Sparkle's dish we can put the milk in it."

She got it and we did.

AND immediately she began an animated chatter about how Sparkle would like this milk and how she had poured them both a drink of milk, etc. Until then, she had barely said one word. In fact, if I had pushed her far enough—"OK, Lisey, get out of the kitchen while I clean up your mess"—she would have probably ended up crying (over spilt milk!).

But the happy ending here did not require too much effort on my part because I wasn't very emotionally involved. My mind could still be objective about the situation to the extent of being able to control and change it.

TESTING ADULTS

In his very good book, *Growing With Your Children*, Herbert Kohl—like just about everyone who writes about children—says that they have to keep testing adults in order to find limits. I absolutely disagree. They do it all the time, no question about that. But I don't think they *have* to do it, or do it primarily for that reason, and I don't think we ought to let them do it. If they want to find out, as they do, the rules of family life and human society, there are other and better ways to do it.

One year, when I was teaching fifth grade, I had a boy in my class who had been kicked out of his local public schools—no small feat. He was a perfectly ordinary-looking, middle-sized, middle-class white kid, didn't pull knives or throw furniture, no *Blackboard Jungle* stuff. It took me a while to understand *why* the public schools had shown him the door. In a word, he was an agitator, always stirring things up. One day, when everyone was trying to do something, I forget what, and he was trying to prevent them, or get them to do something else, I turned on him and shouted in exasperation, "Are you *trying* to make me sore at you?" To my great surprise, and his (judging from his voice), he said, "Yes." It took me a while to understand, or at least to guess, that he had learned from experience that the only way he could be sure of getting the undivided attention of other people, children or adults, was to make them sore at him.

As the year went on, he improved, became only difficult instead of impossible. But he was still a long way from being at peace with himself—the roots of his problem were deeper than I or my class could reach in a year. Our school only went through sixth grade; what became of him later I don't know. Meanwhile, he had taught me something valuable.

At about that time I was beginning to know the interesting but angry and difficult child of a friend. One day I was at their house, talking with his mother about something important to both of us. The boy kept interrupting, more even than usual. I knew by then that children hate to be shut out of adult talk, and tried from time to time to let this boy have a chance to speak. But on this day it was clear that he was trying to keep us from talking at all. Finally, looking right at him, I said, not angrily but just curiously, "Are you trying to annoy me?" Startled into honesty, like the other boy, by a question he had perhaps never really asked himself, he smiled sheepishly and said, "Yes." I said, still pleasantly, "Well, that's okay. Tell you what let's do. Let's play a game. You do everything you can think of to annoy me, and I'll do everything I can think of to annoy you, and we'll see who wins. Okay?" He looked at me for a while—he knew me well enough by this time to know that I would play this "game" in earnest. He considered for a while how it might go. A look at his mother showed that, for the time being at least, he could not expect much help from her if the game went against him. Finally he said, "No, I don't want to play." "Fine," I said. "Then let us have our conversation, and you and I can talk later." Which is what happened.

That was many years ago. From many encounters I have since had with many children, I have come to believe very strongly that children as young as five and perhaps even three are well able to understand the idea of "testing"—doing something to someone else or in front of someone else, knowing they don't like it, *just to see what that other person will do*, and to understand that this is not good. If I thought a child was doing this to me, I would say, "Are you testing me, just doing that to see what I will do?" If the child said "Yes" I would say, "Well, I don't like that, it's not nice and I don't want you to do it. I don't do bad things to *you* just to see what *you* will do. Then it's not fair for you to do that to me."

I think children are perfectly able to understand these ideas, to see that they are fair, and to act upon them. When they do, it will make our lives together much easier.

"OKAY?"

When adults want children to do something—put on coats, take a nap, etc.—they often say, "Let's put on our coats, okay?" or "It's time to take our naps now, okay?" That "Okay?" is a bad thing to say. Our lives with children would go better if we could learn to give up this way of talking.

The trouble with this "Okay?" is that it suggests to the children that we are giving them a choice when we really are not. Whatever people may think about how many choices we should give children, children should at least be able to know at any moment whether they have a choice or not. If we too often seem to be offering choices when we really aren't, children may soon feel that they never have any. They will resent this, and resent even more our not saying clearly what we mean. By giving what we intend as a command and then saying "Okay?" we invite resistance and rebellion. In fact, the only way children *can* find out whether or not we are offering a real choice is to refuse to do what we ask. It is their way of saying, "Do you really mean it?"

Many adults feel that in saying "Okay?" they are only being courteous. But this is a misunderstanding of courtesy. It is perfectly possible to be firm and courteous while making clear to someone that you are not offering a choice but telling them what you want to happen or is going to happen. When I visit friends, I expect to fit myself into their life and routines, and count on them to tell me what they are. So they say, "We get up at seven o'clock," or "We are going to have dinner at six-thirty," or "This afternoon we're going to this place to do such and such." They are not asking me whether I approve of these plans, just letting me know that they *are* the plans. But they are perfectly polite about this.

Some friends of mine have a No Smoking rule in their house. They are in earnest about this. Inside their front door is a sign saying "Thank You For Not Smoking." But every now and then a guest misses the sign, or takes it as a plea and not a command, and starts to light up. My friends gently but firmly inform their friend and guest that if he or she wants to smoke, the porch is the place to do it, but not in the house. No one argues, no one is offended.

Few adults seem to be able to talk to children in this way. In the Public Garden, or airports, or other places where adults and children gather, I hear hundreds of people telling their children to do things. Most of them begin with "Okay?" pleading and cajoling. If this doesn't work, they soon begin to threaten and shout. They can't seem to give a firm request without getting angry first. Then the child is genuinely confused and resentful, doesn't understand why the adults are angry, or what he has done to deserve the shouts and threats.

If a child really resists doing what you want, it may help to say, "I know you don't want to do what I am telling you to do, and I'm sorry that you don't, and sorry that you're angry, but I really mean for you to do it." It doesn't by any means solve all problems, and it may not even stop the child from being angry. But at least it makes clear where things stand. And of course, at such times we must not get angry at the children for being angry with us. We may have a right (as well as the power) to make children obey, but not to demand that they pretend to like it.

◖ John was always alert to the appearance of this dubious word. During the last two years of his life, he went to a great many hospitals and doctors seeking cures or relief from cancer. More than once I'd be sitting near his hospital bed when a nurse would come in and say, "We're just going to roll you over now, okay?" or, "It's time for your medicine, okay?" Sometimes John would shake his head and smile at me, other times he'd offer frustrated glances at the ceiling, and at some point he would just say, "I hate when they say 'okay'!" ◗

TANTRUMS

People who write about tantrums seldom give any strong sense that the anger of two-year-olds is *about* anything. One might easily get the impression that these little children are swept by gusts of irrational "aggression" and rage as the coasts of Florida are from time to time swept by hurricanes. Instead, I would insist that much of the seemingly irrational and excessive anger of little children—"tantrums"—is in fact not only *caused* by things that happen to them or that are said and done to them, but that these things would make *us* angry if they happened or were said and done to us. Even in the kindest and most loving families two-year-olds must be reminded a hundred times a day, perhaps by the words and acts of their parents, perhaps by events, by Nature herself, that they are small, weak, clumsy, foolish, ignorant, untrustworthy, troublesome, destructive, dirty, smelly, even disgusting. *They don't like it!* Neither would I. Neither would you.

On this subject, the mother of J, the little boy whom I described playing with my cello, wrote about his tantrums and how they were both learning how to avoid them.

J is great. No naps now which means he is super go-power all day with a huge collapse about 7:30. He has his room all to himself now, and he really likes to hang out in there alone for an hour and a half most days, driving trucks around mostly. I've never seen a kid more into organizing things. He plays with dominoes and calls them either adobes, for building houses, or bales of hay, and has them stacked, lined up, or otherwise arranged in some perfect order; same with the trucks; he'll scream and yell, as per your theory of two-year-old behavior, if you snatch him up from a group of trucks and carry him off to lunch. But if you give him a couple of minutes to park them all in a straight line then he'll come willingly. Your theory (treat them like big people) works out over and over again; brush past him, leave him behind in the snow when you're hustling up to feed the goats and you get a black and blue screaming pass out tantrum. Treat them "Big" and things roll along. Only hangup is the occasional times you have to take advantage of your superior size and pull a power play. The trick is to learn to avoid the situations that once in a while make that a necessity, like not getting in a rush, and not letting them get so tired they break down completely—like letting dinner be late.

One thing he gets mad about is being left behind by anybody. However, we just went on a trip. . . . I was quite nervous about leaving him with friends as he had been doing his falling down pass out tantrums for our benefit all week whenever anyone went to town without him (in spite of having the other parent on hand). But he just waved Bye Bye and went in the house and had a really good four days. As his father said, obviously he would only bother to pull the tantrum bit for us. He was very calm and very full of new games and words when we got him back, and I know he made progress on all fronts as a result of being away from us and with other interesting people.

. . . Later we were to go on a long trip down the river so we left him with some friends, but decided at the last minute our boats weren't sufficient to carry us and our gear on that rugged and remote a trip, so we picked up J and just went camping on the river, taking our boat and going on short hops along stretches of the river where the road was. Again he was super and loved being with grownups who ate with their fingers and mushed all their food up in one cup just like him. His father wanted him to go in the boat so he put him in a life jacket then tied a rope between them. J hated that and had all kinds of misgivings as water sloshed into the boat and he got wet and cold, but he didn't complain. Amazingly he just sat there and looked pissed off for about two hours. I think he was so glad to be included that he bore with the misery.

Susan Fitch applies this same sensible and respectful attitude to the often difficult issue of bedtime:

My husband and I have always been concerned with having "our" time so our son, Jesse's (4) bedtime was very important to us. Although he was very cooperative, Jesse did not enjoy the limited time he had with his father between his arrival and bedtime. This left everyone frustrated and unhappy.

One evening while I was reading GWS it occurred to me that he was perfectly capable of going to bed when he was tired. The next day we talked about being tired, how much sleep he needed, when to go to bed in order to wake up in time for playgroup, and about our need to talk with one another and have quiet times. The tension evaporated with his father, and he immediately assumed responsibility for getting un-dressed and brushing his teeth. Because of just this one letting go, our time alone and together follows a natural pattern that seems to satisfy everyone. . . .

I can't help noting that no cultures in the world that I have ever heard of make such a fuss about children's bedtimes, and no cultures have so many adults who find it so hard either to go to sleep or wake up. Could these social facts be connected? I strongly suspect they are.

COOKING AT TWO

Children are so much more capable than most adults realize. I sus-pect that children get hurt most often when doing things they are not supposed to do, in a spirit of defiance and excitement, rather than when doing something sensible and natural that they do often and like to do right.

The head of a big adventure playground in London once told me that as long as parents could come right into the playground, the chil-dren often hurt themselves, doing things to impress, scare, or defy their parents, but that once the parents were told that they had to wait for the children outside the playground (in a spot with chairs, benches, etc.) the accidents stopped.

I asked Susan Price, a parent in Florida how Matt learned to cook so young. She replied:

The stove. What could have become my first battle with Matt. He learned to turn the burners on. I said no, dangerous. Effect, naturally: *fun, interesting, do it all the time.* So I slapped his hand, slightly, grabbed him up, me in tears, was he, I don't even remember, holding him on the couch, what to do, what to do. Slowly it dawned on me. There wasn't a damned thing dangerous about him turning them on. I was always with him, could keep the stove cleared, his hand was way below the flames. What was I afraid of? *If people knew*, of course. So I let him turn them on, watched, kept my mouth shut. He turned them all on, went over to the table, stood on a chair and looked at them (he was so far below the flame he couldn't see them standing by the stove). How old was he? Less than sixteen months. Did this for a while, then a couple of times the next day, and *that was all*, never "played" with them again except to turn one on when he saw me getting a pan out to cook something in. Or after Faith was born to turn them on for himself, when he wanted to cook something. No, one other time when he was much older and his friend was over he thought it was funny to turn them on and see how afraid his friend became.

Why did he not respond to my "No, dangerous!"? Because there was no real fear in my voice. Children *will* respond to you when you say something's dangerous if you really are afraid they are going to get hurt *at that minute*. I read somewhere that you have to teach children to do what you say because if you don't they could be out in the street and a car coming and they wouldn't get out of the road when you yelled at them to. That's not the point at all. They're responding mostly to the fear in your voice in that situation, not to the fact that you're telling them to do something.

People are always worrying too much about the future, extrapolating out of the present, with children. They think, if I let them turn the burners on now, they'll always want to turn them on. . . .

My guess is that the main reason Matt no longer needs or wants to play with the stove is that *he can cook on it*. It isn't a toy any more, but a serious tool, that he and the grownups use every day. Before they know how to drive, and can drive, little children love to sit at the wheel of a parked car turning the steering wheel this way and that. But who ever saw a child doing that, *who could actually drive?* It would be baby stuff. And it would be baby stuff for Matt to play with the stove on which he and his younger sister regularly cook food that the whole family eats.

I suspect, too, that one reason that Matt responds so quickly to strong fear or other negative emotion in his mother's voice is that he doesn't often hear this kind of emotion. Children who constantly hear in the voices of adults the tones of fear, disgust, anger, threat, etc., soon take that tone of voice to be normal, routine, and turn it off altogether. They think, "Oh, that's just the way they always talk." Then, when we try to make them pay attention to some real danger, they no longer hear us at all.

◖◗ Jim and Pat Montgomery live in Ann Arbor, Michigan, where Pat has run her well-known Clonlara School for more than thirty years. During a recent weekend I spent with them, Jim explained to me that one of his hobbies was throwing knives, which he learned to do when he was about eight years old growing up in rural Mississippi. His grandfather had a bayonet that he took from a German soldier in World War I, and it became Jim's first, and favorite, knife for him to throw. In his backyard in Ann Arbor are stacks of logs that he uses for targets. So I was not surprised when, after being introduced to six-year-old Felix, their grandson, Felix said, "Do you want to see Grandpa's knives?"

When I said yes, Felix and his younger brother, Simon, almost three years old, fetched a bagfull of knives that Jim kept in the basement. Jim was building a fire in his fireplace, while Pat looked on and the boys showed me the knives. They handled them with great care while telling me to "be careful" as I held each knife, and explained that the edges of the blades were dull but the points were sharp. The young boys demonstrated to me how to find the center of balance for each knife, what makes each knife different from the others, and so on. I was impressed not only with how they handled the knives, but with how Pat and Jim weren't hovering over them, ready to snatch away the knives or fretting aloud, "Be careful!" I also noticed that Pat and Jim did get a bit concerned when the boys started stabbing a cardboard box that Jim was going to use for kindling— and then Jim said, "You shouldn't stab the boxes like that; you should put the point on the box like this and then push firmly." The boys were happy to comply, and they slowly stabbed the box into kindling for a few more minutes before putting away the blades.

Jim then told me that on Wednesdays he comes home at lunchtime so he can meet with students from Clonlara who want to learn knife throwing. It's hard to imagine, particularly for a city boy like me, that knives can be used safely and enjoyably to develop skill and confidence by young children. After all, the way I was raised, when I see a knife I don't associate it with *Little House on the Prairie*; I associate it with *West Side Story*! Of course, children earlier in the past century were probably far more comfortable using knives and other sharp tools than we can imagine. As Holt notes, children "are so much more capable than most adults realize." ☙

INSTEAD OF GOLD STARS

Unless warped by cruelty or neglect, children are *by nature* not only loving and kind but serious and purposeful. Whenever I hear school people say, "The students aren't motivated, how do I motivate them?" I think of the story about Margaret Mead and the Balinese.

This took place in the 1920s, when very few Westerners had ever been to Bali. Margaret Mead was talking to some Balinese, trying to learn about this strange and very different culture. At some point she asked about their art. The Balinese were puzzled by this question. They did not know what she meant by art. So she talked for a while about art and artists in Western cultures. The Balinese considered this for a while. Then one of them spoke. "Here in Bali we have no art," he said. "We do everything as well as we can."

Very little children are like the Balinese. Just about everything they do, they do as well as they can. Except when tired or hungry, or in the grip of passion, pain, or fear, they are moved to act almost entirely by curiosity, desire for mastery and competence, and pride in work well done. But the schools, and many adults outside of school, hardly ever recognize or honor such motives, can hardly even imagine that they exist. In their place they put Greed and Fear.

But what about people who have taken out of school children who have been numbed and crippled in spirit by years of "reinforcement," petty rewards and penalties, gold stars, M&M's, grades, Dean's Lists? How can unschoolers revive in their children those earlier, deeper, richer sources of human action? It is not easy. Perhaps the only thing to do is to be patient and wait. After all, if we do not constantly reinjure our bodies, in time they usually heal themselves. We must act on the faith that the same is true of the human spirit. In short, if we give children enough time, as free as possible from destructive outside pressures, the chances are good that they will once again find *within themselves* their reasons for doing worthwhile things. And so, in time, may we all.

⚬ As a parent I do find some of John's ideas hard to implement—the temptation to externally motivate our girls, using praise and criticism as my primary motivational techniques, is one I constantly find myself fighting against. It is the teaching/learning relationship I'm most familiar with, just as my diet is more familiar with fat and meat than with vegetables and fruit. In both cases, I need to get more comfortable and consistent with new ideas, and in both cases it is difficult to do so.

At our last *GWS* conference, we were fortunate to have journalist Alfie Kohn as the keynote speaker. Kohn has spent most of his adult life documenting the research and controversies surrounding rewards and punishments as common school practices, and he reaches the same conclusion Holt reached: Our intrinsic motivation to learn is warped in school by inappropriate praise and reward. We are all deeply influenced by the ways we ourselves have been raised and taught, often unconsciously so. To catch the spirit of what John Holt or Alfie Kohn have talked about and then acted upon requires a conscious effort on our part, and, sometimes, conscious efforts may seem unnatural or false. But if we fail to make those efforts, we then can only teach the way we've been taught and parent the way we've been parented. ⚬

5

Learning in the World

ACCESS TO THE WORLD

EVEN IN SUPPOSEDLY "FREE" or "alternative" schools, too many people still do what conventional schools have always done. They take children out of and away from the great richness and variety of the world, and in its place give them school subjects, the curriculum. They may jazz it up with chicken bones, Cuisenaire rods, and all sorts of other goodies. But the fact remains that instead of letting children have contact with more and more people, places, tools, and experiences, the schools are busily cutting the world up into little bits and giving it to the children according to some expert's theory about what they need or can stand.

What children need is not new and better curricula but *access* to more and more of the real world; plenty of time and space to think over their experiences, and to use fantasy and play to make meaning out of them; and advice, road maps, guidebooks, to make it easier for them to get where they want to go (not where we think they ought to go), and to find out what they want to find out. Finding ways to do all this is not easy. The modern world is dangerous, confusing, not meant for children, not generally kind or welcoming to them. We have much to learn about how to make the world more accessible to them, and how to give them more freedom and competence in exploring it. But this is a very different thing from designing nice little curricula.

Here is how a family in Washington, D.C., opened up the city to their child:

> We live in Washington, D.C., on Capitol Hill about two miles from the museums of the Smithsonian Institution. Susan and her mother walk there almost every day, observing, playing, meeting people, going to movies, listening to music, and riding the merry-go-round. They see a fantastic variety of nature movies. . . . They know art and history museums exhibit by exhibit. Susan can drag you through the history of the universe, through natural history, on up to the latest Mars landing. They eat lunch near the water fountain, see the latest sculpture, take pictures of their favorite spots, marvel at the beautiful spring and fall days. They attend mime shows, tape record jazz concerts, ride the double-decker bus to their favorite "explore gallery" where things can be played and jumped in. Tuition is very cheap, we all have fun, and we all learn a great deal.
>
> Susan lives in a world of marvelous *abundance*; her resources are unlimited. She has not been "socialized" by school to think that education is a supply of scarce knowledge to be competed for by hungry, controlled children. She doesn't play dumb "Schlemiel." . . . Our home and neighborhood are like a garden full of fresh fruit to be picked at arm's length by all who want to.
>
> She likes to paint, draw, color, cut out and paste. She compares her work to that in the museum. We give our comments and ideas when requested.
>
> We have hobbies in astronomy and camping. Her father is a pediatrician who enjoys working with her in constructing electronic gear. She has excellent soldering techniques and has soldered many connections in our home brew electric computer now used in his office.

It is not just "educated" and middle-class families who can use the city as a resource. In the chapter "The New Truants" in his book *Acting Out*, (see Bibliography, subsection Education and Society) Roland Betts writes:

Today's truants are [New York City's] most misunderstood children. They are also perhaps the most enlightened, aware that neither the schools nor the streets have anything to offer them. They fear both worlds. They sense the futility of the jobs that are available even for those who do finish high school. . . . Most of them are intelligent, sensitive children, far more accomplished in the arts of reading and mathematics than their peers who either attend the schools or lurk outside of them. These truants rarely brush with the law. Their trademark is their solitude.

Randolph Tracey is one of them. He is now (1978) sixteen but he has not been to school since the last day of fourth grade. He is poor and black. . . . [He] is a quiet and meek child, honest in his admission to his mother that he has not been to school in years. He was always a good student, but although he was able to read at a level several years above his grade, he had no tolerance for the continuous noise and confusion that characterized his school. Randolph is never with other children, or with other adults for that matter. He has spent the better part of the past four years in the Metropolitan Museum of Art. Although he has patronized all of the city's museums, he prefers the Met, and humbly claims that he is very familiar with each piece in the museum's standing collection. He recalls being cornered there one afternoon by a class of children he had grown up with from the school he should have attended, a class that might have been his own. He hid motionless behind a Minoan vase for twenty minutes until the danger had passed. Randolph draws and paints on his own, but derives far more pleasure from seeing and studying art in the museums.

Danny Hartman is another dropout. His life is consumed by drawing and tracing figures from comic books and art books, which he borrows from the public library. He can mimic perfectly the drawings of Leonardo and Michelangelo and the most intricate of Rembrandt's etchings. He stayed in school, reluctantly, until the spring of his eighth-grade year [where] he was discovered by an art teacher who encouraged him to apply for admission to the High School of Music and Art. For three years she saw to it that he attended daily classes in English and math, and she allowed him to work in her room while cutting gym, science, typing, and social studies. . . . He was lauded for his talents by his fellow students and was in the eyes of his art teacher a "clear genius." His work was extraordinary. The portfolio he had amassed by Christmas of his eighth-grade year was breathtaking. . . .

But the High School of Music and Art did not admit Danny. His accomplishments on standardized reading and math tests were unconvincing and his cumulative grade-point average was distorted by his many class cuts and subsequent failures. . . . The day that Danny received word that he had been denied admission to Music and Art was the last day he ever spent in school. . . .

What Mr. Betts means when he says that Danny's record was distorted by class cuts and subsequent failures is very probably that Danny's school, like most schools, gave him failing grades for cutting classes, regardless of whether or not he knew that material or could do the work. If this was so, it means that to punish him for cutting classes *the school lied about his academic work*—an outrageous and I would think, if tested in court, probably illegal practice which is common in schools all over the country.

Another of the truants Mr. Betts describes is a voluminous and expert reader; another, an expert on the geography, flora, and fauna of Central Park; another, an expert on television shows and movies; another, a raiser and trainer of pigeons; another, an expert on New York City's enormous transportation system. All of them have learned how to learn from the city what they want to learn. None has ever had any help or encouragement from any adult, or any way to use or get credit for any part of what they know. How easy it would be, and how much less expensive than running giant schools, and jails for those who won't go to them, to find ways to help and encourage the interests and talents of these children, and many others like them. As far as learning goes, they clearly don't need much help; the best help society could give them would simply be to stop treating them like criminals, so that they could do their exploring boldly and freely instead of furtively. They do need, and would probably welcome, help in finding ways to *use* what they learn—which is, after all, one of the things the schools are supposedly for.

Meanwhile their experience shows very clearly that for all its hugeness and harshness, the modern city is rich in resources, and that chil-

dren don't necessarily have to have an adult holding them by the hand
every second in order to make use of them.

Judy McCahill writes from England about a small child's very active
way of using the resources of his world:

> Last Saturday for something to do, because D was out of the country, I
> said to the boys, "Let's go to the art exhibit." S and K thought it was a
> wonderful idea and began discussing what sort of art they would do
> there and what pictures (of their own) they might bring from home.
> Startled, I tried to explain to them what an art exhibit was all about and
> they were genuinely puzzled at my trying to tell them they were just
> going there to look at somebody else's pictures. Puzzled, but not de-
> terred, S gathered his supplies, two sets of paints, a brush, some paper,
> and a jar full of water which he handed me to carry; and K made us all
> wait while he finished a full-color marker pen painting of an army tank.
>
> When we got there, we strolled along the sidewalks near the craft
> shop that was hosting the exhibit, dutifully examining the works and
> passing several fully-grown and wise-looking artists sitting in portable
> lawn chairs, all the while S at my heels urging me to find out how he
> was supposed to enter the show and me ahead of S, stalling.
>
> Finally an old man who works in the shop, who once told me a long
> story about his difficulties getting home to Cobham one night during
> the war when London was being bombed, greeted me. I introduced S
> to him and asked *him* to explain what an art exhibit was. He started to,
> but then he and his daughter, who also works in the shop, saw that S
> was ready to do some work and after a good laugh with a couple of cus-
> tomers over it, gave him a couple of nice big pieces of "card" to paint
> on. He sat on the doorstep of a small office building nearby and
> painted, while the rest of us strolled through the exhibit again, window-
> shopped, and ate ice cream cones.
>
> When he had finished, it was a beautiful picture of a black dog, fur
> flying, running up a hill on a windy day, a glorious sun in the sky. It
> seemed to reflect his mood of magic. He took the picture into the shop,
> where the man said he would put it on sale for 50 pence (and confusedly
> explained about how the artists had to pay rent to the exhibit), and we
> went home.

A few days later, still full of the experience, S told a friend of mine about it. She promptly went out to buy the picture, and it was gone! When I suggested to S that he go and check to see if his painting had been sold, he replied that he already had, the next day (which of course was Sunday), and the shop was closed.

And that was that. He was too busy doing something else to give it another thought.

LIFESCHOOL

A young teenage reader writes eloquently about how much she learns from that part of her life that is *hers:*

I started going to public school right into the second grade and in every grade up to the sixth I was a straight A student. All the teachers were nice to me and I was praised and praised again for my work and I got good grades for it too and that's what kept me going.

When I left school at the end of sixth grade to be out for two years, I learned a new realization. Grades are not what make you a good person. I have a pretty good memory so I remembered all the things I had to, to pass the tests that gave me A's. But I've learned from experience that when I'm not interested in what I am supposed to be learning, I forget everything. Unfortunately, I wasn't interested in anything that I was doing, so my second- through sixth-grade years of public schooling are pretty much blank.

In the two years without any school contact I learned how to live without grades and not to need someone to tell me "It's good" every time I did something. It got so that grades didn't mean anything anymore. Basically, I learned that grades prove nothing. I also learned a lot of different things that I wouldn't have, if I had been in public schools. Public schools can't offer experience. I learned how to deal with and relate to adults better because I was around them so much—all the kids were in school! I learned many practical skills that I never would have learned in public school.

At first I wasn't so sure about the idea of not being in school but I soon adjusted and found it very fun. When I look at kids my age, it makes me glad that we did what we did. I am capable of doing so many more things it amazes me. And it's all because I had the time to learn, and enjoy while I was learning. So things stuck in my mind and they are still there because I am still doing new things, while these kids are doing things just to "get out" and then forgetting them in the meantime *plus* not enjoying much of it anyhow. Whew!

I have such a neat home and lifeschool! I consider myself to be very lucky to be who I am and to have the parents I have for believing in nonschooling!

Jud Jerome writes about the experiences of his daughter in "lifeschool":

One daughter was twelve when we moved to the farm. She finished that year of school on "independent study," living at the farm, turning in work to teachers back at the city. But when fall came she did not want to enroll. To avoid the law we enrolled her in a "free" school in Spokane, Washington, run by a friend, who carried her on the rolls, though she has not yet, to date, seen that city or that school. She spent most of the first year here at the farm, pitching in as an adult, learning from experience as we were all learning. While she was still thirteen we went to help another commune, in northern Vermont, with sugaring, and she loved that place—which was very primitive and used horse-drawn equipment—so asked to stay. This was an agreeable arrangement on all sides—and she has lived there now for over five years, except for one, when she was sixteen. That year she and a young man ten years her senior went to Iceland for the winter, working in a fish cannery. The next spring they traveled, camping, to Scandinavia, hiked the Alps, then flew home—coming back with $3,000 more than they left with, after a year abroad.

Last year she wanted to apply for a government vocational program, for which she needed a high school diploma, so went to an adult education class for a few months, and took the test, passing in the top percentile (and being offered scholarships to various colleges). She "graduated" earlier than her classmates who stayed in school. I think her case illustrates especially dramatically the waste of time in schools.

She is by no means a studious type, would never think of herself as an intellectual, has always been more interested in milking cows and hoeing vegetables and driving teams of horses than in books, and in her years between thirteen and eighteen moved comfortably into womanhood and acquired a vast number of skills, had a vast range of experiences in the adult world, yet managed to qualify exceptionally by academic standards. By comparison, her classmates who stayed in school are in many case stunted in mind, emotionally disturbed, without significant goals or directions or sound values in their lives.

Children can learn a great deal from many of the "unhappy" experiences from which we try so hard to protect them. One mother wrote:

We had one long experience that gave us a different kind of "social" activity. Right after we were approved to homeschool, my father was taken seriously ill with a stroke, so when he had recuperated enough, he was put in a convalescent home for therapy. Because the boys and I were free, we would go in each day to visit him. (They would not have been excused from school for this.) But my father was very depressed and the therapist at the hospital had on his record "uncooperative." This didn't give us much confidence, so we went in each day to make sure they didn't give up on him. It was a good experience for the boys as well as me, for whenever the grandchildren would come my father would get undepressed. He would laugh at their antics and then sink back into depression when they left.

So we agreed that we would take our books (it was now September) to the home and stay most of the day with their Pop-Pop. It worked out well, for the boys had a large place to do their work and they could go outside to play whenever they got tired of being in. They would go to the vending machines and get us things, and several times when the home was short-handed because of the "flu" season, we would sort some laundry and the boys would help take it to the rooms. We made it a game and the patients loved having the boys come in to their rooms and talk to them.

At therapy we kept assuring my father that when he could walk well, we'd take him home, so he really worked hard, and the boys and I would cheer him on, and the other patients, with "You can do it, Pop-Pop. Hurray!" "Great, Pop-Pop!" The other patients enjoyed us cheering them on and when the therapist saw the positive results from this, he was glad we were there. We saw many patients recover in weeks when the therapist had thought it would take months. We don't hope to have this kind of experience again this year, but it showed us that we *could* take a "sad" situation and turn it into one of rejoicing.

CONTROLLING ONE'S TIME

A mother from Washington State writes about freedom from schedules:

We entered the year with no preconceptions or plan of action. I just figured life would go on, and so it has. We go to bed each night and wake up each morning, the day passes and the necessary work gets done. I know that I live in a healthy environment and that I continue to grow as a person, and I trust that is so for my children, as well, though I haven't been "monitoring" their "progress," nor can I point to any tangible proof of "achievement."

About ten days a month I go to the city to work in a printshop. It is my habit, generally, to wake up early and spend an hour or two quietly planning my day according to what needs doing and what I feel like. But on my "work" days I find it very difficult to "get into" that kind of contemplation. Such a large chunk of the day is already planned for me. If I go to work several consecutive days, by the fourth or fifth day I feel very removed from the core of myself, and find it much easier to contemplate doing what at other times would seem irresponsible to me. I seem to have less energy for recycling, conserving fuel, paying good attention to my husband and children, etc. *When I abdicate the responsibility for structuring my own time, a certain moral strength seems to be lost as well* [Author's emphasis]. Who can guess at the degree of personal alienation we as a society cause our children by structuring so much of their time for them? I am beginning to think the greatest harm is not in the "what" or the "how" of this structuring, but in the very fact that five days out of seven, nine months out of twelve, six hours out of the center of those days, we remove from children the responsibility for their time. Perhaps it is not even the length of the time that is crucial, but simply the fact of the interruption. I know from my own experience that even a small interruption—a dental appointment, say, or a meeting or lecture I have to give—can halt the flow of my own creative energies for a length of time much greater than the interruption itself. Once I change from active to passive participant in structuring my time, a certain numbing takes place so that it is much easier to stay passive, "killing time" until the next prescribed activity, like fixing dinner or whatever.

I have noticed that the only periods of real "boredom," when the children complain of having nothing to do, are on days when a chunk of time has been planned *for* them. There is certainly nothing wrong with planning things to do together, but I have grown wary of too much planning *for*, and of removing it from its natural niche in the unique pattern of a particular day to an artificial projection into the future of anonymous days: "Every Tuesday we will . . . "

I have never known how to "stimulate" the children. I know that as a parent I should be raising my children in a "stimulating" environment, so that they will not be "dulled" or "bored," but what is more stimulating: a roomful of toys and tools and gadgets, bright colors and shiny enameled fixtures, or a sparsely furnished hand-hewn cabin deep in the woods, with a few toys carefully chosen or crafted, rich with meaning, time, and care, and intimate with the elements of the earth? The only world I can show them, with any integrity, is my world.

Perhaps that is why field trips were such a disappointment for us. We started off in the fall doing "something special," i.e., "educational field trip," once a week. After about a month we all forgot about taking these trips. They were fun, certainly interesting, but I think we were all sickened by the phoniness. Everyone knew the only reason we all trooped into the city to the aquarium was because Mom thought it would be a "good experience." Of much more continuing interest and, probably, greater educational significance in the truest sense, are the weekly trips into town to do the errands—to the bank (where we all have accounts and are free to deposit and withdraw as we please), the

post office, grocery store, Laundromat, recycling center (source of income for kids outside of parents), drugstore and the comic book
racks—and the evenings at the library and swimming pool. Those
things are real, things I would do even if no one joined me, that just
happen to be important activities for all of us.

When I am trying to "stimulate their interest" in something, the very
artificiality of the endeavor (and rudeness, really—I have no business
even trying) builds a barrier between us. But when I am sharing something I really love with them because I also really love them, all barriers
are down, and we are communicating intimately. When they also love
what I love—a song, a poem, the salmon returning to the creek to
spawn—the joy is exquisite; we share a truth. But our differences are also
a truth. Common thread and fiber we share, but not the whole piece.

And so I do my work each day, work which is full of meaning for me,
and offer to teach it to them: cooking, sewing, splitting wood, hauling
water, keeping house, writing, reading, singing, sailing on the lake, dig-
ging in the garden. Sometimes they are interested, sometimes not. But
if I were to try to "stimulate" them, sugar-coating various tasks, making
games of various skills, preaching, teaching *me* to them, they would not
have the time—great, empty spaces of time—in which to search deep
within themselves for what is most true about them.

And neither, then, would I.

Many parents have written to us about the feelings of liberation
that go with unschooling and unscheduling. Gail Myles and her family
moved to an island to unschool their children:

I never expected the boys to express any appreciation for this experience. I figured they might be sitting at a lunch with some business
friends when they were thirty and mention the year. What I couldn't
have predicted is that they would see the difference so soon. They
learned to dig clams with the clammers of Maine, the salt of the earth,
in forty degrees below chill factors; they lived through situations where
everyone takes responsibility for the lives of each other; they came to
like and understand opera because it was available to us through Tex-
aco broadcasts, an interest none of us had prior to this; . . . and proba-

bly the best thing they learned was to get along with themselves and each other. They had to, because there was no one else, and if you want something from someone you have to give in return. That should take care of this "social life" garbage. To feel your worth in an adult world side by side with hardworking people, is there a better reward? I don't think so. They even had tears at departing from this small coastal community they knew as "in town."

My rewards were beyond measure. No yellow monster took my favorite friends away every morning; when they were exposed to a new vocabulary word I could use it pertinently in everyday happenings; if we wanted to know molecular theory we could work from 9 A.M. to 4 P.M. till it clicked; everything they were exposed to in Calvert Curriculum was learned by all; they spent early evenings putting on operas they made up, shows for Dad's pleasure were presented, sometimes taking three days just to prepare the staging. We read books, books, and books till 1 A.M., and no one had to be up at 6:30 for the monster.

An additional reward was the result of the history, literature, mythology, and architecture we were exposed to; we went to Athens, Greece, in April, a trip we would never have been interested enough in taking or felt a need to take if "doors" hadn't been opened to us. Bud came to love the Parthenon and had to see it. Tim was a walking encyclopedia on mythology and gave Jack and me the tour in the Archaeological Museum, and Mike was our history guide—we didn't even need a Greek service. Mike is also a gifted writer, and after reading his final composition for Calvert the teacher said she wished she could fly up to meet him, said he knew what writing was all about—she wanted to fly to Troy and Greece as his subject was the Trojan War. He had made her *feel* something inside.

I enjoyed the Calvert system. Their writers are excellent and really speak to the kids. It was a personal relationship in which they looked forward to hearing from someone who was writing to them. Letters were scarce and they learned the value of the written word. But I must say we *used* the curriculum to our needs and interests and only took the grading so that the boys would not be denied the credit upon returning to public school. This was completely their choice—they are encouraged to set policies regarding their futures.

The idea I hate most about public schools is that they should have my children all day when I feed, clothe, doctor, transport, and care most for them, and I am denied those hours with them and the sharing of their learning experiences. I cannot reinforce their education if I am denied the subject matter they are exposed to and am only left with tired grumps who eat, do homework, and flop to bed.

REAL WORLD SKILLS

From the cover story of the April 1980 issue of *Home Educators Newsletter:*

These children [of a homeschooling family] form an exclusive student body as they are each born into the school. They take their places according to ability rather than grade level. They listen to works far above their comprehension, just to be part of the present company. In our own instance, we have one child that keeps all vehicles in top running shape, another who provides milk, eggs, and meat for the table, another who displays beautiful artwork, and another who enjoys gardening.

Katrina spends several hours morning and afternoon doing her farm work, but she is the beneficiary of her own labor, keeps all the records for feed, hay, and other purchases so that she can calculate her profit when animals are sold and what man-hours and money have been expended to gain that profit. I personally am not the least interested in any type of farm work and yet I know that this is developing within Katrina an ability far beyond anything that I could teach her. How much barley will a pig eat in a week, a month, till time for the market? What animals have the quickest turnover? What type of labor hours are necessary to operate a farm? I couldn't answer any of these questions, though Katrina can, and for an eleven-year-old girl I consider that quite an accomplishment. She has a reading assignment just like the other children of 200 pages per week plus a written paper every day. She generally turns in a paper that has to do with her present projects.

It is a rare occasion that I do not get the type of workmanship out of my children that I would get out of some adult. We are presently sectioning off a room in the basement and all the partitions will be built by the children. One startling fact is that John, at age seven, has all his own tools, including a power saw and drill. He builds beautiful miniature log cabins and will be in charge of measuring and cutting boards for the partition project. He is also planning on paneling his own room. . . .

Kevin has repaired all my major appliances since he was kindergarten age. Recently I had to hire a repairman to come and fix my furnace motor, which turned out to be shot and had to be replaced. This repairman hadn't been here for several years and his first question was "Why can't Kevin fix this?" When he discovered the problem he knew that the present motor was beyond repair and he went to get another. However, he brought the burned-out one back because he felt that Kevin could use parts from it.

People often ask me how I can tolerate the children doing things that are normally only done by adults, and professionals at that. Well, I watch the children carefully and never expect one to do a job which is over his head. I experiment constantly, finding natural abilities and letting them try their wings in harmless, inexpensive ways. If a child shows an ability in a certain area such as plumbing, I try them out taking apart an elbow and putting it back together without a leak. Next comes faucets, or setting a toilet. Next might come the installation of a shower unit, and finally the child is ready to plumb a bathroom. I would have no qualms about letting my thirteen-year-old plumb my entire house. After all, he wired it for D.C. electricity when he was only eight. Our daughter Cathy is remodeling her own home now (she's nineteen), and she has done all her own plumbing, plastering, wallpapering, and carpentry. Matter of fact, that's how she helped pay for her college education. She worked as a carpenter in an all-male shop!

Handling money is one of the most useful real world skills and one which gets distorted for many children. Louise Andrieshyn wrote us from Manitoba about her children and money:

Heidi and Michael have just bought themselves ponies with their own money. You'll be pleased to learn that Heidi (10) wrote a cheque for hers.

I don't know what other banking practices are like, but at our credit union any child can have a full-fledged account (and *must* be a shareholder in the corporation in order to have an account). Living in the country, we mail-order shop quite a bit and Heidi's cheques have never been questioned. But perhaps the people who receive them don't know her age! I don't suppose they would ever dream that they were accepting a cheque from a ten-year-old. If they knew, I wonder whether they would refuse to accept it or ask for counter-signing?

Since Heidi has a fully personal account, not an "in trust" one, we as her parents are not even allowed to touch her money. We found out the hard way! We went to the credit union to take some money out of her account and they wouldn't let us. They pulled out her file card and showed us her signature saying that only she was able to handle the money in that account. She had signed it when she was 5! I remember distinctly "letting" her sign it, thinking condescendingly how "nice" the experience was for her. Little did I know I was providing her a degree of absolute financial independence.

Another letter shows how a sense of the value of money can start very early:

Thought I'd share with you M's "coming of age" as a consumer. M recently turned three. She received a dollar inside a birthday card sent by one of her friends (a 92-year-old). Last year when he sent a dollar I took it without even showing it to her and bought her some balloons with it. This year she opened all her own mail and instantly recognized that it was money and that it was a present for her. She was quite pleased and put it in her wallet which until now was only for *playing* "grownup," and had held only small change. She discussed the dollar, and that she could buy something—whatever she wanted—for herself.

Next day when she got a five-dollar bill in another card we made a fuss again. We discussed the difference in value—on our fingers—of ones and fives, and I thought, "This is going great!"

Next day, when she got a card with a check for *ten* dollars, I thought, "Oh, no, this learning experience is getting out of hand." I hoped she wouldn't realize what a check was so I could spirit it away, but she was too sharp. "More money!" she exclaimed. So we explained what a check was, and traded it for two fives. M had previously studied the one and the five and pointed out that there were different men on them and asked their names (she's very into everything having a "name").

Then M asked me what she could buy with all her "moneys." I suggested she look in the toy catalogues. She got very excited over a construction set (Tinkertoy), and I told her she could look for one like it next time we went to town. So next time Daddy went to town M grabbed her purse and went along to shop for her present to herself. When she found her "struction set" and went to the counter to pay for it—her first purchase—Daddy told her to give the woman a Lincoln, expecting her to get back two Washingtons. Drats!—she gave her a Jefferson! M took it right in stride. Perhaps we should have left it alone, but at home Daddy traded it for two Washingtons. Controlling it again.

After she played with the Tinkertoy set for a couple of days, she expressed disappointment that she couldn't build a house with it. She checked the catalogues and zeroed in on a Lincoln Logs set. The next shopping expedition to town turned one up—for a Lincoln and three Washingtons. We pointed out that she'd spent a lot of money and didn't have that much left. I sense that she has a very balanced feel for money, a good sense of its value, so I'm not worried that she'll either hoard the rest or blow it recklessly.

With all this concern with cash, M didn't lose track of the fact that the money was sent as presents from people who love her. We took pictures of M posed with her presents and a big smile to send along with the thank-you notes.

SPEECH AND LANGUAGE IN REAL LIFE

The difference between learning in and from real life and learning in schools is perhaps most important of all in speech and language. Ivan

Illich writes about this in "Vernacular Values and Education," in his book *Shadow Work*.

> In most cultures, we know that speech resulted from conversation embedded in everyday life, from listening to fights and lullabies, gossip, stories, and dreams. Even today, the majority of people in poor countries learn all their language skills without any paid tutorship, without any attempt whatsoever to teach them how to speak.

Illich goes on to point out that all over the world many poor people in nonindustrial countries speak more than one language—a goldsmith he knows in Timbuktu speaks *six*—and that on the whole it is only in nation-states that have had several generations of compulsory schooling that we find most people speaking only one language. For in these supposedly advanced nations, people no longer learn their languages from people who talk to them, meaning what they say, in a context of everyday life, but from professional speakers who are trained and paid to say what others have prepared for them. Much is said about how inarticulate today's young are. I suspect that an important reason is that so much of the speech they hear, on TV or in school, is not real speech but canned speech, prepared in advance, and often not even by the speaker. They don't hear many real voices. But it is hearing real voices that makes us want to speak.

A memory. When my sister and I were about four and five, perhaps even less, we visited our grandparents. There was a landing on the second floor, with a railing, through which we could just see down the stairs into the room where the adults sat talking after dinner. After we had been tucked into bed and good-nights said, and the grownups had gone back downstairs, we would slip out of bed, crouch down by the railing, and listen to the grownup voices. We couldn't understand what was being talked about. But the pull of those voices was fascinating. Usually after a while we would sneak back into bed. But one night we fell asleep there by the railing, where the grownups found us when they went up to bed. I don't remember what came of this, whether we were scolded or punished and sternly warned not to get out of bed again, or whether the grownups said nothing about it.

Since then I have seen in many other families that it is very hard to keep young children in bed if a group of adults are having lively conversation not too far away. The children will find a hundred different reasons for coming to check out what the grownups are saying.

But, some might say, that's all very fine for privileged families that have interesting visitors. But what about most families, average families? The answer is, first of all, that all people are interesting. As Studs Terkel and Robert Coles have shown in their (very different) books, everyone has many good stories to tell. As long as real people are talking, not just people on TV, children will want to hear their voices and see their faces, and will learn much from them.

⮜ I first met Ivan Illich in the midnineties and have had the good fortune to spend time in his company since. More than once, I heard Ivan say how much he learned as a young boy simply by sitting under his grandparents' table in their house in Vienna, listening to their conversations. We can't measure such informal learning, but as these stories indicate, people do learn important things about and in the world differently than they can in a conventional school classroom. ⮞

6

Living and Working Spaces

SCHOOL OR CLUB?

To a PARENT WHO WROTE about joining a few other parents in form-
ing their own school, I said:

Thanks for news of your school. One piece of heartfelt advice. People
sending their kids to your school must be made to understand that if
there is something they think those children *must* be taught or *must*
learn, basics or whatever, it must be *their* responsibility to do that
teaching, and to do it in their own home—or at any rate, away from the
school. The school must be a place where people come together to do
the things that interest and excite them most. Otherwise, you will be
torn to pieces with arguments about whether the school should teach
reading or arithmetic, or teach it one or four hours a week, or whatever.
Believe me, I speak from the bitter experience of many people.

And this would be my very strong advice to any group of unschoolers who want to start a school as a way of escaping compulsory attendance laws, or giving their children a place to meet and be with other
children, or for whatever reasons. Okay to have rules which say, more

or less, no fair hurting or bothering other people. Every human society has these, and children expect them and understand them. But the school must not try to *compel* learning. If it does, people will argue endlessly and furiously about what kinds of learning must be compelled. This has happened to small alternative schools again and again. Nancy Plent, a mother in New Jersey, wrote about this:

> One more thing I did want to say is about the other mothers I'm meeting. None of us worry about social adjustment stuff; we all know that kids can keep occupied with friends of all ages and with their own interests. But every one of us feels that our kids need more kids. They are feeling "different" and left out, no matter what their situation. E often greets a sunny day with, "Boy, it's a great day to ride green machines! I'll call Tommy and . . . oh, he's in school today." No big thing, maybe, but it happens often, to all of our kids, and we worry about it.
>
> For this reason, the talk always comes around to "maybe if we started some kind of school." We know it is a problem without an answer right now, but we bat it around wistfully all the time anyway. I can only see an answer when we find more people doing it, convince more people that they should do it. I'm giving it all I've got.

It would be a fine thing if in any community there were more places for children, and indeed people of all ages, to get together and do various kinds of things. I talk about what such places might be like in early chapters of *Instead of Education*, and even more in an appendix describing a remarkable place called the Peckham Family Center, which existed for a while in a part of London in the late 1930s. (People are trying to organize a new one in Scotland.)

In some ways, the country clubs that rich folks belong to are a much better model of what we want than a school. Take away the eighteen-hole golf courses, the elaborate tennis courts and other facilities, the palatial clubhouse, and what's left is very close in spirit to what we are after. You don't *have* to play golf just because you go to the golf club. You don't have to *do* anything. There are certain kinds of resources there for you to use, if you want, but you can spend the day there sitting in a chair and looking at the sky. Why not an inexpensive version of the same thing? A country club without the country—or perhaps a different kind of country, just a little patch of field or woods or whatever is handy.

If we can keep the idea of a family club in mind, we will probably make more sensible choices and decisions.

Some years ago a good friend of mine, Peggy Hughes, then living in Denmark, decided to make a 16mm sound film about the Ny Lille Skole (New Little School), a small "school" in which she was working, which I describe in *Instead of Education*. She had done a small amount of black and white photography, but had never even owned a movie camera, let alone made a film with sound.

In time, working almost entirely alone, with occasional advice from the more experienced, she produced a film, about forty-five minutes long, called "We Have to Call It School." I am not unbiased about it; she and I are old friends, I loved the school and the people in it, and for some of the footage I was her sound man. But I think it is the most vivid, touching, and true film portrait of children that I have ever seen. Anyone who likes, enjoys, and respects children will surely be charmed and delighted by it and may learn much from it.

Why should unschoolers want to see a film about school? The answer is in the title. Early in the film is a shot of the children arriving at school in the morning. Over this we hear the voice of one of the teachers, Erik, saying, "We have to call it school. The law in Denmark says that children have to go to school, and if we didn't call this a school, they couldn't come here." But it is not a school in any way that we understand those words. It is a meeting, living, and *doing* place for six or seven adults and about eighty children, aged about six through fourteen. It is more like a club than anything I can compare it to. The children come there when they feel like it, most of the time during the winter, not so often when spring and the sun arrive. Once there, they talk about and do many things that interest them, sometimes with the adults, sometimes by themselves. In the process, they learn a lot about themselves, each other, and the world.

The film is important for unschoolers for many reasons, among them this one. What we need in our communities is not so much schools as a variety of protected, safe, interesting *spaces* where children can gather, meet and make friends, and do things together. Such spaces might include children's libraries (or sections of libraries), children's museums (a wonderful one in Boston), children's theaters (children *making* the drama, not just watching it), children's (or children's and adults') arts or craft centers, adventure playgrounds, and so on. One such space was the Peckham Center. Another such space could be something like the Ny Lille Skole. It's not a matter of copying it exactly, but of catching the spirit of it.

GREENHOUSE

Beth Hagins writes from Illinois about still another child space, the best of the lot, because it is not primarily for children at all, but has its own real and serious work.

. . . We are working to create a biological research setting for children in the south Chicago area. It's a large solar greenhouse that we have built with people in the black township of Pembroke, Illinois. It's a very rural, low-income community. The quality of life is superbly suited to growing without schooling.

I don't know how to describe the place without sounding like a grant application. I've been "learning" there for the past four years, largely being taught by the older people. They've taught me how to grow, how to make compost, how to conserve, how to slaughter, how to cooperate. I've never been happier learning anywhere. It's even helped put my own formal academic instruction in perspective . . . (Kindergarten through Ph.D.).

The greenhouse manager is a 67-year-old man who's been selling and growing all his life. Our experiments are economic and biological. We are raising laying hens, getting eggs, saving chicken manure, growing worms, fertilizing starter plants, and watching our chickens and plants *flourish* in all the sunlight. We would love to have a few children to work with. We are working to get a few local children involved actively, but it is always more exciting for them to have friends from outside the area coming to learn, too.

. . . It's funny. As I think back on school, the one thing that I feel most molded by was the reward structure for getting A's. Apart from a "B" in sociology as a sophomore in college, I don't think I got anything but A's since fourth grade. I discovered I could get A's in anything, although I am to this day not very quick on my feet in terms of thinking. I suppose that the A's were what opened doors for me, got me into more exciting learning situations—like regional orchestras, national debate forums, and other kinds of special "larger than life" experiences that can stimulate and impress if they do not intimidate. I don't know enough about the deschooling movement to know if this kind of larger association of children is possible. We hope to be able to do something like this with the greenhouse experiments, and to introduce the children to some of the schooled, practicing experimenters who nonetheless share the values of the deschoolers. Many of the solar societies are organized and powered by very wonderful scientists and researchers who would like the opportunity to work on a limited basis with children outside a formal school context.

SPACE UNLIMITED

Harold Dunn of Oregon writes of the hazards of calling any kind of children's space a "school," and about traveling in Mexico with children:

My primary interest is in building nonschool alternatives for kids. Two years ago, when I still believed that Free Schools were the answer, I started a mini-school, with five kids and two adults living with me in my home, a converted school bus parked way out in the Oregon woods beside a small lake. Tuition was free, teaching nonexistent, curriculum based on survival since we had less than $100 a month for all eight of us to live on.

Two of the boys, aged 14 and 15, had spent much of the summer out at my place, always busy and creative in their play. They dreaded the return to public school in September, so we called ourselves a school and just continued on as we had all summer. Only it didn't work out. They became bored, restless, and complained they weren't learning anything.

It took me quite a while to realize that since they were now in "school," they expected somebody to *do* something *to* them. It didn't matter that all summer they had been exploring new realms and expanding their limits with no adult supervision. Now they demanded to be told what to do. Somebody was supposed to learn them something, or else it wasn't a real school and no damn good after all.

I realized then how much we had destroyed for these two boys just by calling ourselves a school. Of course, the destruction happened gradually during all their previous schooling, as they were conditioned to believe that learning is a passive thing, and that school is where it happens.

The three other kids in our school, age 5, 10, and 12, had never been to school, so had no preconceived ideas of what to expect. What a joy it was to watch them explore the world and themselves. Their greatest treasure was my library card, which allowed them to read hundreds of pages each day. They never seemed to get their fill of books, yet they still had energy to cook, bake, chop wood, wash dishes, and clean house. The two oldest girls did far more than their share of the work needed to sustain us all—because they *wanted* to. They were alive, eager, and incredibly inventive. They saw the whole world as open to them, because nobody had taught them there were things they couldn't do.

In a month's time, M (12) went from being a virtual nonswimmer to being the first kid to pass the "Mountain-Man Test," a challenge I had put up to a group of boys that hung out at the lake all that summer. The test consisted of swimming out to the middle of the lake (about 100 yards), alone, at midnight, and diving to the bottom (12 feet), bringing back some mud to prove it. Several boys had tried it, but they all chickened out, even those that were much better swimmers than M. But she stuck with it, working hard to overcome her fears. (It's *dark* down in that lake at night.) And the night she passed the test she announced that since she was now the only member of the Mountain-Man Club, she was changing the name to Mountaineers!

The incredible contrast between these girls, who had no previous schooling, even in free schools, and the two boys so conditioned by their years of public school dogma, was a powerful lesson for me. For many years, I had dreamed of starting a new kind of free school, run entirely by the kids themselves, rather than controlled by the parents or the teachers, as is usually the case. Finally my dream had come true, only to teach me its own absurdity. Any kids truly free to run their own school exactly as they see fit, will immediately declare a permanent vacation, and that will be the end of it. They may get together as before, and do the same things, but they won't call it school unless you make them—and then *you're* running the show, and that's not freedom, even if you're doing it, as I was, "for their own good" to keep them out of public school.

FARM SPACE

An article by Jerry Howard in *Horticulture* tells about a food-raising space in a rich Boston suburb:

Bill McElwain, a Harvard man who had taught French, run a Laundromat, and become a discouraged farmer, moved to the prosperous town of Weston, Mass., and saw a lot of fertile suburban land going to waste, on the way to and from his work in Boston (rehabilitating houses in the South End).

He saw suburban teen-agers with few alternatives to football, tennis, drama or boredom, and he saw poor city people paying more for food in Roxbury than he was in Weston. (Bill surveyed the cost of twenty-five identical items in both areas and counted a 13% difference.)

In April, 1970, Bill began with borrowed hand tools and donations of seed and fertilizer. With a handful of dedicated helpers, he cultivated almost an acre; the produce was trucked into Roxbury and distributed free to a children's food program and a housing project. There, residents collected donations that found their way back to the farm.

Within a year, Bill was hired as project director of the new Weston Youth Commission. In 1972, he convinced the town to buy the farmland. He ignited a small but dedicated cadre of supporters, including enough people in the volunteer government to insure the continued support of the town. More kids got involved with the farm, and with the proceeds from the vegetables (now sold in Boston for a nominal $1 a crate) he paid workers a minimum wage. The town put more money and equipment into the project, and by 1975, the farm was growing as much as 100 tons of produce a year. About 25% of this was sold locally; the rest went into Boston.

Bill McElwain was fifty years old when the town bought the farm. He is still project director for the Youth Commission, despite his cavalier view of keeping fiscal records, and he still writes a column for the *Weston Town Crier*, in which he proposes dozens of other activities for the young to take part in.

One fall, for instance, Bill counted 600 maple trees along Weston roadsides. In a year and a half, he and a crew built a sugarhouse near the junior high school (using pine boards milled from local trees); scrounged buckets, taps, and evaporating equipment; and produced a cash crop of 250 gallons of grade A maple syrup. There was cider pressing, orchard reclamation, firewood cutting, crate making, construction of a small observatory, and an alternative course at the high school with regular field trips to Boston's ethnic neighborhoods, and to rural New Hampshire.

Virtually all his plans, large or small, have these common ingredients: they provide young people with paying jobs that are educational, socially useful, and fun; they operate on a small scale, need little capital, and use readily available resources, preferably neglected ones; and they bring a variety of people together to solve common problems in an enjoyable context. Building community is one of Bill's more crucial goals, and he'll seize any opportunity—planting, harvesting, "sugaring off," a woodcarving workshop, or May Day—to bring folks together for a festive occasion.

❧ Many homeschoolers try to run family businesses out of their homes as a way to make it all work, but this is often no less stressful, and, sometimes, more financially burdensome than trying to balance a traditional job with homeschooling. However, homeschoolers tend to be more entrepreneurial than the general population, and home businesses as a primary or secondary source of income are probably more common among homeschooling families than the general population. I personally know computer programmers and organic farmers, symphony conductors and general contractors, who figure out ways to arrange their schedules to allow for homeschooling in their lives, and many others would be able to, as well. Children at any age can be involved in discussing how they spend their time. Suggest to your children resources, schedules, and ideas for achieving what you want, individually, and as a family, and listen to what your children say—or don't say. Goals and schedules will emerge as the discussion occurs, and this will be an ongoing, not a one-time, process, because goals and schedules do change, particularly for young people. Think of this as a strength of homeschooling: There is more time to have these talks and to listen to children's observations. Lessons can be compressed and expanded as needed, performance can be evaluated in dynamic situations, and families can take a break or vacation whenever needed. Homeschooling families can have a different rhythm than families that listen to the beat of school (more about this in Chapter 12). There are many ways to make homeschooling work once all parties see learning as an activity that may sometimes involve classes, rather than as just "classroom activity."

Children have always been welcome at the Holt Associates offices, but after John died and staff members started having families, the offices, at times, just teemed with kids. We usually worked while the children played, though sometimes they'd ask if they could help pack books, answer phones, stuff envelopes, or stamp letters. They'd work alongside us for a while, and then either drift into a new activity or conversation with a friend or, sometimes, they'd ask for more work when they completed a task. Sometimes one or two kids would walk into my office and ask questions about what I was doing; sometimes they'd just play hide-and-seek in my office, while I pretended not to see them. However as the kids became older, ages eight to twelve in particular, they wanted to have their own space for play or privacy. We allowed the younger ones to ride small bikes in our basement storage area, and the older ones to create a clubhouse in the back-issue storage room.

If you came into our office in those days you would see evidence of children everywhere. Our walls were filled with their drawings and projects, and the air would sometimes be filled with their games and talk;

during good weather we found it useful to pay a colleague to take the kids to a nearby park so we could work quietly or hold important meetings without interruptions. Seeing a child sitting on their mom's lap while she read a book to him or her during a break was a common sight in those days, and something we encouraged. Many of the delivery people who came to our office would wonder aloud if they were delivering to a day-care center instead of a place of business! Yet, somehow, all the work that needed to be accomplished got done. It wasn't the most efficient and cost-effective way to run a business, but it was a lot more interesting than your typical office, particularly if you liked being around kids.

As the children got older, many staff members found that they were involved in serious schedule conflicts, picking up and dropping off the older ones at classes and meetings all around town during business hours. Sometimes staff members pooled their homeschooling driving, so our office often became a hub for pick-ups and drop-offs for kids, particularly the older ones. Sometimes teens scheduled meetings or workshops with adults they wanted to learn with in our office during business hours, which worked just fine. We had enough office space to accommodate such events.

My three girls, in particular, enjoyed playing with makeup and doing "dress ups," so our office had a good stash of costumes, plastic jewelry, and accessories stored in an old toy chest near the shipping area. Phil Cranshaw, my father-in-law, who worked as our shipper/receiver, once was teasing the girls by taking a big feather boa out of the chest and wearing it while he packed orders, refusing to give it back to them because he "looked so good with it on." The girls loved seeing "Papa Phil" wear the boa while he worked, and there was much laughter to be heard. However, when the UPS man made his delivery that day, he caught sight of Phil prancing before the girls with the boa around his neck. Just as Phil started to explain what was going on, the UPS man stopped him with this remark: "Don't apologize. I shouldn't be surprised by anything when I come to this place!" ❧

7

Serious Play

IN THIS CHAPTER PARENTS give us a few glimpses of the ways in which children use play, fantasy, make-believe, poetry, song, drama, and art as a way of exploring and understanding the world. This is a very important part of their life and growth. People have done some persuasive studies to show that children who are good at fantasizing are better both at learning about the world and at learning to cope with its surprises and disappointments. It isn't hard to see why this should be so. In fantasy we have a way of trying out situations, to get some feel of what they might be like, or how we might feel in them, without having to risk too much. It also gives us a way of coping with bad experiences, by letting us play and replay them in our mind until they have lost much of their power to hurt, or until we can make them come out in ways that leave us feeling less defeated and foolish.

For a healthy and active fantasy life children need time, space, and privacy, or at least only as much companionship as they choose. Obviously school, or any other large-group situation—day-care center, nursery school, play group, etc.—does not allow much of this. Perhaps worst of all, they are usually under the eye and control of adults who, even if they will allow children a fantasy life, feel they have to watch it, understand what it means, judge it, make use of it. It was for just this reason that a well-meaning and quite highly praised book, written about ten years ago, called *Fantasy and Feeling in Childhood*, seemed and still seems to me deeply mistaken. The gist of it (and there may well be many books like it) was that if we, i.e., people who work in schools, paid enough attention to the fantasy lives of children, we could learn to understand them and bend them to our own purposes.

This would be a great mistake and a great wrong. Instead, we should be content to watch and enjoy as much of children's fantasy lives as they will let us see, and to take part in them, if the children ask us to and if we can do so happily and unselfconsciously. Otherwise, we should leave them alone. Children's fantasy is useful and important to them for many reasons, but above all because it is *theirs*, the one part of their lives which is wholly under their control. We must resist the temptation to make it *ours*.

We must also resist the equally great temptation to think that this part of children's lives is less important than the parts where they are doing something "serious"—reading, or writing, or doing schoolwork, or something that we want them to do—or to think that we can only allow them time for fantasy after all the important work is done, as we might give them a little piece of candy after a meal. For children, play and fantasy are one of the main courses of the meal. Children should be able to do them, not just in what little tag ends of time remain after all the "important" work is done, but when they are most full of energy and enthusiasm. We talk these days of "quality time." Children need quality time for their fantasy and play as much as for their reading or math. They need to play well as much as they need to read well. Indeed, we would probably find if we looked into it that children who are not good at playing, dreaming, fantasizing, are usually not much good at reading either.

At any rate, here are some nice accounts of this part of the lives of children.

FANTASTIC WORLDS

A mother writes about the world her son created:

But at the same time we are, deep inside, ready to "un-school." I am
absolutely convinced of its rightness. My problem is my children, especially the older one (10). After five years of schooling he has made
it palatable and even enjoyable by creating a world within a world
there with a couple of his friends. The schoolwork is no problem; he
goes so that he can get together easily with 2 or 3 other boys for playing baseball or whatever. Also, their world contains its own society of
"weepuls"—scores of Ping-Pong-ball-sized fuzzy creatures of different colors with big feet and tiny antennas. For almost a year they had
their city covering our 20'×12' sun porch (forced to be dismantled because we are remodeling). I haven't read *Gnomes*, but doubt if it
could be a more complete study than these kids have with weepuls:
the cast of characters, layers of their society, their soccer and football
fields, space-ports and ships, disco, museum, school, movie theater,
transportation system, all made in detailed miniature with great care
and skill; their diet of only bananas and banana juice, their death by
contact with water, and so on. When J went on a scout trip to the
snow, the weepul King Eeker went with him on skis made out of
tongue depressors. The weepuls go to school and hide in the desks
until break time when they come out and make school their place and
the boys can do what they want with and through them. Homework
and boredom are put up with for the chance to meet A and K and play
with weepuls.

Candy Mingins, a teacher, writes about a similar game called Atlas:

The family didn't have much money, and did have plenty of German
thriftiness—hence the children were not swamped with plastic toys and
gadgets. . . . They had to create their own play, so C and his brother and
two sisters (all older) played this ongoing game (invented mostly by his
brother) for 8 years or more. It was a game of the World. Each child
had tribes of people made from: toothpaste caps glued to marbles (the
Lilliputians); Hi-Q game pieces (the Microscopians); used Magic Mark-
ers with toothpick swords and aluminum foil shields (the Sudanis);
cooking oil bottles decorated with paper (the Criscoeans); etc. The
tribes fought battles in the garden, conquered territories, kept maps

and records, held art shows, had a newspaper, and had their own languages and money systems.

It was an ingenious invention of play, which the children created entirely by themselves, and which lasted through time, always encompassing new interests and ideas as the children grew.

COPS AND ROBBERS

A mother writes about a perennial child's game and her own memories of it:

Nobody ever told me not to play guns. But, when I was a kid, and the gang played cops'n'robbers, I had a problem because I couldn't "die." Some kid would shoot me, and I would want to fall down and die, but somehow I couldn't, and I would just stand there and look dazed. And if I shot somebody, he would just ignore me because he knew I hadn't really killed him.

After I grew up and had kids of my own, and they had taught me *how* to play cops'n'robbers, I realized that I had been a very schizoid child, very uptight, totally lacking in spontaneity, frozen out of the NOW—and playing guns is a kid's way of getting really "with" other kids and into a very fast-moving, action-packed *present*.

My observation (of about 15 years watching such games) is that only very free-spirited kids can play a really good game of cops'n'robbers, and that many games of cops'n'robbers are ended by a child who *does* have feelings of violence and cruelty and causes an "accident" to happen in which someone is hurt. Usually that child wants to put an end to the game because of jealousy—he *can't* share in the fun; not because he has been excluded by the others, but because he isn't capable of playing.

I don't think "playing guns" usually has anything to do with guns, violence, hostility, or cruelty; it is a game of awareness. Feelings, other than joy, get in the way of awareness, and you can explode your feelings by experiencing the sound of the cap exploding in a cap pistol, for instance.

In playing guns, I believe it goes like this: If I am *aware* of you first, I can shoot you, and you have to die! If I get surprised by you, then I

KNOW you are more aware than I am because *you* surprised *me*, so I've got to die. I just give up all awareness (falling in the process) until I feel a surge inside me that says I'm ready to be born again—MORE alive than before! Sometimes you and I catch each other at exactly the same time, and then we have to battle it out—Bang! Bang! Pow! Pow! I got YOU! NO you didn't, I got you FIRST!—until we both know that one of us has bested the other. One of us must die and be born again!

If, instead, one of us gets MAD—then the game quickly ends.

Oh, I love a good, noisy game of cops'n'robbers!

I am an old fossil of almost forty who couldn't play guns now to save my soul, but at least I still remember that I learned something from some kids a long time ago.

I'm trying to *tell* you something that can only be experienced, which tells me that I'm a fool. So, my suggestion is that you find a free-spirited kid (maybe you have one in your home?) and see what you can learn from him.

I believe that it's best to learn to look at the spirit—the feelings expressed—in what your child does, and see through the material object. After all, a child can express his feelings of cruelty and hostility when he pets the dog, and he can express his joy and delight when he shoots his gun. If your child is a joyful child and he WANTS a gun, I think you can trust in his joy, because the Bible says the things of this world are perishable, but the things of the spirit are everlasting, and I, personally, think kids are born knowing this.

Even if a child uses his toy gunplay to drain off his anger and hostility, without hurting anything or anyone in the process, what's the harm in it? My husband says he can remember having those feelings when he played guns as a kid (whereas I never saw such feelings expressed when our kids played guns). He said he thought it was a good thing that he had that outlet, as he had a very unhappy home.

Theo Giesy, a mother of four in Virginia says about this:

Darrin and Danile were introduced to guns by a friend K when they were 2 and 4, respectively. K was 4. One of them would stand on a hassock, the others would shoot him and he would die very dramatically.

Then someone else would climb up to be shot and die. K died most dramatically and was most fun. This was repeated as fast as someone could climb up, always with high spirits, fun, and friendliness. Darrin immediately wanted guns and built up quite an arsenal. Shortly after that we moved from California to Michigan. Without K the game changed entirely. Now Darrin and Danile would play house. She would stay home and take care of their babies (her dolls and his dolls) and he would ride the scooter to go off to the woods with his gun to hunt a bear to bring home for them to eat. (All imagination—no one we knew was a hunter.) Darrin was then 2½. At the same time when Darrin was really angry he never thought of guns. His expression of violence was "I'll throw a shoe at you." Guns were part of the world of fun and imagination and had nothing to do with real violence. The "death" of K and Danile and Darrin had nothing to do with hurting anyone.

I thought of that often the next year when Darrin's best friend was not allowed to have guns and they were not allowed to have guns at nursery school. So they built guns out of Tinkertoys or snap blocks. Parents who forbid guns are neither preventing violence nor gunplay and parents who allow guns are not encouraging violence.

HOMEMADE STORIES

The mother of a two-year-old boy told me that she had made up a story in which he was the hero, and all the other characters the animals on their small farm. He loved the story. Later she wrote it down and sent me a copy, saying, "You may find it a bit cute but a five-year-old boy wondered—in a whisper—all the way through, 'Is it true?'"

Children, whether in city or country, are more likely to be interested in stories in which they play a part, and which are full of things drawn from their everyday life. Parents, or other people who know the children well, are the ideal people to make up such stories. Even if they are not very polished, such stories are likely to be much more interesting than most of the stories in books for little children.

A. S. Neill, at Summerhill, used to make up stories for the children there, in which they were the leading characters, chasing or being chased by various spies, crooks, and villains. And as many know, *Alice in Wonderland* was made up for the real child who was the Alice in the story. So, take a shot at making up stories for your children. As with everything else, as you do it you'll get better at it.

Here is part of my friend's story:

PIG IN THE BED

On Tuesday last week a strange thing went on;
Jack came home early and his parents were gone.
He knew right away that something was up
When he took a look at his friend the pup.
(He was drinking a Coke, taking sips as he spoke.)

. . .

"Hey Jack! Look out! Better step aside.
The horse and her colt are going for a ride!"
Jack turned around when the pickup truck
Made the sound that it makes when it's just starting up.

. . .

The horse put it in gear and sputtered past,
Then before she started going too fast,
She yelled, "Sorry, Jack, to be taking your car,
But it's been a long time since we've gone very far."

. . .

Jack stared, then he wondered, then he said, "O.K.,
But will you try to get back by the end of the day?"

. . .

He shrugged and went on down to the kitchen,
But when he got there it was full of his chickens!
"Just fixing a little midday treat.

We get awfully tired of old corn to eat,"
Said the hens as they mixed and blended and baked
Until they came up with banana spice cake.

Everywhere Jack looked in the house, he found animals—even in his bed! How to get them out before his parents came back? Then he hit on the solution:

"I've got it!" said Jack, and he started to scream:
"Up in the barn there's chocolate ice cream!"
The chickens took wing, the pig climbed out of bed.
The cow left the tub and the goats quickly fled.

•   •   •

Up the road the horse was parking the truck.
Jack ran to the freezer. "Whew! I'm in luck!"

•   •   •

He got out two gallons of chocolate ice.
"Plenty for everyone! As long as you're nice."
He passed it out fairly to all on the farm,
To the pig in the pig pen and the cow in the barn.
"Thank heavens you knew just what to do,"
Said the dog, passing his plate. "May I have some too?"
"Certainly," said Jack. "But what will mom say
When she sees I ate two gallons of ice cream today?"

Most parents, whether on a farm or in a city, could spin such a homemade epic. It doesn't need to scan or rhyme as well as this—the children who see themselves in the story won't be fussy.

REQUIEM FOR A TURTLE

Small children when left on their own love to make up their own songs and chants. One mother told me about a chant that her daughter, when two years and nine months old, had made up one day while swinging on the swing, and seeing something disappear with a crunch into the mouth of her cat. The chant went like this:

> Oh, we went downtown . . .
> Downtown my mother
> and Mary Jean went.
> We saw some pretty turtles,
> some pretty little turtles.
> Yes, we did. O yes we did!
> Pretty, pretty little turtles . . .
> They wiggled and wiggled,
> They wiggled their heads,
> They wiggled their legs,
> And their tails they wiggled, wiggled . . . O!

.   .   .

> My mother buyed me
> Two little turtles
> Two little turtles *and*
> One little turtle made
> The *other* little turtle
> Not lonesome . . . O!
> He was s'posed to make him
> Not lonesome . . . O!

.   .   .

> Did he make him not lonesome? NO!
> He climb out, out . . .
> He fall on the ground . . . O!
> Oh, oh, oh, OH!
> He climb out
> Over and over AGAIN!
> I just can hardly believe it!

.   .   .

Poco-cat
Ate him all UP!

However, it turned out later the cat *hadn't* eaten the turtle, who was found under the child's bed.

A VERY YOUNG ARTIST

A father writes about a "precocious" artist:

> We have one of the happy stories about unschooling. Before M was born we had decided not to send her to school. We moved to the country thinking it would be easier there. Now I realize it might sometimes be more difficult.
>
> We were lucky. The teacher and school board of our local school, where I am janitor, have been tolerant and helpful. The teacher is one of the good ones. M goes once a week on a day of her choosing. Any more than once a week, she thinks, would be awful. One defense that we have thought might help if we are given any trouble about not going to school is that she is bilingual and does learning in her other language at home. (There are laws protecting bilingualism in California schools.) M's mother is Japanese.

Unfortunately, the law no longer protects bilingual education in California, and this is becoming true in other states as well. Although many parents would agree that using a one-size-fits-all approach to teaching children is wrong, it appears that sentiment doesn't pertain to foreign children learning English. Speaking only English or being bilingual in the classroom do not have to be mutually exclusive. Teachers and students both need options when things aren't working rather than ensuring by law that only one method can be used.

> M began to draw when she was 6 months old. Everything she did was treated as important art. By the time she was one year old she could draw better than anyone around her. Knowing that she could do

something better than anyone, even better than the ever-competent gi-
ants around her, emboldened her strokes. In other areas it gave her the
confidence to try something difficult, then to continue until she could
do it well.

At one year of age she was given an easel and some tempera paints.
On her second birthday she got nontoxic acrylics, the medium she has
preferred since. She enjoyed painting so much that she began calling
herself an artist.

We became curious about other children artists so we checked out
the children's art scene in San Francisco where we were then living. We
made the surprising discovery that M is a child artist who does not
paint children's art. Her work would look absurdly out of place in a
show of children's art. Especially so since she began using acrylics because it is always assumed that children's art should be done with wa-
tercolors. For obvious reasons acrylics are easier to use than poster
paints or tempera but they cost more. I know people who make 5 or 6
times my subsistence wage who tell me they can't afford acrylics for
their children. What this really means is that they think children can't
do anything worth that much.

Probing deeper in this direction via an understanding of adultism
might begin to explain what I mean when I say that much of what is
known as children's art is an adult invention.

In all the contacts we have had with the children's art establishments
in San Francisco and Tokyo we have had nothing but unpleasant experiences. They are amazed but they are even more skeptical. I think they
are hoping she'll turn out to be the 40-year-old midget in one of your
books. [Author's note: This refers to an episode in *Escape From Childhood*.] Finally we know they are the enemy. We avoid them, scorn their
nonsense books on children's art ("Children will generally not be ready
to paint before they are 5 years old"), frown back at the saved mission-
ary smiles they are in the habit of turning on their flock. When they used
to say M's work was very good for her age I asked them if they would say
Picasso's erotic drawings, done in his latter years, were good for his age.

It is recognized that children have their original imagination destroyed in the socializing process and that as adult artists they must

struggle to regain it if they are to create an original vision. There must be some way for people to grow up without losing this although it rarely happens. The most obvious thing to do is to stay out of school and maybe to prevent their exposure to phony children's art. One indication of what might have happened to M if she had been forced to go to school full-time is that when she draws at school her drawings are stiff and uninteresting. They are like children's drawings are supposed to be, cute and easy to patronize. She also prints her signature on them like the other children do. She has always signed her name in cursive and has used nothing but cursive at home since she learned it when she was 4 years old. She's 7 now.

M's conversations about what was going on in the paintings while she was doing them were so interesting that I decided when she was 4 years old to get some of her old paintings out to talk about them with her. She enjoyed seeing her treasures again. About the same thing she said originally was repeated but more concisely. She called them poems. During her fifth year she began writing her poems and stories by herself. One of her 4-year-old poems about a painting described what she imagined she did when she was wandering around the world with us five years before she was born: "When I was in Mama's stomach it was very dark so sometimes I wanted to get out. From a secret door I was looking out of Mama's stomach through her navel. Everywhere Mama went I was watching from my secret door. Each time I looked out she came to a new town. I saw the whole world. That's the place I was born."

With his letter the father sent me some reproductions of M's early work, five paintings done between the ages of twenty-six and thirty-eight months. They were printed in Japan, perhaps by some museum in connection with a show on children's art. I am guessing, but they look like the postcards of paintings that one can buy in museums. The paintings themselves are stunning. Three of them would stop you dead in your tracks if you saw them in an exhibition of "adult" art. The colors, the shapes, the drawing, the design, the underlying idea of the paintings, are extraordinary.

I am ready to believe that M is an exceptionally talented child. But that is what I felt when I first heard four- to six-year-old children, students of Suzuki in Japan, playing difficult music by Bach, Vivaldi, etc., in perfect time and tune. Perhaps other children might do work of equal beauty and power if their talents were taken seriously and given scope.

8

Learning Without Teaching

MUCH OF THE MATERIAL in this chapter could have gone into Chapter
5, "Learning in the World." I put it here to make a different point.
There I was talking about children (and others) learning outside of
school. Here I am talking about them learning without teaching—
learning by doing, by wondering, by figuring things out, and often in
the process resisting teaching when well-meaning adults try to force it
on them. A letter from Judy McCahill in England describes this kind
of learning very well:

> I do have the worst time explaining to people how I teach the kids. The
> trouble arises from the very basic concept, which most people can't
> grasp, that the kids actually teach themselves. I find it impossible, both
> timewise and because of my live-and-let-live nature, to give any sort of
> formal lessons. Recently I thought I would begin giving myself system-
> atic lessons in basic science so that I could teach the kids better, but af-
> ter three days that failed because I always seemed to have something
> more important to do than study. So I continue with my major tech-
> nique of just answering questions as well as I can and helping the kids
> to ferret out information when they want it.

It interests me, though, how quickly the kids latch onto my *real* enthusiasms and, without anybody intending anything, begin to learn. Last summer I visited the Tate Gallery (a big art museum in London) with a girl who had just finished a year-long course in the history of art. She infected me with her enthusiasm, I attended a slide-illustrated lecture that day, and I examined incredulously the calendar of (free!!!) events the Tate had set up—all sorts of lectures, films, special exhibitions, and guided tours.

I've only been back to the Tate once since then, but I brought home a couple of books and gloatingly circled all the events I would attend if I could. (Next week I am going to a performance of *Julietta* by the English National Opera which is connected to a film and lecture on Surrealism at the Tate.) Last month our 18-year-old niece came to stay with us and she and Colleen have gone to the Tate three or four times. She [Colleen] has checked an art book out of the library (never having been interested in art before). And the boys often page through the books, studying the pictures. We have many discussions arising from what the girls have seen at the Tate; Colleen takes notes on the lectures for my benefit. So something new has entered our life, and it was completely accidental.

NO WORDS TO THE WISE

As many may know, in the Suzuki method of violin instruction, at least as first conceived and practiced, the parents of a child, while it is still a baby, begin to play for it, and often, recordings of the easy violin pieces which it will itself learn to play at the age of three. Kathy Johnson and I have talked often (in letters) about Suzuki. Recently she wrote:

> You asked me last December to let you know how my home adaptation of Suzuki violin with my two-year-old daughter is working. I hadn't actually brought home the ¹⁄₁₆-size violin then, but in self-defense had to get her one to keep her from having tantrums when my dad and I played. Her being well into the "No" stage now is living proof of why they don't organize a class of young Suzuki violinists until age three.

But I feel you *can* do more at an early age than merely play the record. With no big fanfare, one day when a tantrum started during our duet, I simply suggested she play her own violin—that little one over there in the corner. She gave me a look as if to say, "Oh yes, but of course!" And before the duet was over, she had figured out how to open the case, get the violin out, and saw the bow upside-down over the strings a few times. She was delighted.

In the past four months, whenever we saw such a gross mistake on her part, either my dad or I (whoever was closer) would *very briefly* reach down and show her a better way to play as we went along. Of course, she had to learn some rules: not to carry her instrument around the house, especially on noncarpeted surfaces, not to handle the bow hair (or it won't make any sound on the strings), etc. We were amazed how fast she learned to respect her instrument. She even keeps the bow rosined!

She hasn't mastered the technique of playing just one string at a time yet, but she has darn good position, and a wonderful time developing those long full bows.

We were amazed when out-of-town relatives came to visit and our *shy* little daughter brought out her violin to squawk on the strings in front of a roomful of adults. We were all proud—but not as proud as she was! I think the important thing my dad and I learned very quickly was to recognize that moment when she needed help, capitalize on it briefly, then leave her alone to experiment. Praise is used, but in not much greater amounts than Dad and I praise each other. We play for enjoyment. I think she does, too.

She won't stand for a "lesson." Help that is a few seconds too long or in the wrong tone of voice brings loud "No-No's" followed by her putting her violin away and being angry. At this age, there's a fine line between happiness and tears. When she wants, if she wants, we'll see an expert.

A mother writes about another child resisting teaching:

My daughter (3) is in the kitchen teaching herself addition and subtraction on the Little Professor Calculator—a machine I don't really approve of—and every time I give her a gentle hint, she flies into a rage, but when I leave her alone and watch her out of the corner of my eye, I see her doing problems like 3 + 5 = 8!

Years ago I went to a meeting of Catholic educators, where I heard a talk by a wise, funny old man who had been teaching all his life. One thing he said made us all laugh, and has stuck in my mind ever since: "A word to the wise is *infuriating!*" Yes it is, because it is insulting, and little children pick up this expression of (often loving and protective) distrust or contempt, even when we're not conscious of sending it.

Some years ago I was reading aloud to a small child, as yet a non-reader, perhaps three or four years old. As I read aloud I had the bright idea that by moving a finger along under the words as I read them I might make more clear the connections between the written and the spoken words. A chance to get in a little subtle teaching. Without saying anything about it, and as casually as possible, I began to do this.

It didn't take the child very long to figure out that what had begun as a nice, friendly, cozy sharing of a story had turned into something else, that her project had by some magic turned into *my* project. After a while, and without saying a word, she reached up a hand, took hold of my hand, and very gently moved it off the page and down by my side—where it belonged. I gave up "teaching" and went back to doing what I had been asked to do, which was to read the story.

A father writes:

It is not possible for an inquisitive child to delve deeply into dinosaurs without wondering about, and learning, how big they were (measure-ments), how many roamed a certain area (arithmetic), where they lived (geography), what happened to them (history), etc. And, after daddy's knowledge of dinosaurs was exhausted, which happened pretty quickly, a lot of reading was necessary. In short, it simply isn't possible to learn a lot about dinosaurs or anything else without along the way learning and using knowledge and skills that are intellectually prerequisite. After all, the reason that we call "the basics" by that phrase is that they *are* basic, and to worry that a kid will learn just about anything without learning and using the basics is like being worried that he might decide to build a house starting with the roof.

It's hard work, of course, for us to adjust ourselves to the kids' interests. They wake up every morning curious but, alas, rarely curious about the particular topics that we might be prepared to talk about or might prefer that they be curious about—that's when temptation rears its head and must be suppressed. It's a waste of time and quickly degenerates into intellectual bullying to try to sidetrack a kid onto topics *you* think he should be learning. Of course, going along with the kids' interests may, as it recently did in our family, find you subjected to six straight days of inquiry into space exploration. But, if you will just be patient and observant, the time comes when the kid, because *he* realizes that it's pertinent to learning about his primary interest, will, almost off-handedly (but it sticks), add rocket thrusts, multiply fuel loads, distinguish ellipses from circles, etc. Keep your mouth shut when you are not needed, and be ready to help when you are. The kid will learn.

Perhaps the reason that so many adults—including, I confess, myself—find it hard to refrain from "helping" kids is that it wounds our egos to see how well they get along without us! How can that dumb kid of mine learn so much without a smart fellow like me to teach him? We try in effect to horn in on the kids' sense of pride in accomplishment and, all too often, particularly in schools, we succeed. The results are psychologically and intellectually catastrophic for the victims.

Another father writes:

I have read the books you have written, and between them and Bob (4), I've found, for me, the best way to teach is by example, and the best way to learn is by doing. (Bob continually tells us, "I don't want to know that" when we try to teach him something he doesn't want to learn.) Linda and I are impressed how quickly he picks things up, but what impresses me the most is his ability to just sit and think. I never knew young children did that until Bob showed me. He also repeats and repeats things until he has them. We put him to bed at 9 P.M., and often at 11 we can hear him talking to himself as he goes over things he wants to get straight. This is how he learned the alphabet and how to count to

129. That's his favorite number and he counts to it over and over and over. Somehow he has picked up the idea that a number means a quantity of objects, and I am amazed he has learned that level of abstraction so quickly and completely.

I've tried to let Bob and David learn what they want to at the rates they set, but sometimes it is hard not to teach. There is one story I enjoy, simply because it was the only time I've been successful at teaching when Bob wasn't interested. When Bob was learning to count, he asked me what comes after 113. I didn't answer his question, but instead asked him what comes after 13. Well, he got mad because that's not what he wanted. I remained stubborn and he finally said, "14 comes after 13, what comes after 113?" very indignantly. I immediately said, "114." At first he was disgusted because I didn't answer his question the first time, but then he understood what I had just done. He broke out in a big grin and covered his face. We like to trick each other, and I had just gotten him.

One summer I was visiting an eight-year-old friend and her mother. They lived in a little house on a small side street, really more an alley. Cars seldom come through so kids can play there safely. In one part of the street there are high board fences on both sides, which makes it a good place for small ball games. My young friend and her friends often play their own version of baseball here. For a bat they use a thin stick about three feet long. The ball is a playground ball about six inches in diameter. The rules fit the space perfectly; with that stick, no one can hit that ball over those fences.

The day I arrived, after dinner, she asked me if I would pitch some batting practice. I said, Sure, and we had about forty-five minutes' worth in the alley. Next morning after breakfast she asked again, and we had about an hour more. Some of the time she very kindly pitched to me. I was amazed to find how hard it was to move that squishy ball with that skinny stick.

The point of the story is that in all this I did something about which I felt quite pleased, that I don't think I could or would have done even five years ago. In our almost two hours of play I did not offer *one word* of coaching or advice. The words were more than once on the tip of my tongue, once when she tried batting one-handed (she did better than I thought she would), once when she tried batting cross-handed (she gave it up on her own), and now and then when she seemed to be getting careless, not watching the ball, etc. But I always choked the words back, saying to myself, "She didn't ask you to coach, she asked you to pitch. So shut up and pitch." Which I did.

Nor did I give any praise. Sometimes—quite often, as a matter of fact—when she hit a real line drive, I let out a word of surprise or even alarm, if it came right at me. Otherwise we did our work in silence, under the California sun. I remember it all with pleasure, and not least of all the silence. I hope I can be as quiet next time.

A mother in Ontario describes an extraordinary day in which she and another mother let the children lead the play:

Last fall we had a school group meeting [of children who on most days were learning at home] twice a week. Mostly 2–4-year-olds and mostly girls with one five-year-old girl and a six-year-old boy. Altogether there were about twelve children. It was quite a delightful group.

This is the day I remember best from that time. We began painting, and working with clay, and playing in the yard in front of the house. As lunch time neared we decided to have a picnic in the little pine forest. (This was one of the favorite nice weather activities.) The little pine trees are about twelve years old and a wonderful size for little people to climb and create fantasy worlds within.

As we were eating, I noticed some tiny green plants growing within the browns, reds, oranges of the fall leaves. I looked closer at the little plants and suggested that the children near me help me look for the various tiny plants growing around us. We found my favorite spring greens—sorrel and peppergrass—and some clover and a couple of plants none of us were familiar with. We nibbled the greens and were pleased with our discovery.

Soon the wonderful game of "roaring lions in the forest" began. The other mother and I sat to rest for a while. One child (3) stayed with us looking at the plants. She was a very quiet child and often stayed by herself very absorbed for long times with her interests while all the others very easily related and played and talked with each other. Sometimes I wondered if she wanted help getting to know others, if she was lonely and frightened in her solitude. But from observing her I'd decided she was actually quite happy on her own a lot. She almost never talked at school, but I knew she could talk because I'd heard her talk to her older sister quite freely. So when she began talking to me about the plants I was delighted. We looked very slowly at many little plants and she pulled some out to look at the roots. Then she looked at the different levels of dead leaves—the brand new, bright crunchy ones were pushed away by her delicate finger, next there were softer brown ones, then black matted ones, then dirt. We talked throughout this examining of the magic of plants and earth.

When that was complete we moved off to join the others who led us through the pines to the edge of the swamp—cedars and black gooshy mud and water. Someone took shoes and socks off and within a very short time all shoes and socks came off. There was a great deal of splashing and stamping and singing and joy. Someone fell down and got his pants mucky. (I thought—What are his parents going to think?) They were obviously having way too much fun to stop them. Soon all clothes were being taken off and put on the moss under the cedars. And the jolly dance continued. The little girl I described earlier was joining right in with all the others looking quite radiant. One child stayed back from the muck and the wet. He didn't seem disturbed by the others dancing in the muck, but obviously it didn't appeal to him. Exploring the swamp went on until it was time to dry off, get dressed, and go home.

I thought about that day and wondered how most of the parents would have responded. Some might not have allowed the naked water play—others probably would have. Some probably would have felt there wasn't much happening that day as much of it was spent on a long walk. But I was glad that the other mother who was there was as willing as I to follow the little people on their adventure and I loved that day!

FINDING OUT

. . . A three-year-old has moved into a new house and has played in the sunshine on the new roof. He goes downstairs to supper and when he comes back steps into a changed and darkened world. With a wondering glance he says, "The big shadow is all around." Another three-year-old sees a thin cloud float across the moon. She watches intently, then says to herself, "Like ice, like ice."

This child's vision, quoted in a Colorado (Boulder) magazine called *Outlook*, is echoed by Hanna Kirchner, writing in Poland about the work of the physician Janusz Korczak:

He always stressed that by means of learning the everyday expressions from the obscure language of adults, the child tries to fathom the mystery of life. The child's fragmentary and incomplete knowledge of the world, welded together by imagination, creates a specific "magic consciousness" which, as has been discovered in the twentieth century, exists among children and primitive people and may be associated with the origins of poetry.

She then gives this wonderful quote from Korczak's book *How to Love a Child* (not yet translated into English):

[one child says], "They say there is one moon and yet one can see it everywhere."
"Listen, I'll stand behind the fence and you stay in the garden." They lock the gate.
"Well, is there a moon in the garden?"
"Yes."
"Here too."
They change places and check once again. Now they are sure there must be two moons.

And yet they figure out, sooner or later, and *by themselves*, that there is only one moon.
And Theo Giesy tells this nice story:

When Danile was 6 or 7, she was lying in my bed thinking about money and wondering how $1 would divide among 3 children. She thought about it a while and said, "You could break it into dimes and give each one 3, that leaves 1 dime, you break that into pennies and give each one 3, and I get the extra penny." That was all her own, I made no comments or suggestions.

When I first taught fifth grade, before I had "taught" the children anything about fractions, or even mentioned the word, I used to ask them questions like this: "If you had three candy bars, and wanted to divide them evenly among five people, how would you do it?" Most of them could think of one or more ways to do this. But after they had "had" fractions, and learned to think of this as a problem that you had to use fractions to solve, most of them couldn't do it. Instead of reality, and their own common sense and ingenuity, they now had "rules," which they could rarely keep straight or remember how to apply.

Since to so many people "learning" means what happens in school, or what is supposed to happen, I would rather use other words to describe what we humans do as a natural part of our living. "Finding out" seems to fit pretty well. Here, a reader talks about this continuous process:

I am almost a caricature of the congenital unteachable. It may have been something I picked up from imitating my father, for I notice he shares the trait to this day. He is very quick to learn, but utterly resists being taught.

I began to see how much this unteachability pervaded my life when I began about a year ago to see how much of my childhood I could remember distinctly. Probably the extreme example was learning to play the piano. I am told that I started banging away on the family upright at about age four. One day my dad got tired of the noise and said something to the effect of "If you're going to play, why don't you play *something*?" Well, I quit until my parents left the house, and when they came back that afternoon I was already picking out tunes. In a year I played "Silent Night" at church Christmas ceremonies.

So much has been like this. I started drawing at about four, also holding the pencil the wrong way. People said that I would never be able to draw that way. After selling dozens of paintings and drawings, I still hold it that way—I don't like the other way, as it produces a more unsteady hand for me. When, at about twelve, I wanted to write books, my dad gave me an old Royal and left me alone. I learned to type at good speed with one right-hand finger.

Then there were swimming lessons, which almost permanently made me hate swimming. A couple of years afterward, when I *wanted* to swim with my friends, I jumped in and swam as if I had always done so.

I taught myself auto mechanics on my first car, after being told for years that I was low in mechanical ability. I became a good carpenter's apprentice in two months, building one and a half houses with just one carpenter working at the same time. I surprised them all (except my parents—who had been listening) when I switched from an undergraduate education in pre-law to master's work in engineering, putting to rest the old thing about how artsy-booksy types cannot cope with numbers.

How did I get through schools? Only one way—by taking the offensive. Way back around fifth grade, my parents supplied us kids with the *Golden Book Encyclopedia*. I lapped up each book as it came home from the supermarket. Not long after that I was tested for reading at school and was found to be reading five years ahead of my grade. What is more, the *Golden Book Encyclopedia* gave me two invaluable things which freed me from much of the meaningless work the schools had cut out for me. One, I acquired from the encyclopedia a working familiarity with many aspects of science, history, geography, and art—such that I still "leaned on" this knowledge during exams as late as, say, tenth grade. Moreover, it taught me an understanding of how the world works, so that I could figure out what I did not actually know.

I recall what I did in fifth grade to free up more time to study airplanes, which I was then immersed in as a subject. The teacher wanted us to come up with five new words a week which we were supposed to define as a vocabulary lesson [Author's note: as if anyone ever learned words this way]. Trouble was, words did not come to me at this steady pace. So, one day, I reached into the dictionary for two hundred-odd words and did a year's assignments in one bored stroke. Then I went back to gobbling up new and historical words as part of the new book I was writing on airplanes.

When I went back to grad school I again entered on the explicit understanding that I would take some required courses and do some required research for the chance to be allowed hunks of free time to pursue an area that no one at the school even understood. It worked. So well, in fact, that I literally walked into a job working with the guy who my previous research had shown to be tops in the field.

And now I find some strange truths. With the top-notch people that make up our company, *what counts is the ability to teach oneself* [Author's emphasis]. As my employer puts it, "Though we may seem to know a lot around here, we succeed because we start out by admitting our ignorance, and then setting out to overcome it."

This points up one important idea, the "need to know." People often say of me that I "know" a great deal about this or that; but often I have only average knowledge or less. In any given context, however, I can identify what I need to know next, and self-reliance has taught me to immediately acquire the knowledge in ways which do not essentially differ from one case to the next. Thus it occurs to me that if people recognized knowledge as being important *only in relation to actual goals*—narrow or broad in scope—rather than being some kind of unquestionable goal in itself, they might better know how to go about acquiring it.

I know more than a few individuals who share my experience. Their existence assures me that a market exists for free schools offering not "teachers" but *the resources necessary for self-teaching*.

THE SHORT, HAPPY LIFE OF A TEACHING MACHINE

When the Santa Fe Community School was just starting, a young inventor, who hoped to market one of the "teaching machines" then in fashion, lent one of his models to the school. It was a big metal box, that sat on top of a table. Through a window in the front of the box, one could see a printed card. Beside the window were five numbered buttons. On the card one might read something like this: "An apple is a (1) machine (2) animal (3) fruit (4) fish (5) musical instrument." If one pushed button #3, a little green light went on above the buttons, and a new card appeared behind the window. If one pushed any of the other buttons, a red light went on. Like most teaching machines, it was only a fancy way of giving multiple choice tests.

On the day the inventor brought the box to school the children, aged five through eight, gathered around to see how it worked. The inventor showed them how to use it, and for a while the children took turns pushing the buttons and answering the questions on the cards. This only lasted a short while. Then the children began to say, "Open the box! We want to see inside the box!" Someone opened up the front panel, showing the cards, mounted on a revolving drum. Beside each card were five little holes, and a metal plug to stick into the hole matching the "right answer" to the question on the card.

The children considered all this a minute, and then fell to work— *making cards.* After a while they all had some cards to load into the machine. Bargains were struck: "I'll play using your cards if you'll play using mine." One child would load up the machine with his cards, and put in the answer buttons, then another child would come and take the test, then they would trade places. This went on for perhaps a day or so, all very serious.

Then, so the friend told me who was teaching there at the same school and saw all this, the game began to change. There was much loud laughter around the machine. The teachers went to see what was going on. What they saw was this. A child would load the machine, as before, and another child would take the test. Up would come a card saying something like, "A dog is a (1) train (2) car (3) airplane (4) animal (5) fish." The child taking the test would press button #4, the "right answer," and *the red light would go on.* The child who had made the card, and others watching, would shriek with laughter. The child being tested would push the buttons, one by one, until he hit the "right" one and the drum turned up the next card. Then, same story again, another right answer rewarded with the red light, more laughter. When one child had run through all his rigged cards, the other would have a turn, and would do exactly the same thing.

This happy game went on for a day or two. Then the children, having done everything with the machine that could be done with it, grew bored with it, turned away from it, and never touched it again. After a month or so the school asked the inventor to take his machine away.

This little incident tells us more about the true nature of children (and so, all humans) than fifty years worth of Pavlovian behaviorist or Skinnerian operant conditioning experiments. Maybe Psychologist and Pigeon is a good game, for a while at least. But all human beings soon want to play Psychologist; no one wants to be the Pigeon. We humans are not by nature like sheep or pigeons, unquestioning, docile, happy to work the machine as long as it lights up its green lights or rolls out its food pellets. Like these children, we want to find out how the machine works, and then *work it*. We want to find out how things happen, so that we can make them happen. That is the kind of creature we are. Any theory of learning or teaching which begins by assuming that we are some wormlike or ratlike or pigeonlike creature is nonsense and can only lead (as it has and does) to endless frustration and failure.

LEARNING A NEW LANGUAGE

Young children who come into contact with people who speak more than one language will learn to speak all of those languages, usually without much trouble. Older people, who have a great deal of trouble, are amazed by this. To explain it, they invent fancy theories about children having a special aptitude, or their brains being somehow different from adults'.

The real explanation is simpler. The child, who in his home speaks language A, but meets outside the home other children who speak language B, does not in any way set himself the task of "learning language B." In fact, he does not think of himself as "speaking language A," or indeed any language. He just speaks. He tries to understand what people are saying, and to make them understand what he wants to say, and the more he does this, the better he gets.

Now, all of a sudden, he meets some people whom he can't understand at all, and who can't understand him. What he wants and tries to do is understand those people, at least a little, *right now*, and to make them understand him, at least a little, *right now*. That is what he works at, and since he is smart, tireless, ingenious, not much discouraged by difficulties, and not at all worried about "failing" or looking foolish, and since he gets instant responses to tell him whether or not he is understanding or being understood, he very quickly gets good at it.

His parents think how wonderful it is that he is learning language B so quickly. But he is not trying to do that. He would not understand what it meant to "learn a language," and would not know how to do such a task even if people could explain to him what the task was. He is just trying to communicate with those people he meets.

After my father had retired from business, he and my mother began to spend the winter half of each year in Mexico. My father, who had been—just barely—a good enough student to graduate from a "good" college, told himself sternly, and kept telling himself for six years and more, that he ought to "learn Spanish." My mother, who had not gone to college, and had been a poor student—she had always been terribly nearsighted, but beyond that was bored to death by the tasks of school—could not have cared less about "learning Spanish." What she wanted, like little children, was to be able to talk to these people around her, who were not at all like any of the people she had ever known, and who interested her very much. She had always had a small child's keenness of observation and sharpness of mind, and now, like a young child, she began to try to talk to the people around her, to ask the names of things, to ask *how* to ask the names of things. The people she talked to, enchanted as people always are by someone who makes a real effort to speak their language, talked back, showed her things and told her their names (as they did to me when I visited), gently corrected her mistakes in pronunciation or usage, not so that she would speak "correctly" but only so that she would be better understood, and helped her in every way they could. The result was that very soon she could talk easily and fluently with people on many subjects.

At the same time, my father, who thought of himself as trying to "learn Spanish," which meant to learn to speak it correctly, so that *then* he could talk to the people around him, never learned more than twenty or so words in all the years he lived in Mexico. Now and then my mother tried to get him to say a few words to the people he met.

He couldn't do it. He was struck dumb by his school-learned fear of doing it wrong, making a mistake, looking foolish or stupid. He backed away from all these human contacts, telling himself all the while that he really ought to learn Spanish but was just too old, didn't have the aptitude, and so on.

LEARNING MUSIC

The October 5, 1977, issue of *Manas* magazine quotes, from the book *Piano: Guided Sight Reading*, by Leonard Deutsch, this interesting fragment:

> The famous Hungarian and Slovak gypsies have a centuries-old musical tradition. This colorful folk has brought forth numerous excellent instrumentalists, notably violinists. They learn to play much as an infant learns to walk—without teaching methods, lessons, or drills. No written music is used. The youngster is merely given a small fiddle and *allowed to join the gypsy band* [Author's emphasis]. He gets no explanations or corrections. He causes no disturbance, for his timid efforts are scarcely audible. He listens: he tries to play simultaneously what he hears, and gradually succeeds in finding the right notes and producing a good tone. Within a few years he has developed into a full-fledged member of the band with complete command of his instrument.
>
> Are these gypsy children particularly gifted? No, almost any child could accomplish what they do. The band acts as teacher talking to the pupil in the direct language of music. The novice, by joining the band, is immediately placed in the most helpful musical atmosphere and psychological situation; thus, from the beginning, he finds the right approach to music activity.

In contrast, an extremely intelligent and capable friend, not at all daunted by most forms of learning, and a lover of music, once told me that she wished she could read music, but that ever since she had been taught music in school, the task had seemed hopelessly mysterious, terrifying, and impossible. I asked her if she could think of any special part of it that seemed harder than the rest. Like most people in that position who are asked that question, she made a large gesture and said, "All of it. I just don't understand *anything* about what those little dots mean on the page." I asked if it was the rhythm or the pitch that seemed most mysterious. After some thought, she said, "The pitch." I then said (there was a piano handy), "If you like, I think I can show you in a few minutes how to find any written note." She agreed. Within half an hour she was very slowly playing, by herself, a piece out of a beginning piano instruction book.

Five things made it possible for me to help her find out how to do this. (1) It was her idea, her interest; *she* wanted to do it. (2) I was at all times ready to stop if she wanted to. She knew I would not, in my enthusiasm for teaching, push her into the confusion, panic, and shame into which eager or determined teachers so often push their students. (3) I accepted as legitimate and serious both her anxiety and her confusion. Even in the privacy of my own mind, I did not dismiss any of her fears or questions as silly. (4) I was ready to let *her* ask all the questions, to wait for her answers, and to let her use my answers as she wished. *I did not test her understanding.* I let her decide whether she understood or not, and if not, what to do about it, what question to ask next. (5) I was not going to *use* her to prove to her or myself or anyone else what a gifted teacher I was. If she wants to explore written music further, fine. If she wants to ask me for more help, that's fine too— though even better if, as I suspect, she can do it without my help. But if, having proved to herself that she *can* figure out what notes mean, she doesn't want to do more of it—well, that's fine too.

In an article entitled "Violinist Par Excellence," in *Music Magazine*, February 1980, a great violinist talks about teaching:

Nathan Milstein says his own family in Odessa was not particularly musical. "They became musical eventually," he laughed. "But I don't think a musical family makes much of a difference." His mother wanted him to play violin not because she was musical, but because, as he said once, she "wanted to calm me down and she thought the violin would do it."

Later, he taught his younger brother how to play the cello. "It wasn't difficult. If somebody's smart and knows music, he can do it. I could teach him because I played the same family of instrument: violin, cello, it's the same, only you put your fingers further apart. People exaggerate everything."

Like many artists, Milstein suspects that even the role of teachers is exaggerated. "A teacher doesn't help much. Not many teachers do. Young people often think that if they go to a teacher, the teacher will tell them how to play. No! Nobody can tell you. A teacher may play very well in one way, but his student might not be able to play as well if he is taught to play the same way. That's why I think that the teacher's business is to explain to the pupil, especially the gifted ones, that the teacher can't do very much except to try to open the pupil's mind so that he can develop his own thinking. The fact is that the pupils have to do it. They have to do the job; not the teacher."

Looking back, Milstein admits that none of his teachers were particularly helpful in this way. "But you see," he explains, "I was always very curious and experimenting. Instinctively I thought that if I will not help myself my teacher will not help me."

. . . The worst teachers, in Milstein's opinion, are those who are not performers themselves. "Performers can give students more than any professor who is in the Curtis Institute or in the Juilliard School," he says vehemently. "Because you can only give something to a young person from your own experience. Teachers who don't perform, who never studied for a career, how do they know? I know of famous teachers in America that are ruining young people. Ruining!" By contrast, Milstein does not think that a very gifted person will be ruined by not having a teacher. . . .

SELF TEACHING

A teacher in Vancouver writes:

I saw an interesting thing this past week. I was down at a little storefront place called the Community Computer Institute (a small business which rents time on computers—the little personal ones—for very good rates: they also have self-teaching programs which you can use to have the computer teach you how to use the computer). While I was there an older man and a young boy, about 11, came in and were looking around. The kid was fascinated and the man was a little perplexed and amazed, "They're finally here . . . my, my . . . . " However, the kid began to show the man some games on one of the simpler computers and within a few minutes both were engrossed in a major "Star Trek" game. After the game the kid explained some rudimentary principles of programming to the man, who by this time was very interested.

So was I, because here was a classic example of a teaching/learning situation between two people without regard for age, roles, or formal structure. I felt very good watching this whole episode and wondered what kind of things we could invent to facilitate this kind of thing happening throughout the city. I tried to explain this to some of the teachers I work with and they just ignored me. "That's not real learning and it just gets in the way of teaching them math skills." Here was an 11-year-old kid who had taught himself more about computers than I know, just by hanging around this place before it officially opened (so they let him use the computers for free) and by reading simple articles about programming. And they tell me that it's not real learning!

A mother writes more about "real learning:"

The best thing I wanted to share with you is that E is reading. I was prepared to see him a nonreader still at the age of 10, 12—who could tell? He was fascinated with the shapes of letters on his father's truck when he was two, picked out letter shapes in sidewalk cracks, read short words on signs, played games with beginning sounds (his idea, not mine), and generally always liked words.

Getting from that stage to actually reading books left a blank in my mind. If he didn't want me to help him, didn't sit down and work at it, how was he going to read beyond the shopping center signs stage? It must be at this stage that school people nervously rush in with methods and phonics rules, and at times I had to stop myself from doing the same. Teaching habits die hard. He knew so much! But he wasn't pulling it all together, wasn't even interested in opening a book to see if he could read the whole thing. I was dying of curiosity to see if he could, but I kept biting my lip every time a "lesson" threatened to come out.

He started about three months ago curling up with a comic book in the magazine section of the supermarket every week. Sometimes he'd buy one, and after we read it to him once, he'd take it off to a corner and study it for a while. He began "reading" them in bed. I knew something was happening because he got very quiet at these times, never asked me what a word was, and never made comments on the pictures. It became clear to me that reading was a private thing to him. After a while, he picked out easy books for bedtime reading and offered to read them to me. There were very few words he didn't know, and I'll never know how he learned the others. But it doesn't matter. He did it because he wanted to. I just hope I can keep on resisting all the pressures to do otherwise and let him set his own priorities.

One of our readers tells us about his brother's learning:

My brother is an electronics technician, by trade, and an electronics whiz by vocation. While still a teenager he *taught himself* all the mathematics, language, etc., necessary and built many complicated things—an oscilloscope, a computer, etc. He is now making a lot of money (I am not!) as a skilled technician (I am not!) while continuing to develop his own very creative ideas in electronics in his free time, with his own equipment, at home.

TEACHING VS. LEARNING

In "Vernacular Values and Education," a chapter in his book *Shadow Work*, Ivan Illich wrote of a man he had visited:

This man . . . had ceased to be a parent and had become a total teacher. In front of their own children this couple stood *in loco magistri*. Their children had to grow up without parents, because these two adults, in every word they addressed to their two sons and one daughter, were "educating" them—they were at dinner constantly conscious that they were modeling the speech of their children, and asked me to do the same.

Vol. 3, nos. 5 and 6 of *The Home and School Institute Newsletter* talks about things people can do with children at home. At first glance, many of them seem very sensible and pleasant, things that many loving and observing mothers have been doing for years. Thus:

BEDROOM—READING

Dress Me and Body All (vocabulary builders). There are words that attach to clothing—shirt, blouse, sock, shoe, etc.—and there are words attached to body parts—foot, arm, head, knee, etc. The bedroom is a fine place to learn these words; say the words aloud as clothes go off parts of bodies, print the words on large pieces of paper and label clothes in closets and drawers. . . .

Well, yes, perhaps. It all depends on the spirit in which this is done. If you like babies and little children, and on the whole I do, it is fun to talk to them about the things you are seeing or doing together. In *How Children Learn* I said that many mothers (or other adults) getting a small child ready to go out might say something like:

". . . Now we'll tie up this shoe; pull the laces good and tight; now we'll get the boots; let's see, the right boot for the right foot, then the left boot for the left foot; all right, coat next, arms in the sleeves, zip it up, nice and tight; now the mittens, left mitten on the left hand, right mitten on the right hand; now comes the hat, on it goes, over your ears . . . " This kind of talk is companionable and fun, and from it the child learns, not just words, but the kinds of phrases and sentences they fit into.

But I'm afraid that the real point of this, that the talk *was* companionable and fun, a way for the mother to express in words some of her love for the child and pleasure in its company, may have been lost. In this mother's voice, as I hear it in my mind's ear, I can hear tones of pleasure and excitement, the words matching the action, perhaps a sympathetic grunt as she tugs at a stuck zipper or pulls on a boot, the whole thing underlined with many an affectionate squeeze or pat. This is not at all the same thing as saying, as we put on the child's coat, "Coat! Coat! Coat!" so that the child will "learn that this is a coat." The difference is between talk which is done for the pleasure itself, with learning only a possible and incidental by-product, and talk which has no purpose other than to produce learning.

From what I read elsewhere in this *Home and School Institute Newsletter*, it looks as if they have fallen solidly on the wrong side of this line. Thus:

> *Subject Bounce.* Over a fast breakfast or a sit-down dinner, play this "talk" game that prepares children for putting their thoughts into writing. Toss out a subject, start with simple ones that children know about—summer, friends, breakfast, school. The child then comes up with a statement about it; examples, "Summer is the best season," or "Friends like the same things you do." As children build sophistication, their subjects and statements get more sophisticated, too.

Awful! Reading this, I understand and share the real horror that Illich felt at his friend's dining room table. Years before I began teaching, I spent an evening with parents of young children in a home in which nothing was said or done without some kind of "teaching" purpose. Every word or act carried its little lesson. It was nightmarish, the air quivered with tension and worry. I could not wait to leave.

Life is full of ironies. I wrote *How Children Learn* hoping to help introduce the natural, effortless, and effective ways of learning of the happy home into the schools. At times I fear I may only have helped to bring the strained, self-conscious, painful, and ineffective ways of learning of the schools into the home. To parents I say, above all else, don't let your home become some terrible miniature copy of the school. No lesson plans! No quizzes! No tests! No report cards! Even leaving your children alone would be better; at least they could figure out some things on their own. Live together, as well as you can; enjoy life together, as much as you can. Ask questions to find out something about the world itself, not to find out whether or not someone knows it.

THE PRICE OF TEACHING TRICKS

Dr. Gregory Bateson, one of the most learned and creative intellectuals of our time, who in his life studied and wrote a great deal in anthropology, psychology, and other fields, summed up much of his life's work and thought in the book *Steps to an Ecology of Mind*. In one chapter, discussing the difficulties of communicating with dolphins and other animals, he says,

> . . . [There are] very special difficulties in the problem of how to test what is called the "psychology" (e.g., intelligence, ingenuity, discrimination, etc.) of individual animals. A simple experiment . . . involves a series of steps: (1) the dolphin may or may not perceive a difference between the stimulus objects, X and Y. (2) The dolphin may or may not perceive that this difference is a cue to behavior. (3) The dolphin may or may not perceive that the behavior in question has a good or bad effect upon reinforcement, that is, that doing "right" is conditionally followed by fish. (4) The dolphin may or may not choose to do "right," even after he knows which is right. Success in the first three steps merely provides the dolphin with a further choice point. . . .
>
> Precisely because we want to argue from observation of the animal's success in the later steps to conclusions about the more elementary steps, it becomes of prime importance to know whether the organism with which we are dealing is capable of step 4. If it is capable, then all arguments about steps 1 through 3 will be invalidated unless appropriate methods of controlling step 4 are built into the experimental approach. Curiously enough, though human beings are fully capable of step 4, psychologists working with human subjects have been able to

study steps 1 through 3 without taking special care to exclude the confusions introduced by this fact.

In other words, as a rule, when psychologists ask a human subject
to do some task, and the subject does not do it, they tend to assume it
is because he cannot do it. This makes it quite easy for subjects, especially if they are people from whom the psychologists expect little, to
fool their testers. In *Dibs In Search of Self,* Virginia Axline tells about
a very capable six-year-old boy who had been able to make a number
of experts in such matters think, wrongly, that he was autistic, illiterate, and all but incapable of speech. In *The Naked Children,* Daniel
Fader tells of some black students in a Washington, D.C., junior high
school who by their behavior and test scores had tricked their teachers into thinking, again wrongly, that they could barely read, could not
speak Standard English, and indeed could speak little English of any
kind.

Bateson goes on to say:

> Let me now consider for a moment the art of the animal trainer. From
> conversations with these highly skilled people—trainers of both dol-
> phins and guide dogs—my impression is that the first requirement of a
> trainer is that he must be able to prevent the animal from exerting
> choice at the level of step 4. It must continually be made clear to the
> animal that, when he knows what is the right thing to do in a given con-
> text, that is the only thing he *can* do, and no nonsense about it. In other
> words, it is a primary condition of circus success that the animal shall
> abrogate the use of certain higher levels of his intelligence.

My uncle by marriage, Grove Cullum, an officer in the U.S. Cav-
alry, expert horseman and lover of horses, made this point more
bluntly. One day in conversation I happened to make some remark
about horses being intelligent. "Goodness, no," he laughed, "they're
not intelligent. If they were, they'd never let us ride them."

In 1959 or so, teaching fifth graders in a very exclusive private
school, which with rare exceptions would not even admit children
with I.Q.'s of less than 120, I wrote, "School is a place where children

learn to be stupid." I could see it was so, but didn't know why. What was it about even this very high-powered, child-centered, "creative" school, that made children stupid? I came to feel, as I wrote in *How Children Fail*, that it was fear, boredom, and the confusion of having constantly to manipulate meaningless words and symbols. I now see that it was that, but far more than that, the fact that *others had taken control of their minds*. It was being *taught*, in the sense of being trained like circus animals to do tricks on demand, that had made them stupid (at least in school).

On the basis of much experience, Bateson says this is true of all creatures, and I agree. The elephant in the jungle is smarter than the elephant waltzing in the circus. The sea lion in the sea is smarter than the sea lion playing "My Country, 'Tis of Thee" on some instrument. The rat eating garbage in the slums is smarter than the rat running mazes in the psychology lab. The crawling baby, touching, handling, tasting everything it can reach, is smarter than the baby learning, because it pleases his mother, to touch his nose when she shows him a card with NOSE written on it.

The most important question any thinking creature can ask itself is, "What is worth thinking about?" When we deny its right to decide that for itself, when we try to control what it must attend to and think about, we make it less observant, resourceful, and adaptive, in a word, less intelligent, in a blunter word, more stupid.

This may be the place to answer a question that by now many people have asked me: what do I think of baby training books—teach your baby this, teach your baby that, make your baby a genius. I am against them. The tricks they tell parents to teach their babies to do are not necessary, not very helpful, and if continued very long, probably very harmful. The trouble with teaching babies tricks, even the trick of reading, is that the more we do this, the more they think that learning means and can only mean *being taught by others to do tricks*, and the less they want to or can explore and make sense of the world around them in their own ways and for their own reasons.

I don't doubt for a second that the experts in teaching babies tricks can indeed teach them an impressive variety of tricks while they are still quite young. But this has little or nothing to do with true learning or the capacity for it. Intelligence, as I wrote in *How Children Fail*, is not the measure of how much we know how to do, but of how we behave when we don't know what to do. It has to do with our ability to think up important questions and then to find ways to get useful answers. This ability is not a trick that can be taught, nor does it need to be. We are born with it, and if our other deep animal needs are fairly well satisfied, and we have reasonable access to the world around us, we will put it to work on that world.

9

Learning Difficulties

DISABILITIES VS. DIFFICULTIES

I HAVE INCLUDED THIS short chapter, which may someday be part of a longer work on this subject, for several reasons. In the first place, parents who teach their children at home may find now and then that some of them do things like writing letters or spelling words backwards or showing some confusion about right and left. Such parents should not become alarmed, or assume that something serious is wrong with their child, or that they must throw the whole matter into the hands of "expert" specialists. In the second place, parents who have already sent children to school may be told that their children have such problems. Such parents, again, should not panic, and should be extremely skeptical of anything the schools and their specialists may say about their children and their condition and needs. Above all, they should understand that it is almost certainly the school itself and all its tensions and anxieties that are causing these difficulties, and that the best treatment for them will probably be to take the child out of school altogether. In the third place, parents should resist the general claim on the part of schools that only they are competent to teach children because only they are able to tell which children have learning disabilities and if so, what must be done about them.

To school people and others who talk to me about "learning disabilities," I usually ask a question something like this:

"How do you tell the difference between a learning *difficulty* (which we all experience every time we try to learn anything) and a learning *disability*? That is to say, how do you tell, or on what basis does someone decide (and who is the someone?) whether the cause of a given learning difficulty lies within the nervous system of the learner, or with things outside of the learner—the learning situation, the teacher's explanations, the teacher him/herself, or the material itself? And if you decide that the cause of the difficulty lies within the learner, who decides, and again on what basis, whether or not that inferred cause is curable, in short, whether anything can be done about it, and if so, what?"

If any readers ask these questions of schools, I would like very much to know what answers they get. I have never received any coherent answers to these questions. What I usually get instead are angry insistences that learning disabilities are "real," that is to say, built into the nervous systems of children. Here are some of my reasons for thinking they are not, and instead, what may be some of their true causes, and what we might sensibly do about them.

NOBODY SEES BACKWARDS

A few years ago a national magazine ran a full-page ad for some organization dealing with so-called "learning disabilities." At the top of the ad, in large letters, were the words, SEE HOW JOHNNY READS. Then a photo of an open children's book printed in very large print, large enough so that people reading the ad could read the book. The story was "The Three Little Pigs." But many of the letters in the story had been shifted and turned around in odd ways. Some were upside-down or backwards. Sometimes two adjacent letters in a word had been put in reverse order. Sometimes an entire word was spelled backwards. Then, beneath the photo, again in large letters, the words

THINK HOW JOHNNY FEELS. Then some text about all the children suffering from "learning disabilities" and all the things the organization was doing to cure or help them.

The message was plain. We were being asked to believe that large numbers of children in the U.S., when they looked at a book, saw something like the photo in the ad, and so, could not read it. Also, that this organization could and would do something about this—it was not clear just what—if we gave it enough support.

I looked again at the children's book in the photo. I found that I could read it without much trouble. Of course, I had two advantages over this mythical "Johnny": I could already read, and I already knew the story. I read it a bit more slowly than I ordinarily would; now and then I had to puzzle out a word, one letter at a time. But it was not hard to do.

This was by no means the first time I had heard the theory that certain children have trouble learning to read because something inside their skins or skulls, a kind of Maxwell's Demon (a phrase borrowed from physics) of the nervous system, every so often flipped letters upside-down or backwards, or changed their order. I had never taken any stock in this theory. It failed the first two tests of any scientific theory: (1) that it be plausible on its face; (2) that it be the most obvious or likely explanation of the facts. This theory seemed and still seems totally implausible, for many more reasons than I will go into here. And there are much simpler and more likely explanations of the facts.

The facts that this theory set out to account for are only these: certain children, usually just learning to read and write, when asked to write down certain letters or words, wrote some letters backwards, or reversed the order of two or more letters in a word, or spelled entire words backwards—though it is important to note that most children who spell words backwards do not at the same time reverse all the individual letters.

I was too busy with other work to take time to think how to prove that this theory was wrong. But for a while I taught in a school right next door to what was then supposed to be one of the best schools for "learning disability" (hereafter LD) children in New England. I began to note that in that particular learning hospital no one was ever cured.

Children went in not knowing how to read, and came out years later still not knowing. No one seemed at all upset by this. Apparently this school was felt to be "the best" because it had better answers than anyone else to the question, "Once you have decided that certain children can't learn to read, what do you do with them all day in a place which calls itself a school?" Later, when I was working full-time lecturing to groups about educational change, I had other contacts with other LD believers and experts. The more I saw and heard of them, the less I believed in them. But I was still too busy to spend much time arguing with them or even thinking about them.

Then one morning in Boston, as I was walking across the Public Garden toward my office, my subconscious mind asked me a question. First it said, "The LD people say that these children draw letters, say, a P, backwards because when they look at the correct P they *see* it backwards. Let's put all this in a diagram.

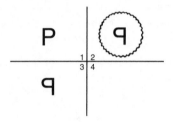

"In space #1 is the correct P which the child is asked to copy. In space #3 is the backwards P which he draws, because (we are told) this is the way he sees it. All right; in space #2 we will put what the child supposedly sees when he looks at the correct P in space #1." (The wavy line represents perception.)

Then came the $64 question.

"Now, what does the child see when he looks at the backwards P in space #3, the P that he has drawn?"

I stopped dead in my tracks. I believe I said out loud, "Well, I'll be d——!" For obviously, if his mind reverses all the shapes he looks at, the child, when he looks at the backwards P in space #3, *will see a correct P!*

So our diagram would wind up looking like this:

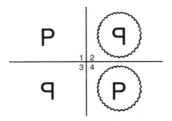

This imaginary child, if he did what the LD experts say he does, would look at P#1, see P#2, draw P#3, and *looking at that, see P#4.* What he had drawn would not look *to him* like what he was trying to copy. He would think to himself, "I made a mistake," and would draw his P the other way around. At least, he would do so if, as the LD people claim, his drawing was an accurate copy of what he perceived. Even if his mind reversed every shape it saw, *a backwards P would still look backwards to him!* To put it still more broadly and fundamentally, we cannot tell by looking at the shapes people draw whether they perceive shapes backwards or not, *since they would draw the same shapes in either case!*

So the "perceptual handicap," "he-draws-backwards-because-he-sees-backwards" theory goes down the drain. It does not explain what it was invented to explain. Nor does it explain anything else—this event, the child drawing the letters backwards, is all the evidence that supports it. Why then does this obviously false theory persist? Because, for many reasons, it is very convenient to many people—to parents, to teachers, to schools, to LD experts and the giant industry that has grown up around them—sometimes even to the children. The theory may not help anyone learn to read, but it keeps a lot of people busy, makes a lot of people richer, and makes almost everyone feel better. Theories that do all that are not easy to get rid of.

But then, why does the child draw the P backwards? If he is not, as I have shown, reproducing the shape that he perceives, what is he doing?

The answer is plain enough to anyone who has watched little children when they first start making letters. Slowly, hesitantly, and clumsily, they try to turn what they see into a "program," a set of instructions for the hand holding the pencil, and then try to make the hand carry out the instructions. This is what we all do when we try to draw something. We are not walking copying machines. When we try to draw a chair, we do not "copy" it. We look at it a while, and then "tell" our hand to draw, say, a vertical line of a certain height. Then we look at the chair again, then back at the paper, then "tell" our hand to go halfway up the vertical line, and from that point draw a line of a certain length in a certain direction. Then we look back at the chair for more instructions. If, like trained artists, we are good at turning what we see into instructions for our hand, we will produce a good likeness of the chair. If, like most of us, we are not good at it, we will not.

In the same way, the child looks at the P. He sees there is a line in it that goes up and down. He looks at the paper and tells his hand, "Draw an up and down line," then draws it. He looks back at the P, then tells his hand to go to the top of the up and down line and then draw a line out to the side. This done, he looks back at the P, and sees that the line going out to the side curves down and around after a while and then goes back in until it hits the up and down line again. He tells his hand to do that. As you can tell watching a little child do this, it may take him two or three tries to get his pencil all the way around the curve. Sometimes the curve will reverse direction in the middle, and that will have to be fixed up. Eventually he gets his line back to the up and down line.

At this point, most children will compare the two P's, the one they looked at and the one they made. Many of them, if they drew their P backwards, may see right away that it *is* backwards, doesn't look quite the same, is pointing the wrong way—however they may express this in their minds. Other children may be vaguely aware that the shapes are not pointing the same way, but will see this as a difference *that doesn't make any difference,* just as for my bank the differences between one of my signatures and another are differences that don't make any difference.

In thinking that this difference doesn't make any difference, the children are being perfectly sensible. After all, they have been looking at pictures of objects, people, animals, etc., for some time. They know that a picture of a dog is a picture of a dog, whether the dog is facing right or left. They also understand, without words, that the image on the page, the picture of dog, cat, bicycle, cup, spoon, etc., stands for an object that can be moved, turned around, looked at from different angles. It is therefore perfectly reasonable for children to think of the picture of a P on the page as standing for a P-shaped object with an existence of its own, an object which could be picked up, turned around, turned upside-down, etc. Perhaps not all children feel this equally strongly. But for those who do, to be told that a "backwards" P that they have drawn is "wrong," or that it isn't a P at all, must be very confusing and even frightening. If you can draw a horse, or dog, or cat, or car pointing any way you want, why can't you draw a P or B or E any way you want? Why is it "right" to draw a dog facing toward the left, but "wrong" to draw a P facing that way?

What we should do, then, is be very careful *never* to use the words "right" and "wrong" in these reversal situations. If we ask a child to draw a P, and he draws a T, we could say, "No, that's not a P, that's a T." But if we ask him to draw a P, and he draws one pointing to the left, we should say, "Yes, that's a P, but when we draw a picture of a P we *always* draw it pointing this way. It isn't like a dog or a cat, that we can draw pointing either way." Naturally, there's no need to give this little speech to children who never draw letters backwards. Indeed the chances are very good that children who start off drawing certain letters backwards would, as with errors in their speech, eventually notice the difference between their P's and ours and correct it, if we didn't make such a fuss about it. But if we are fainthearted and feel we have to say something about backwards P's, it ought to be something like the above.

However, I strongly suspect that most children who often reverse letters do not in fact *compare* shapes. Like so many of the children I have known and taught, they are anxious, rule-bound, always in a panicky search for what the grownups want. What they do is turn the P they are looking at into a set of instructions, memorize the instructions, and then compare the P they have drawn against the instructions. "Did I do it right? Yes, there's the line going up and down, and there's the line going out sideways from the top, and there it's curving around and there it's coming back into the up and down line again. I obeyed the rules and did it right, so it must *be* right."

Or perhaps they may try to compare shapes, but are too anxious to see them clearly. Or perhaps, as with anxious people, by the time they have shifted their eyes from the original P to the P they have drawn, they have forgotten the original P, or dare not trust the memory of it that they have. This feeling of suddenly not being able to trust one's own memory is common enough, and above all when one is anxious. Now and then I find myself looking up a phone number two or three times in a row, because each time I start to dial the number I have the panicky thought, "Did I remember it right?" Usually I can only break out of this foolish cycle by saying to myself, "Right or wrong, dial it anyway." It usually turns out to be right. But I can understand how a certain kind of self-distrusting person (by no means rare) might go through this process a great many times. I am sure that many of the failing students I have taught have had somewhere in their minds the permanent thought, "If I think of it, it must be wrong."

It is possible, too, that a child, making up a set of instructions for his hand, might try to use the ideas of Right and Left, but with some of the confusions I will talk about later in this chapter, so that "right" when he was looking at the P might mean the opposite of "right" when he was drawing it. The fact remains that whatever may be children's reasons for drawing letters backwards, there is no reason whatever to believe that seeing them backwards is one of them.

STRESS AND PERCEPTION

We can tell a good deal about the competence of a particular group of experts by the kinds of research they do or do not do.

In World War I we first began to see evidence that prolonged anxiety, stress, and fear can have great destructive effects on the human nervous system. The trenches were a kind of satanic laboratory of stress. More soldiers than ever before lived for much longer times than ever before in cold and wet, under the constant threat of death, often under continuous heavy bombardment. Under these conditions many suffered a disorder which doctors called "shell shock." Some became totally blind, or deaf, others became paralyzed, shook all over, lost all control over their muscles and limbs. The authorities first suspected faking, but it was soon clear that these soldiers were not faking. The only cure for these ailments, which in many cases looked like "physical" disorders, was to take these men out of stress, away from the front. After some time in a safe and calm place, they regained to varying degrees their sight, hearing, and use and control of their limbs. Many were even able to go back to the front.

In World War II this happened again. Many of the British troops who spent days on the beaches at Dunkirk, under continuous bombardment from both guns and planes, broke under this stress in exactly the same way. The doctors of World War II called their condition "psychoneurosis." The cure was basically the same—to remove the afflicted men from the scene of stress and danger.

In the years since then, all kinds of other evidence has begun to accumulate that stress can cause what seem to be physical disabilities. In my own work I began to see, not only among the children I taught, but in myself as I struggled for the first time to learn a musical instrument, that anxiety could make it much harder for the children, or myself, to think, to remember, or even to see. In *How Children Fail* I described how one day, under pressure, I totally lost for a short time the ability to see meaningfully. Five years later, in *The Lives of Children*, George Dennison described, in the most painful and almost clinical detail, the effects of stress and fear on one of his pupils.

So it was reasonable to suppose, when educators began to claim that some children might be having trouble learning because of "perceptual handicaps," that they might look for possible connections between such inferred handicaps and children's fears and anxieties. As far as I have been able to learn, very few of them have yet done so.

Not long ago I was one of many speakers at a large conference of specialists in "learning disabilities." Before more than a thousand people I reviewed the evidence for a connection between anxiety and perceptual or other learning disorders. I spoke of the medical experience of two world wars, and of my own experience as a teacher and as a beginning learner of music. Then I asked for a show of hands response to this question: "How many of you have heard of—only heard of, not done—any research on possible connections between perceptual handicaps in children and their anxiety, however measured? How many have heard of any research to find whether and to what degree lowering measurable anxiety in children might lessen the incidence of perceptual handicaps?"

In that roomful of over a thousand experts in this field, *only two people* raised their hands. What the others may have known, I do not know. But only two raised their hands.

I asked what they knew. One told me of research I had long known about, done by a man who, at least until very recently, had no degrees in psychology and no standing whatever in the educational "establishment." He had found high correlation between children's anxieties and perceptual handicaps, and that lowering the anxieties did indeed greatly lower the incidence of such handicaps. (He also found that diet was very important.)

The other man who raised his hand did not speak. But later, he wrote me a letter. He is, and has been for some time, a professor of education at a leading university in the very city in which this conference was held. He too had suspected the kind of connection I talked about. He then had worked out a way of teaching reading that he thought might lessen this anxiety, had used this method to teach a group of students officially labeled "perceptually handicapped," and had found that after quite a short time in his class, in the opinion of their regular teachers, his students were much less handicapped than they had been before. This, I would add, in spite of the fact that his classroom was nowhere as stress-free as others I have known, or as he himself might have made it if he had not been under pressure to show some fairly quick results.

There were other questions I have asked at other places and times, but did not think to ask there. When I first heard that boys were supposed to be four or five times as likely to have "perceptual handicaps" or "learning disabilities" as girls, I asked in a letter published in a national magazine whether any research had been done to look for possible connections between this four- or five-to-one ratio and the sex of the teacher. I have yet to hear of any. And it would surely be interesting to see what connections there might be between the incidence of "perceptual handicaps" in children and the measurable anxiety *of their teachers*. But again, as far as I know, no such research has been done.

Meanwhile, we have every reason to be very skeptical of the expertise of people who fail or refuse to ask such questions.

One more note about the LD conference. On one of the many tables displaying books and pamphlets were copies of a newsletter published by one of the leading LD associations. Reading one, I came across a most extraordinary sentence, in an article by a former president of the association. In it she said that LD "professionals" should insist very strongly that the causes of these disabilities were always neurological. She admitted that there was so far very little evidence to support this idea. Then she added these remarkable words: "We must not take the absence of evidence as the evidence of absence." In other words, just because there is no evidence to support our theory doesn't mean that we shouldn't continue to push it.

⋘ The "seeing-backwards" hypothesis is no longer used to describe dyslexia by learning disabilities specialists, and many studies are still being conducted as to why some people have difficulty learning to read, so no definitive answer has been reached as to whether learning disabilities should be considered solely a neurological problem. Nonetheless, Holt's call to consider the learning environment is still, at best, a footnote in LD studies, even though many studies note how LD, ADD, and AD/HD behavior is often not visible outside the classroom setting. Before putting your child on drugs like Ritalin, if you can, try homeschooling or enrolling him or her in a school that has patience and experience working with late readers or high-energy kids. There is now a considerable body of literature by psychiatrists, such as Johns Hopkins University's Dr. Peter Breggin (*Talking Back to Ritalin: What Doctors Aren't Telling You about Stimulants and ADHD*), educational psychologists, like Dr. Thomas Armstrong (*The Myth of the A.D.D. Child: 50 Ways to Improve Your Child's Behavior and Attention Span Without Drugs, Labels, or Coercion*), and others, who are concerned about the tenfold increase in Ritalin prescriptions for children, primarily boys, since the mid-1980s. These doctors,

like Holt, are not arguing that there aren't children who are overly energetic, wild, or difficult; they are just saying that drugging these children
shouldn't be the primary or preferred way of helping the kids learn to
cope with their learning difficulties. ☙

RIGHT AND LEFT

Many adults get very upset and anxious about right and left. If a child
writes a letter backwards, or reads off some letters in the wrong order,
or does anything else to suggest he is confused about right and left,
adults begin to talk excitedly about "mixed dominance" and "perceptual handicaps" and "learning difficulties." The child is quickly labeled as "having a serious problem." Specialists (if the family or
school can afford them) are called in and told to take over.

A child once asked me a question that not only completely surprised me, but also suggested that when children are confused about
right and left, the reason may not be in them but in us, the adults, and
the way *we* talk about right and left. In short, the child's confusion
may make sense, and if we only understood that, we might easily
straighten it out.

I was in an early elementary classroom, working on something with
some children in a corner of the room. I needed something in my
desk, and asked a child please to get it for me. He said okay, and asked
where it was. I said, "In the top right-hand drawer." There was a
pause. Then he said, "Whose right hand, mine or the desk's?"

For an instant I was baffled. Then I saw, and understood. When he
looked at the desk, it was as if he saw a living creature looking at him.
So I said, "*Your* right hand." Off he went, brought back what I had
asked for, and that was that.

Later, I thought that many young children must be animists, and
see objects as if they were living creatures. I wondered how many of
them might have had that same question in their minds, without ever
asking it. And if they didn't ask it, how did they ever learn the answer?
Probably from experience. They went to the desk, looked in *its* right-
hand drawer, found nothing, looked in *their* right-hand drawer, found

what they wanted, and so learned which was meant, like the infant I described in *How Children Learn*, who at the table asked people to pass the salt, pepper, butter, etc., so that by seeing what was passed she could find out what those words meant.

But some children might not interpret the desk experience in that way. They might assume that the adult had made a mistake about the drawer. Or they might think that they themselves had made a mistake about which was right and which was left. The kind of children who worried about mistakes, because their parents or teachers worried, might be particularly ready to blame themselves for any confusion.

Only recently, as I began to think more about this, did I realize that our adult rules about right and left are even more confused than I had thought. Thus, when we ask a child to get something out of our right-hand coat pocket, we mean the coat's right hand, not the child's. When we talk about the right headlight of a car, we mean the car's right hand. But the right-hand entrance to a house is *our* right hand, not the house's. We adults talk sometimes as if things were people, and sometimes as if they were not, and there's little rhyme or reason in the way we do this. Why should a car or boat or train have its own right side, but not a house?

In the theater, of course, the confusion about whether the audience's or the actors' right or left is meant led people to invent the words "stage right" or "stage left" to mean the right or left of the actors as they looked at the audience.

Under photos of groups of people we see, "Reading from left to right, Jones, Smith, Brown, etc." A child being shown such photos might hear someone say, "That's me over on the right." Our right as we look at it? Or the right of the group? So the people on the right are *really* on the left, and vice versa. Some children might see this as more of the world's delightful nonsense. But other children might think in panic and terror, "Why don't they make up their minds which way they want it? How do they ever expect me to get it straight?"

We might well ask, how do any of us ever get it straight. Most of us learn it the way we learn the grammar of our language, which is so subtle and complicated that (I am told) no one has yet been able to teach it to a computer. Children learn very early that the words "I, you, she, etc." refer to different people depending on who is saying them. Not an easy thing to figure out, when you come to think about it. Yet no one ever explains that to them. Nor do they say to themselves, as they grow up, "*I* refers to the person who is talking, *you* to the person or persons talked to, *we* to both of them together, and *he, she, they, or it* to the people or things talked about." They just use the words that way, and it works.

In the same way, most children don't think to themselves, "Cars, boats, coats, trains, planes, all have their own right hands, while books, photos, desks, houses do not." They just learn from experience which is which, and don't worry much about the contradictions, just as most French children don't worry about why a house should be feminine and a building masculine, or a coat masculine and a shirt feminine.

In short, most children master the confusion of right and left because they never become aware of it, any more than I did until just a few days ago. Others may become aware of the confusion but are not troubled by it and don't feel any need to set it right or make sense of it—it's just the way things are. But some children are philosophers. They examine everything. They expect and want things to make sense, and if they don't, to find out why not. Still others are threatened and terrified by confusion and paradox, above all, by seeing people act as if something made sense when it obviously doesn't. At some deep level of their being, they wonder, "Am I the one who's crazy?"

I suspect that most of the children who have persistent trouble with right and left in school or in life are of this latter kind. After a few right-left mistakes, which they make only because they have not yet learned our crazy right-left rules, they begin to think, "I must be stupid, I never can figure out right and left." Soon they go into a blind panic every time the words come up. They work out complicated strategies of bluff and avoidance. When people ask about right and left, they learn to get other clues—"You mean the one by the window?" etc. (Since this article appeared in *GWS*, many adults have told me about the tricks and devices they must rely on to keep from mixing up right and left.) In general, they assume that there is something wrong with them.

If this is true, what might we do about it? One thing we should *not* do is to set out to "teach" the rules of right and left. Most children have always figured out right and left without much teaching, other than being told when very little, "This is your right hand, this is your left foot, etc." Let them go on learning it that way. But if a child seems to be confused or anxious about this, then we can begin to make the rules more explicit. We can say, "I mean *your* right hand, not the desk's," or "I mean the *coat's* right hand, not yours," perhaps adding, "I know that sounds a bit crazy, but that's just the way we say it, don't worry about it, you'll get used to it."

EAST AND WEST

Thinking about right and left brought back an old memory. Years ago a teacher of geography told me of a most interesting and surprising discovery. Teachers who teach young children about maps and directions find that some pick it up quickly. But others, when shown a map and asked to point east, act like the children I described in *How Children Fail*—wave their hands in all directions while carefully reading the teacher's face for cues, watch their smart classmates, bluff, fake, wait it out, and so on. Most teachers let it go at that, thinking, "Good students, bad students, you get all kinds."

But somewhere a teacher noticed something. A few children, shown a map and asked to point east, almost always pointed wrong, *but always in the same direction.* Looking into it further, people found that a small percentage of people, some children, some adults, had a very strong sense of direction. It was as if they had a compass in their minds, or as if under their feet the ground was everywhere marked with direction lines. Whether their compass and direction lines were correctly labeled, whether the east they pointed was in fact true east, my informant did not tell me. But, asked to point a given direction, they always pointed the same way.

My mother had that kind of sense of direction. Driving without a map on strange, winding, suburban roads, when the rest of us had long since lost our bearings, she always knew about where we were, which way we were headed, and which way we needed to go to get where we wanted. An inborn gift? Perhaps, though it can probably be learned. At any rate, for children with such a gift, the question, "Which way is east?" can only mean, "Which way is *true* east, or *world-east*?" If we understood this, we could make the distinction (which we ought to make anyway) between *world-east* and *map-east*. Once children understood the relation between maps and the territory being mapped, which we could help them see by making maps of their room, the house, the yard, the block or neighborhood, etc., we could then ask questions like, "If you were here"—showing a point on the map—"and began to walk east, show me on the map where you'd be going." Or we could take the walk first, and then see on the map where we had walked. After doing this a few times, a child would be able to show map-east, map-north, etc.

I talked to a teacher friend (math) about this. He laughed and said that when he was a child he thought for quite a few years that north, world-north, was straight up, and world-south straight down, since all the maps he had seen were in school, on the walls. In time, he figured it all out for himself, *by* himself.

Recently these thoughts about east and west have led to a new thought. Suppose there were some people who thought that right and left, like east and west, referred to something in the world itself, in short, that right meant world-right and left meant world-left. How could they ever figure out, from our talk about right and left, which was which? One minute world-right would seem to be this way, the next minute that way. We can hardly imagine their confusion and, probably, terror. Most of them would soon decide that they were just too stupid to figure out what seemed so easy for everyone else. Yet they, or we, might quickly clear up all that confusion by just asking a couple of the right questions.

What to do, if children seem to have these confusions? Above all, keep calm. If a child shows confusion about right and left, don't panic, give him plenty of time to work it out for himself. Some small things we could do might help. When we first start telling children which is our right hand and which our left, it would probably be a good idea for both of us to be facing the same way, the child standing in front of us or sitting on our lap. At some point, facing the same way, we might both hold a toy in our right hand, and show that when we are facing the same way, the right hands are on the same side, but that when we turn to face each other, the right hands are on the opposite side. It would probably be better not to talk much about this as we did it. Just show it now and then, as another interesting fact about the world.

Beyond that, we should not assume, just because children do know that this is their right hand and this their left, that they understand all about right-hand drawers and coat pockets—all our strange rules about right and left. For some time, when we talk about such things, we should be sure to point out which side we mean. If the child seems to take all this in stride, we don't need to say anything and would be wiser not to. But if the child seems unduly puzzled or anxious about this, then we could make the right-left rules more explicit.

10

Children and Work

ON FINDING ONE'S WORK

IN HIS BOOK *Growing Up Absurd*, Paul Goodman asked (italics his): "But *the question is what it means to grow up into such a fact as 'During my productive years I will spend eight hours a day doing what is no good.'*" Later, in an essay printed in a collection of his works entitled *Nature Heals* he wrote:

> Brought up in a world where they cannot see the relation between activity and achievement, adolescents believe that everything is done with mirrors, tests are passed by tricks, achievement is due to pull, goods are known by their packages, and a man is esteemed according to his front. The delinquents who cannot read and quit school, and thereby become still less able to take part in such regular activity as is available, show a lot of sense and life when they strike out directly for the *rewards* of activity—money, glamour, and notoriety. . . .
>
> It is disheartening indeed to be with a group of young fellows who are in a sober mood and who simply do not know what they want to do with themselves in life. Doctor, lawyer, beggar-man, thief? rich man, poor man, Indian chief?—they simply do not know an ambition and

cannot fantasize one. But it is not true that they don't care; their "so what?" is vulnerable, their eyes are terribly balked and imploring. (I say "it is disheartening," and I mean that the tears roll down my cheeks; and I who am an anarchist and a pacifist feel that they will be happier when they are all in the army.)

Paul Goodman was writing here about poor boys. But even in the more hopeful '60s it was just about as true of affluent youth. In those days I was often asked to speak to high school assemblies, mostly in rich suburbs of big cities. What I almost always talked about was the difference between jobs, careers, and work. A job, I said, was something that you did for money, something that someone else told you to do and paid you for doing, something you would probably not have done otherwise, but did only to get the money. A career was a kind of ladder of jobs. If you did your first job for a while, made no mistakes and caused no trouble, whoever gave you that job might give you a new job, better paid, maybe slightly more interesting, or at least not so hard-dirty-dangerous. Then, if you did that job okay for a while, your boss might then give you a slightly better job, and so on. This adds up to what is called "a career."

By "work" I meant and still mean something very different, what people used to call a "vocation" or "calling"—something which seemed so worth doing for its own sake that they would gladly choose to do it even if they didn't need money and the work didn't pay. I went on to say that to find our work, in this sense, is one of the most important and difficult tasks that we have in life, and indeed, that even if we find it once we may later have to look for it again, since work that is right for us at one stage of our life may not be right for us at the next. I added that the vital question, "What do I really want to do? What do I think is most worth doing?" is not one that the schools (or any other adults) will often urge us or help us to ask; on the whole, they feel it is their business only to prepare us for employment—jobs or careers, high or low. So we will have to find out for ourselves what work needs to be done and is being done out there in the world, and where and how we will take part in it.

As I said these things, I looked at the faces of my hearers, to sense how they felt about what I was saying. What I saw, and usually heard in the question periods that followed, made me feel that most of these students were thinking, "This guy must have just come from Mars." Work worth doing? Work that you would do even if you didn't need money, that you would do *for nothing*? For most of them it was not just impossible, it was unimaginable. They did not know, hardly even knew *of*, any people who felt that way about their work. Work was something you did for external rewards—a little pay, if you were like most people, or wealth, power, fame if you were among the fortunate.

Among all the young people I talked to, there was never, anywhere, a hopeful, positive, enthusiastic response to what I said. I cannot remember even one among all those students, the most favored young people of the (then, at least) most favored nation in the world, who said or later wrote to me, "Mr. Holt, here's what I am interested in and care about, how can I find a way to work at it?"

FINDING TRUE WORK

I was on my submarine, the U.S.S. *Barbero*, heading west for Pearl Harbor, when we first heard the news about the atomic bomb. I knew enough to know that before long any country that wanted could and would make them. It seemed clear to me that the only way to prevent the worldwide spread of nuclear weapons, and in the end nuclear war, was to have some sort of world government. When we came back to the U.S. in October, to "mothball" our sub, I tried to find out about any other people who might be working in some way for world government. By the middle of the following summer I decided that I had to find a way to do this work full-time. I went to the three world government organizations to ask for a job. Two had nothing. The third had nothing at the moment, but said that in the fall the young man working in their mailroom would be going back to college and that I could have his job for $35 a week. I said I would take it. In the fall I began work, making up and sending out packages of literature, stamping the mail, keeping the membership card files, running the Addressograph machine, and doing any other odd jobs that turned up. One day I was told that the Junior Chamber of Commerce in Bayonne, New Jersey, had just asked for a speaker, on a day when all our other speakers were busy. Would I do it? I gulped and said I would. It was the first of about six hundred speeches that I was to give for the organization. Later I left the mailroom and began to work as a "field organizer," traveling about, giving speeches and trying to start local chapters.

In 1952 I left the organization, spent much of the next year living and traveling cheaply in Europe, and came home, thinking that I might try to go into farming, since even then I was very interested in what we now call ecology. My sister, who had been trying without success to persuade me to be a teacher, did persuade me to visit a small co-ed boarding school, the Colorado Rocky Mountain School, that John and Anne Holden had just opened in Carbondale, Colorado. Since the school planned to do much of its own building and food-raising, she thought I might be able, while working and being paid, to learn many things I would need to know if I did go into farming. Thinking, "It can't hurt to look," I went to the school two weeks after it had opened and spent a day there, living the life of the school, going to some classes, talking to the students, helping some of them with their work, and playing informal soccer with them.

I liked it. My insides sent me the same message they had sent years before, when for the first time I went down into a submarine: "Right now, this is the place for you." Next day, just before I left, I said to John Holden, "You know, I like it here, and I'd like to stay and work here." He made what some might have taken as a rather negative reply: "Well, we'd be glad to have you, but the trouble is, we haven't any place to put you, and we haven't any money to pay you, and we haven't anything for you to do." In return I said, "Well, if you get some sort of roof over my head, I don't much care where you put me, and if you're feeding me I can probably live without money, for a while at least, and I'm pretty sure I can find something to do." It was an offer he couldn't refuse. He laughed and said, "If you're willing to come out here on that basis, come ahead."

Two weeks later I was back. For a month or two I lived in a little building, once a granary, that they were turning into an infirmary. I slept on a cot near a table saw, stepped over piles of sawdust to get to it, lived out of my suitcases. I found plenty to do. I began cooking breakfast for the school every day, tutoring individual students in economics, trigonometry, reading, and coaching soccer. When another teacher left to get married, I took over her room and salary (about $1,750/yr.) By the next year I was teaching regular classes in English and math, and was the school business manager. A year later they hired a full-time business manager, but I then started teaching French as well as English and math. I taught there four years, worked very hard, had a good time, learned a great deal.

The point of these stories is that many of the people who are doing serious work in the world (as opposed to just making money) are very overworked and short of help. If a person, young or not so young, said to them, "I believe in the work you are doing and want to help you in any and every way I can, and I'd be glad to do any kind of work you ask me to do or that I can find to do, for very little pay, or even none at all if you can give me room and board," I suspect that many of them would say, "Sure, come right ahead." Working with them, the newcomer would gradually learn more and more about what they were doing, would find or be given more interesting and important things to do, might soon become so valuable that they would find a way to pay her or him. In any case, he or she would learn far more from working with them and being around them than in any school or college.

A FALSE START

I have a close friend whom I have known since he was in high school. His marks were good, his parents had money, so when he finished high school he naturally went to a "good" college. Since English had been his best and easiest school subject, he majored in English. Four years and $20,000 later he had his B.A. degree. What next? Well, his marks were still good, he still had time, his parents still had money, so he went to a "good" graduate school to get a Ph.D. in (now necessarily) English. During these years we remained good friends. One day, when he had completed all the course requirements for a Ph.D. and was finishing his thesis, I asked him, "When you get through with all this stuff, what are you going to do?" The question seemed to surprise him. After a pause, he said, "I don't know, teach English in some college, I guess." I said, "Is that what you really want to do?" This question surprised him even more. After another pause he said, "No, not particularly, but what else *can* I do?" That surprised *me*. Is that what a Ph.D. is supposed to do for you?

He began to teach English at a small state university, in the Western mountain country he loved. He soon found that his students were at college only to get the ticket, and were not in the least interested in anything he had learned and wanted to teach. All they wanted to know, and very politely asked, was, "What do we have to do to pass the course?" This took all the point out of teaching. For a while he tried to put in his class time, collect his paycheck, concentrate on the farming, hunting, fishing, hiking, camping, and skiing that he really loved, and not worry about his students and what they liked or didn't like. It didn't work. He stuck it out for some years, every year hating it more. Finally he quit. Today, after some difficult years, he is a carpenter and small builder and contractor, doing careful and skilled work in a town where there is enough demand for it to keep him busy. He has found his work. But it still seems too bad to have spent fifteen years of his life and $40,000 of his parents' money just to find out that he didn't want to be an English professor.

◖◖ The cost to do this now would be more than $100,000. ◗◗

Even then, he was fortunate in having enough money behind him so that he could run the risk of leaving his job and looking for work worth doing. Most people can't. A young woman about to graduate from a school of education once said to me, "Well, I've learned two things here, anyway—that I don't like children and I don't like teaching." I asked why she went on with it. She said, "I have to, I've spent too much time and money learning to do this, I can't turn around and start learning to do something else."

Ten years ago many students used to ask me whether they should go to, or stay in, or go back to college. I used to say, and say now, that a college degree isn't a magic passkey that opens every door in town.

It opens only a few, and before you spend a lot of time and money getting one of those keys, it's a good idea to find out what doors it opens
(if any), and what's on the other side of those doors, and to decide
whether you like what's on the other side, and if you do, whether
there may not be an easier way to get there.

GROWING UP, PERHAPS NOT ABSURD

How much it can mean to a young person to feel that there is work
worth doing out there in the world can be seen from these excerpts
from letters from a Massachusetts high school senior. During the
summer after a very unhappy and unsuccessful year in eleventh
grade, she wrote:

> I developed a very negative attitude about school but I was still very
> distressed and concerned about my performance in school. I was still
> very interested in learning but in the classroom I found learning very
> dull. I was enrolled in classes in which everyday attendance was manda-
> tory, but I began cutting classes. I was not alone. A whole crew of us
> used to hang out in a dingy girl's room. The school doesn't have a
> lounge so this room had to do. Well, my whole school year was a disas-
> ter. I dropped out of all my classes except for two when the 4th term
> rolled around. I scheduled these classes for the morning and so I could
> leave the school before 11:00 nearly every day. . . .
>   I was studying my third year of Spanish but I dropped out at the end
> of the third term because I could not learn in an atmosphere which I
> felt was hostile (toward me).
>   . . . I often resorted to smoking marijuana during school. It broke up
> the monotony of a school day. Pot didn't interfere with my studying. I
> found I could concentrate remarkably well while I was high. But I must
> say it totally ruined my attitude, especially when it came time to decide
> whether or not I should go to the next class.
>   . . . My relationship with my family suffered. . . . I was going around
> with older kids outside of high school. . . . My parents felt these kids
> were responsible for my attitude change. Perhaps they were to some

extent. A few of them had dropped out of high school and none of them went to college except for one kid who stopped going after two years. They didn't seem to be headed anywhere. . . .

Well, here I am. I hope to go on to college yet with my high school record I don't know. Kids have a tendency to goof off during their senior year. I am going to have to work hard to make up for last year's mistakes. But . . . I feel alienated in school, at home, and even with my "friends."

. . . I would like to know if you have any suggestions. I am interested in ecology, conservation, English, writing, history, gardening, photography (I don't have a camera, though), silver jewelry making (I have already completed a beginner's course), alternative energy sources (solar energy especially). . . .

In reply, I suggested that during the summer she visit the New Alchemy Institute in Woods Hole, Massachusetts. The New Alchemists, as they call themselves, are a group of people, led or perhaps I should say assembled, guided, directed, inspired, and coordinated by John and Nancy Jack Todd, who are trying to find ways in which human beings can live, in modest comfort, in a gentle, stable, and enduring relationship with the earth. The Institute is a small experimental farm and research facility, in which people experiment with solar greenhouses, fish-farming, intensive food-raising, tree raising, windmills, composting, biological pest control, worm raising, etc. As small as it is, it seems to me one of the most important groups of people working anywhere. It is not at all an exaggeration to say that the health and happiness of our country, our planet, and the human race, may depend a great deal on what they are able to learn there.

At any rate, the student did visit them. In December of that same year she wrote again:

My main purpose for writing you is to thank you for your advice. I had written that I was interested in organic gardening and you suggested that I should visit the New Alchemy Institute. Well, my mother and I took you up on your suggestion one Saturday and although I did not get a chance to talk with any of the Alchemists, I thoroughly enjoyed exploring the farm. I went to a seminar on raising earthworms and saw a movie about the present plight of small farmers in this country.

Last spring an article on the New Alchemy Institute was featured in the *Boston Globe*. . . . I brought it into the Alternative School Room to show my friend and Alt. advisor. I also showed him your letter and I must say with no exaggeration the man was delighted. . . . He had not visited the Institute but in spring he may arrange to take a group of Alt. students for a visit. . . .

During the summer I suffered from an extremely bad attitude about school. I wanted to complete my last year of high school by means of a totally alternative learning process. But I decided upon entering school in September that if I was to have a satisfactory academic record for college, I must work within the system. The trip to the New Alchemy Institute made a permanent impression on me and influenced my decision to major in Life Sciences and Agriculture in college. Well, not only did I wish to improve my academic standing for college, but I also wished to prove to myself that I was still capable of being a good student despite my changed attitudes toward a structured and traditional education. Last year's failures in school nearly ruined my self-esteem.

I enrolled in five major subjects (not including physical education) though I needed only five credits and a year of gym to graduate. I'm presently enrolled in an honors Spanish III Course, Latin I, Marine Biology and Animal Behavior, Economics, and an advanced placement English course! Believe me, that is quite a change in academics from the previous year. In order to carry this workload I had to quit Alternative School. No one told me that I had to leave the program, but I decided it was best. . . . Well, I've survived and after the first term I had earned a place on the honor roll.

THE MOST DIRECT WAY

An article from *Sports Illustrated* (December 17, 1979) shows how a person can zero right in on his chosen work:

One of the youngest and most successful design teams in contemporary ocean racing [has] Ron Holland, 32, as its equally unlikely chief. Holland failed the most elementary public exam for secondary schools in his native Auckland, New Zealand, repeatedly flunked math (considered by many to be a requisite in yacht design) and has no formal qualifications whatsoever in naval architecture. He even elected not to complete a boatbuilding apprenticeship. Yet today everybody wants a Holland design.

. . . At 16 he walked out of secondary school—"too academic," he says—and told his mother later. Even then he seemed to know that his future lay in boats. Until a primary-school teacher introduced him to Arthur Ransome's *Swallows and Amazons*, a classic children's tale about a sailing holiday off England's Norfolk Broads, Holland had read nothing. Teachers had sent him to remedial reading classes. But after *Swallows and Amazons* he became a bookworm. He had been sailing since he was seven, when his father bought him a seven-foot dinghy, undaunted by the fact that in his first race he finished fourth and last.

Holland got into the boating industry as an apprentice, and quickly chucked that job because the boss would not give him time off to go ocean racing. . . .

He spent nearly three years working with American designers, first Gary Mull and finally the flamboyant Charlie Morgan.

It was in 1973, after less than three years of intermittent design experience, that Holland changed course again. He left Morgan to campaign his own quarter-tonner, *Eygthene*, in the world championships at Weymouth, England. It was a radical design—based, Holland admits now, on intuition, not "plain arithmetic." *Eygthene* won.

And just in time. With Laurel, whom he had married in 1971, he was living aboard the cramped quarter-tonner. A potential sale had just fallen through. He had no money in the bank.

Ron Holland sets a good example for people trying to find their work. If you know what kind of work you want to do, move toward it *in the most direct way possible*. If you want someday to build boats, go where people are building boats, find out as much as you can.

When you've learned all they know, or will tell you, move on. Before long, even in the highly technical field of yacht design, you may find you know as much as anyone, enough to do whatever you want to do.

Of course, if none of the people doing your chosen work will even let you in the door without some piece of school paper, you may have to pay time and money to some school to get it. Or, if you find out that there are many things you want or need to know that the people working won't tell you, but that you can find out most easily in school, then go for that reason. At least, you will know exactly why you are there. But don't assume that school is the best way or the only way to learn something without carefully checking first. There may be quicker, cheaper, and more interesting ways.

Here are some other examples. This from *Solar Age*, December 1979:

> At age 22, Ken Schmitt is head of Research and Development for Alternative Energy Limited (AEL), a small new company . . . which plans to sell [alcohol] stills beginning some time next year. . . .
>
> At 17, he owned a construction company, which "gave me the capital to experiment." Schmitt has experimented with solar energy systems for the last two years. His pilot plant for methanol (wood alcohol) synthesis may be the forerunner of a plant that will produce half a million gallons per day for Los Angeles motorists; and five foreign countries may buy rights to use a pyrolysis process he developed.

And from *The Boston Monthly*, December 1979:

> The head of the Boston Computer Society, a group that regularly publishes a newsletter and holds meetings to learn and exchange computer ideas and information, is 16 years old. Technicians for many of the local computer stores are high school students. Computerland in Wellesley has a volunteer expert with a terrifying knowledge of computers who works with their customers in exchange for unlimited computer time— he is twelve years old.

SERIOUS WORK

A family I know has been traveling around the country in a converted bus, staying for a while in towns that interest them or where they know people they like, then moving on. Not long ago the father wrote:

A friend had just become "owner for a week" of a grocery store because the owner needed a vacation. S, the friend, decided he would capitalize on the opportunity and try to get a month's worth of "ownership" out of a week. He hired me to do several electrical and carpentry jobs while the boss was gone. An impression must be made. Many improvements. Check writing power—hire—fire—chief for a day!

We had to be there early and work before the store opened. I shook the kids up at six, we unplugged the bus, and were off. The kids followed me into the store toting tools. S said they could play in the store and the idea of having a supermarket all to yourself carried quite a charge. Supermarkets almost always come fully equipped with people—most of whom are adults. Children who are there are seldom wanted or welcome. They are usually being admonished by mother for handling the sacks of candy placed carefully within their reach by knowing management.

Well, not the case this morning—the store was theirs. They roamed the aisles for a while contemplating the space. Within half an hour everyone felt at home and C sat down with K at a table in the deli and started reading her a book they had brought from the bus.

Soon S arrived in a panic! The fresh juice-making operation in the back room was two hours behind because the shipment of containers hadn't come. A big selling item for the store was fresh-made juices of several kinds, made from fresh produce early each morning. Panic— the crowds would hit and there would be no juice. Money would be lost, good will would slip. Being "owner for a week" S had fewer learning sets than your average supermarket manager so he said, "Who wants a job?" F and G (the boys) were low on funds—"We do." "Wash your hands and come with me." They went back to the little juice factory in the back room and S introduced the new help to the juice man.

I stopped by about half an hour later and saw an amazing operation. I have never seen F and G work so hard with such enthusiasm. F was filling bottles with carrot juice and G was wiping, labeling, and pricing. The juice man was pouring bushels of carrots into a big peeling machine and then on to a grinder and then to a two-ton hydraulic press. Gallons and gallons of carrot juice were flowing and the boys' eyes were wide and their hands were a blur. Before today carrots existed either one every few inches in a row in the ground or in one-pound plastic-wrapped bundles. These machines ate carrots like a giant dinosaur. The pace was intense. The juice man had his routines down pat and the kids picked up the rhythm. It was a dance and you had to keep in step. Commands came in three-word sentences and they were obeyed. No time for discussion or explanation—real work—a real product—a real classroom. Sacks of carrots became 85¢ bottles of juice in minutes. G said, "I don't care if S pays us or not, this is fun."

Three hours later I was done, the store was open, and they were still having fun. Three large garbage cans of dry carrot pulp sat outside the juice room door. F's shirt and pants were orange and drenched. G was restamping a case of bottles he had marked 58¢ instead of 85¢. No hassle over the mistake—just stamp them again. After all, the juice man had to throw out a whole batch of carrots that got to the shredder before they were peeled. Mistakes are part of what people do. Unfortunately in schools full of desks, they are forbidden.

I was having my breakfast on the bus when they finished and they popped in, each carrying a fist full of three dollars. They had worked harder in that three hours than I had ever seen them work before and they were ecstatic. They had new knowledge, new dignity (they saved the day), and some negotiable legal tender. My prize was to have been there to see it.

From a mother:

J (4) took another quantum leap. We're market gardeners. He asked for and has his own plot, marked off with string (to his specs) for which he raised plants in the greenhouse and in which he's raising radishes for money. This is all on his own, but we try to help carry out his suggestions and ideas. Including when he's asked me to thin his radishes as he was "too tired." However, yesterday while I was working steadily transplanting, he took up a hoe and hoed every part of the garden that needed it *because he saw it needed to be done* [Author's emphasis]. It took about an hour of hard work in which he did as good a job as I. Usually when he does something well I find myself commenting with some praise, but this time it would have been obviously, even ridiculously, superfluous. As if I would tell my husband he was a good boy for working so hard. J was at that time in that enterprise my equal. I was thrilled.

A mother writes from Manitoba:

One of the best times we had in the euphoric first two months out of school, was a marathon session in the biochemistry lab where I work. I had a 48-hour experiment going which had to be checked in the middle of the night. J went in with me the first night and we had trouble with one of the machines, a fraction collector which moves test tubes along under the end of a length of fine tubing which slowly spits out the stuff to be collected. We stayed there until 5 A.M. and J occupied himself almost the whole time with a stopwatch checking the rate of drips from the tubing, the rate of movement of the tubes, and the rate of a monitoring pen on another machine—all work that was necessary for getting the job done—and he revelled in it.

We left the building just as the last stars were leaving the sky. Sheep and cattle were grazing quietly on nearby university pastures. Only the birds provided sound. J was amazed that he had really passed through all the dark hours without sleeping. I thought of all the kids who could not have the kind of exhilaration he had just had because of their confinement to hours dictated to them by schools.

We slept all that morning and went back to the lab for checks during the afternoon and again at night and the following day. J wanted to stay with it right to the end and did. He learned all sorts of things in that short span of time about units of volume and time, about multiplying and dividing, about fractions, about light absorption, magnets, solutions, and probably other things. The same boy had been completely

turned off by school math and was regarded by some as "slow" and
"lazy."

A mother writes from New Hampshire:

T, A, and I . . . earn almost all of our money by seasonal orchard work—
picking apples 2 months in the late winter. We leave home and work in
various parts of [apple country].

   . . . A started picking of her own accord one day when she was 5. She
put her raincoat on backwards, using the hood as a bucket to hold the
fruit until she emptied into the boxes. She was very proud of herself.
She worked all day and picked 3 bushels. The next rainy day we made a
quarter-size bucket out of a plastic waste basket and a pant leg. The
cloth bottom opened up for emptying like our buckets. T made her a
10-foot ladder (he makes and sells apple-picking ladders). She picked
from the bottoms of our trees and we paid her what we earned per
bushel before deductions for food and rent.

   Now, 5 years later, she has a custom-made half-size bucket and a 14-
foot ladder. She works 2 hours or more most days, picking to the same
quality standards we use. She keeps her own tally. She pays about half
of her own living expenses from her earnings when we're on the crew.
She handles the ladder well, picks as much of the tops as she can.

   How much to pay her and how much to expect her to work have
been areas of confusion. It didn't seem right to continue to pay her, in
effect, more per bushel than anyone else by not deducting any expenses. But if we deducted her full expenses, she wouldn't earn anything (yet). So we compromised. Earning money is not her main
motivation but she likes to get paid and it seems good for her to have
money to spend. If she continues to increase her production she'll soon
be able to pay her full expenses on the crew and have a good amount
left over.

   In many poor cultures the kids' earnings help support the whole
family. We have to earn enough to live on the rest of the year. So it
seems possible that as she gets older she might pay her expenses the
rest of the year too, or contribute toward things we'll all use. We are
not part of a tradition where the kids work a lot or contribute much to

the family's survival. And we are not so close to the line that our survival depends upon her contributions. So when we're in doubt we take the more regular (like our own upbringing) course. I believe she's working a good amount of her own accord when we're on crews. She says she wants to get so she's paying all of her expenses on the crews.

I don't believe in compelling kids to study some subject they don't want to, but I do believe in insisting they do some work, in relation to their abilities and the needs of the family. Since they start with a compelling desire to do what the older family members do, this is no problem. Now sometimes she objects to some chores (it's boring, so-and-so doesn't have to). We insist. If you want to be warm, too, you have to carry firewood, too. She seems to see the justice of it and gives in pretty easily.

She helps with pruning, too. Has her own saw and with direction will sometimes prune a whole tree. But it is a harder skill to learn.

I think living on a work crew has been really good for our family. It helped me set limits and encouraged us to accept time away from each other, but still allowed us to be together when we needed it. Very young, A accepted that I had to work and learned to amuse herself very well. I think that kind of solitude is very important for everyone. She became less clinging and demanding and I learned I could choose which demands I would meet. Before crew life I felt I should give her everything she was asking for. As a result of working with her near I learned that she could accept it and *benefitted* when I sometimes let her work it out herself. This led to both of us feeling our own individuality and made our close times closer. And brought my way of being with her into accord with T's way. Her attitude toward work (and mine) have benefitted from the work situation. Most of the crew, most of the time, are working with a willing attitude and there's a lot of enthusiasm that is catching. She works harder and longer with T, who enjoys pushing himself, than with me.

Since I have been the bookkeeper on the last few crews her interest in math has grown sharply. She helps with the payroll and counts out everyone's final net pay. She seems to have a good solid concept of reading and math. She doesn't gobble them up in quantity but when she's interested in something she follows it through.

I wrote in reply:

You wonder how A compares with other kids her age? My guess would
be that she compares very well, probably smarter, more self-reliant,
more serious, considerate, self-motivated, independent, and honest.

People get smart by giving constant attention and thought *to the
concrete details of daily life*, by having to solve problems which are real
and important, where getting a good answer makes a real difference,
and where Life or Nature tells them quickly whether their answer is
good or not. The woods are such a place; so is the sea; so is any place
where real, skilled work is being done—like the small farm where Jud
Jerome's daughter worked, like your own orchards.

Two summers ago I spent some time working with a small farmer in
Nova Scotia, the neighbor and friend of the friends I was visiting. He
had a large garden where he grew almost all his own vegetables, had
about 20 acres in hay, raised Christmas trees. He also owned woodlots,
from which he cut wood, for his own use and to sell. He was 72 years
old, and did all this work himself, with the help of two horses. The skill,
precision, judgment, and economy of effort he displayed in his daily
work were a marvel to see. The friend I was visiting, a highly intelligent
and educated man, no city slicker but a countryman himself, who had
long raised much of his own food and killed, butchered, and cured or
frozen much of his own meat, said with no false modesty at all that if he
farmed for fifteen or twenty years he might—with plenty of luck and
good advice—eventually learn to farm as well as this old neighbor.

LEAF-GATHERING

Children show me again and again that they love to be really useful, to
feel that they make a difference.

Two years ago, as I write this, I began a mini-experiment in urban
agriculture. Each fall, when the trees in the Public Garden have lost
their leaves, men blow them into big piles and later take them away.
While the leaf piles are still there, I collect several garbage cans full
and make a packed-down pile of them in the little sunken patio be-

hind my basement apartment. Every day I pour over them the water I use for washing, dishes, shower, etc., and use the rotted leaves to feed the worms I am raising.

As soon as the leaves were thick on the ground this fall I began collecting. Many early mornings, I put two plastic garbage cans on a small garden cart, took a leaf rake, trundled the cans into the Public Garden, raked up a pile of leaves, and filled the cans, jumping up and down in them from time to time to pack the leaves well down. Then I rolled cart and cans to the sidewalk behind my apartment, dumped the leaves over the wall into the patio, and later gathered them into piles which I packed down with weights.

One morning I collected and piled up more than a dozen loads. Feeling rain in the air, I thought I would make a couple of trips and bring in four more cans full, while the leaves were still dry. When I reached the Public Garden I saw four boys (8, 9, 9, and 10, as I later found out), gathering leaves and putting them into the now dry sunken pool that surrounds a small monument. They spotted me and rushed over to ask if they could borrow my garbage cans to fill up with leaves, which would be quicker than dumping one armful at a time. I said that was a good idea, but that I needed the cans, because I was going to fill them up with leaves and take them home. What for, they asked. To make them into rich dirt, I said. They thought about this for a moment. Then they asked if they could borrow the "wheelbarrow." I said, Sure, but that when my cans were full I would need it back. They agreed and went off with the cart, which they used to take their leaves to the empty pond. When I was ready I called to them and they brought the cart back. I took the cans home, dumped the leaves over the wall, and went back for more.

This time the boys came over to ask if they could help by loading into my cans some of the leaves they had put in the pond. I said that there were plenty of leaves left on the ground, and that I didn't want to take leaves away from their nice pile. They insisted that they wanted to do it, so I thanked them and said to go ahead. While they filled the cans, I raked up more leaves. Back they came in a few minutes with full cans, all talking and asking questions. I jumped up and down on the leaves inside the cans; the boys were amazed to find how much the leaves packed down. Then I began to fill the cans with the leaves I had raked. The boys asked if they could help me do that. I said, Sure. As we worked I told them I was going to use the leaves to feed the worms I was raising. They were fascinated by this. What kind of worms? How many did I have? Where did I get them? How much did they cost? What did they eat? How did I feed them? What did I keep them in? Why was I doing this?

When the cans were full and loaded on the cart the boys asked if they could help me take them home. I thanked them again and said, Fine. With very little arguing, they organized a four-man cart-pushing team. Two pushed, and two stood up at the front corners holding on, "guiding it," as they said. By this time they were so curious about the leaves and the worms that I decided to show them to them. They had been told to stay in the Garden, but I said that since I lived only a couple of blocks away we would be right back and I was sure their mothers wouldn't mind. So they pushed the cart to the wall where I unload. One asked me to lift him up so he could see the leaf pile in the patio. I did, and he was amazed to see how big it was. Soon they all climbed or were lifted to the top of the wall, and watched while I dumped the leaves. When the leaves stuck a bit in the can, one of them helped pry them loose. All the while they asked questions about me. What did I do? I said I wrote articles and books. What kind of books? Books about children and school. And so on.

When we went indoors two boys insisted on carrying the empty garbage cans downstairs, while a third pulled the cart up some steps—a hard struggle—and put it away. Then we went out to look at the leaf pile. I found a worm and showed it to them. There was a chorus of "Yuk! Slimy!" But in only a second or two they all wanted to hold one. I also found and showed them some egg cases, and one of them spotted a tiny worm, newly hatched, hardly bigger than a thread. They were fascinated by this, all four talking and asking questions at once. Soon they asked if they could each have a worm. I said, Sure, got one for each, gave each a little hunk of dirt to keep the worm in, some leaves to wrap the dirt in, and a paper bag to carry it.

As we walked back to the Public Garden they asked about how worms made more worms. I told them that worms were bisexual, boys and girls at the same time, and that any two worms could come together and fertilize each other, after which both of them could produce egg cases. Soon we were back at the monument and their leaf pile. After a bit more talk I said that I was sorry but that I had to go home and do some other work. I hated to leave these bright, friendly, curious, enthusiastic, helpful children. I loved working with them and showing them things and answering their questions. I think they were just as sorry to leave me. I remember, when they were pulling the loaded cart (which was quite heavy) toward my apartment, one of them said, to the others, not to me, and in the kind of voice that can't be faked, "This is *fun*, doing this!" They all agreed—much more fun to be helping a grownup do serious (even if mysterious) work than just playing around in a leaf pile. I hope they may have more chances to work with me, or some adult who cares about what he or she is doing. I hate to think of them ever becoming like the bored, sullen, angry, destructive teenagers who hang out every day at the Boylston Street entrance to the Public Garden.

The other day a young person wrote me saying, "I want to work with children." Such letters come often. They make me want to say, "What you really mean is, you want to work *on* children. You want to do things *to* them, or *for* them—wonderful things, no doubt—which you think will help them. What's more, you want to do these things whether the children want them done or not. What makes you think they need you so much? If you really want to work with children, then why not find some work worth doing, work you believe in for its own sake, and *then* find a way to make it possible for children—if they want to—to do that work with you."

The difference is crucial. The reason my work with the leaves and worms was interesting and exciting to those boys was precisely that it was *my* work, something I was doing for *my* good, not theirs. It was not some sort of "project" that I had cooked up because I thought they might be interested in it. I wasn't out there raking up leaves in the hope that some children might see me and want to join in. I never asked them to help, never even hinted; they *insisted* on helping me. All I did for them—which may be more than many adults might have done—was to say that if they really wanted that much to help me,

then they could. Which is exactly the choice I would like to see the
adult world offer to all children.

VOLUNTEER WORK

A twelve-year-old wrote us about being an office volunteer:

In July 1978 my mother was asked to work at the Childbirth Education
Association office. At that time we had a three-month-old baby named
C. So my mother asked me if I would like to go to the office to mind C
while she did her work. But when I went in, it seemed that C slept most
of the time except when she was hungry. So I started to do a little work.
Mrs. L. gave me some little jobs to do. Her daughter R (who is now a
very good friend of mine) helped me to get into bigger things. She
taught me to make registration packets. Even now I do about 100 a
week at home. She taught me to run the folding machine so that we
were able to fold the papers for the registration packets and also for the
Memo. We enjoyed that a lot. I can even do it better than my mom because she gets the papers stuck sometimes. I also learned what to say
when I answered the phone, even though I had a hard time getting
"Childbirth Education Association" out in one breath and I sometimes
disconnected people instead of putting them on hold.

I can't forget the literature orders. That was the best. We really had
fun doing those. Finding the right papers and counting them out. Writing out bills and addressing the envelopes was lots of fun. R and I both
knew what literature was there and what wasn't, so we could answer
questions about what was in stock better than our moms.

I also had to do the postage meter at the end of the day. I always
tried to use Mrs. L's adding machine to figure out the totals, but sometimes I would have to use my brain; then I didn't like it so much.

But it wasn't all work; sometimes R, her brother, and I would play a
game or go to the library. I really looked forward to coming in to the office. But soon the bad part came. I had to go back to school. So as soon
as I got my school calendar I sent in a paper with all the days I had off
from school so I could come into the office.

Now I am waiting for the summer to come so I can go into the office and help out.

Not long ago in our office we had so many letters from people asking about *Growing Without Schooling*, and about teaching children at home, that we could not answer them all. In the magazine I asked readers if some of them, who could type and also had a cassette tape recorder, would help with this. Many offered to do so, among them the mother of L, a Down's syndrome child. She asked if it would be okay, for the letters she was doing, if L addressed (in handwriting) the envelopes. I said, Fine. I sent them a tape of letters, which came back soon afterward, the letters typed, the envelopes neatly addressed. Then I sent them a big stack of letters from all over the country, that we had already answered, but that now needed to be broken down by states so that we could send them to people in the various states for a closer follow-up. Along with these I sent a tape of instructions. About this, L's mother wrote:

> . . . L was thrilled with the whole project, and most impressed with being addressed by name on the tape. She took to the sorting and filing with gusto. I hadn't mentioned that this was another part of our "program," again one where I had tried to convince the schools to do something "real." They kept trying to get her to alphabetize on paper, and I wanted them to give her index cards, recipes, etc., or folders. No use. So when we started our planning this year, I had her make up a bunch of file folders, for each course or planned activity, and she puts receipts, brochures, and stuff in them. Also we keep her papers for figuring out money, arithmetic problems, sentences, etc. Also, since I need some shape for my days and am a chronic list-maker, we'd make up daily schedules (especially so she could go about her work without having to check with me every minute, something she really enjoys—the independence, I mean). These schedules, if more than routine, go into the folders.
>
> So she was already used to that. She made up the folders (with my help in listing the states and assorted abbreviations). The first round, I went through the letters and underlined the state. The second time

around I just screened them to be sure there *was* an address and that it was legible, but didn't note them—she figured them out herself. Anyway, L loves the job, and can't wait to get started, at night even, after supper. All this seems ideal for L's purpose—some work experience, plus the exposure to the filing, alphabetizing, state names and abbreviations, etc., all without any formal "instruction," just doing it—the perfect way, but hard to find, especially for her. [Author's note: In a later letter, she said that L had a paying part-time job.]

11

Homeschooling in America

◖❦ ONE OF THE THINGS about *Teach Your Own* that I've rediscovered is how much it is not just a polemic and a practical guide for how and why to homeschool, but that it is also a major attempt to address the political, legal, and legislative issues homeschoolers faced in the early eighties— and are likely to face now and in the future. Holt writes about the need for allies; about how schools and homeschoolers can work together for society's good and how different groups can work together, even though they may have different visions about education, and so on. This was not just a rallying call but an action plan, as well. However, some readers were intimidated by Holt's lengthy legal descriptions, even though Holt, by explaining the intricacies of homeschooling and the courts, wished to demystify the law and not to intimidate the public with it.

Holt wanted people to feel that the law was something they could understand on their own, and he spent a lot of time in the original edition describing various federal, state, and local court decisions that uphold the right to homeschool. When Holt wrote *Teach Your Own*, homeschooling occupied a gray area in the law, and in some states it still does. Contrary to popular myth, there have never been statutes forbidding homeschooling anywhere in the United States. If homeschoolers are taken to court, it is usually for disobeying the compulsory education laws or some charge of educational or child neglect, not for the act of homeschooling. Indeed, some states still haven't a single law regarding homeschooling, whereas others have reasonable laws and some have laws that are restrictive. There is room for disagreement about how homeschooling occurs and how it is described in each state, but teaching your own children is legal everywhere even if it isn't explicitly called "homeschooling."

For instance, in Alabama you can homeschool only if you qualify as a certified tutor or if your home qualifies as a church school. Many families simply register their home as a church school, and some even enroll other families in their church schools, because such schools are exempted from all Alabama state education code requirements, with the exception of filing enrollment and attendance forms. In California, there are several ways to homeschool, including registering your home as a private school, but for some strange reason the California State Department of Education's legal department refuses to acknowledge homeschooling as an official practice—even though California has one of the largest populations of homeschooling families in the nation. To them, home schooling does not exist: You are either doing tutoring, independent study through a public or private school, or you have registered your home as a private school. So if you were to ask "Is homeschooling legal?" of a California or Alabama education state official, you might get the surprising answer, "No," even though homeschooling is flourishing in both states. The best source of information about the regulations and laws regarding homeschooling in your state is an active homeschooling group in your local community or state; I provide advice about getting this information in Chapter 12, and more resources at the end of the book.

As Holt notes, and as the semantic tap dancing of education regulations demonstrate, not even the schools themselves are widely aware of a family's right to choose the sort of schooling they want their children to receive. The situation is less confusing today than it was when Holt first wrote *Teach Your Own*, but some of Holt's observations about how to fight for and preserve our right to homeschool are more important now, as we enter the twenty-first century, than when he first wrote them.

Charter schools, distance learning, and all sorts of for-profit tutoring and education services are blurring the line between home and school, on-campus credits and off-campus credits, service learning, and community service. The positive side of this is the multitude of flexible options these services can provide to homeschoolers. The negative side is that many of these options are beholden to schoolish ideas of when, what, and how children should learn. Lists and schedules of what and when to learn already dominate our schools, and the more we allow regulators to pressure our homes into being like schools—following the same lists and schedules for learning, being evaluated and held responsible in the same way—the less likely we are to try something different than what the law, or school regulations, dictates for our children. One of the great legal issues homeschooling will face in the coming century will be the ability of homeschooling to remain distinct and well protected from other forms of private and public education, not only for the sanctity of family and personal privacy, but so that an option will always remain for teachers and students in school, too: the option to "unschool," not to be like a school at all in their approach to learning.

I have edited Holt's three chapters dealing with the courts, legal strategies, and legislature into this one chapter to bring it up to date. ᴑᴗ

Not long ago I spoke to a large meeting of educators from southeastern Massachusetts. This is fairly affluent country, so the school people there are probably about as well informed as anywhere. At one point I asked people to raise their hands if they had even a rough idea of what was meant or referred to in the phrase *Pierce* v. *Society of Sisters*. I had expected to see perhaps a dozen hands. Not one was raised. But this U.S. Supreme Court decision of 1925 is perhaps the most fundamental of all rulings on this question.

More recently, when I was testifying before the Education Committee of the House of Representatives of the Minnesota legislature, a member of the legislative staff read to the committee a summary she had prepared of court decisions on compulsory schooling. It was not bad as far as it went, but it was at least *two years* out of date. And it left out some very important earlier rulings in favor of homeschool families.

Most judges in family or juvenile courts, where many unschooling cases will first be heard, probably don't know this part of the law either, since it is not one with which they have had much to do.

This means that when we write up homeschooling plans, we are going to have to cite and quote favorable rulings. The more of this we do, the less schools will want to take us to court, and the better the chances that if they do we will win. Under our adversary legal system the task of courts is not so much to decide what "justice" is, as to decide which of the parties before them, in terms of existing laws, court decisions, etc., has the strongest argument. The courts will not do our legal work for us. If we don't cite favorable court cases in our plans or briefs, judges (who may very well not even have heard of them) are not going to put them in their rulings. But once we put before a court an argument or a legal precedent, the court cannot ignore it, but must either agree with it or find a stronger argument to oppose it. Otherwise, it runs the risk that its ruling will later be reversed by a higher court.

Now and then I discover a wonderful book, which I want to recommend to all homeschoolers, only to find that it is long out of print. One such book is *The End of Obscenity* by Charles Rembar. (It might be in a library or law library.) It is the best book for laymen, at least that I have seen, about how constitutional law *works*. I learned an immense amount from it about how judges think, and about how lawyers go about making cases that they think may convince judges.

Rembar was able to persuade the courts to overturn definitions of obscenity that had been established in statutes and upheld by courts for many years. In other words, he was trying to persuade the courts essentially to reverse themselves on an important point of law—something they very rarely do. And by an amazingly ingenious series of arguments he was able to do it.

The chief lesson of Rembar's book is that if you want the courts, or a court, to reverse rulings that have been well settled in law, you have to present them with arguments they (and the courts before them) have not heard before. You can't go before them and say what has been said before, in the hope that *this* time they will say Yes where previously they had always said No. You have to give them a reason for saying Yes that the earlier courts did not have.

THE LAW ON SCHOOLING SUMMED UP

Here, in sum, is the meaning of these rulings:

1. Parents have a right to educate their children in whatever way they believe in; the state cannot impose on all parents any kind of educational monopoly of schools, methods, or whatever. *Pierce* v. *Society of Sisters* (1925), *Farrington* v. *Tokushige* (1927), *Perchemlides* v. *Frizzle* (1978).

2. The state may not deprive parents of this right for arbitrary reasons, but only for serious educational ones, which it must make known to parents, with all the forms of due process. Again, *Perchemlides;* also *Michigan* v. *Nobel* (1979).

3. A state that would deny parents these rights by saying that their home education plan is inadequate has a burden of proof to show beyond reasonable doubt that this is so. Parents are assumed to be competent to teach their children until proved otherwise. This Assumption of Competence is kin to and part of the general Assumption of Innocence (of the accused) which holds in all criminal proceedings. *State of Iowa* v. *Sessions* (1978).

4. In order to prove that the parents' education plans are inadequate, the state must show that its own requirements, regulations, etc., are educationally necessary and do in fact produce, in its own schools, better results than the parents get or are likely to get. *Hinton et al.* v. *Kentucky* (1978); also *Nobel.*

⊲Q The cases Holt cites in the previous paragraph can be looked up in a law library. They have formed the basis of many subsequent decisions that affirm a constitutional right to homeschool. Because homeschoolers are far more likely to be dealing with their local school officials rather than courts today, I've cut much of the legal information. However, there are good resources you and your children can use to look up the law, including Lipson's *Everyday Law for Young Citizens* and Elias and Levenkind's *Legal Research: How to Find and Understand the Law.* Many homeschooling groups will have copies of the relevant case law or education regulations about homeschooling in your respective state, sometimes in a special vertical file at a public library, thereby making this information even easier to access than it was in 1981. Most state homeschooling groups, and state departments of education as well, post their homeschooling laws or regulations on the Internet. A good search engine can give you all you need to know if you like to search for information this way.

Parents who wish to assert their rights or bring about change would do well to emulate Holt's broad-minded political tactics. He recognized and sought legal precedent and protection for homeschooling from all over the political spectrum in order to keep the field diverse and vibrant. He worked hard to keep homeschooling from being cast as both a primarily conservative or a liberal issue, angering partisans of all stripes who want to claim homeschooling as "their issue." For instance, conservative homeschoolers often refuse to use arguments to protect homeschooling that rely on the right of family privacy because they feel this will further entrench *Roe* v. *Wade* in case law. Liberal defenders of homeschooling often refuse to use arguments about the rights of children not to go to school, for fear that will bring ruin to the public school system. Holt never hesitates to mention these and many other legal arguments that support homeschooling, both broadly and specifically.

One of the most striking legal points Holt makes is one most parents aren't aware of, though most children are: If you learn, the schools get the credit; if you don't, the student gets the blame. In short, you can't sue a school for educational malpractice. Holt explains the situation this way: ᕍᕤ

A DOUBTFUL CLAIM

We have already discussed the claim of the schools that they alone know how to teach children. Most of the time, they make this claim with no reservations whatever. Yet when they are sued in court for not having done what they say they and they alone know how to do, they suddenly become very modest.

A most revealing article on Teacher Malpractice in the *American Educator*, journal of the American Federation of Teachers, said, in part:

In 1972, parents of a graduate of the public school system in San Francisco brought a $500,000 suit against the school district charging that after a total of 13 years of regular attendance, their son was not able to read.

During his years in school, according to information compiled on the case, he was in the middle of his classes, maintained average grades, and was never involved in anything which resulted in major disciplinary action. His parents claimed that during their son's years in the public school they were rebuffed in their attempts to get information on the progress of their son, but were assured by school officials and teachers he was moving along at grade level.

Shortly after the youth's graduation, he was given a reading test by specialists who concluded the youth was only reading on a fifth-grade level. . . .

The California State Court of Appeals rejected the parents' claim of the school system's failure to educate their son. The court declared it was impossible for any person, most of all the courts, to set guidelines for "proper" academic procedures which must be followed by all schools and all teachers.

"Unlike the activity of the highway, or the marketplace, classroom methodology affords no readily acceptable standards of care, or cause, or injury. The science of pedagogy itself is fraught with different and conflicting theories of how or what a child should be taught, and any layman might, and commonly does, have his own emphatic views on the subject," read the court's opinion.

The court was, of course, quite right in saying this. But what then becomes of the claim, which the schools make all the time, that they alone know how to teach children? Parents in conflict with schools might find it very helpful to quote those words from the California ruling.

This very issue came up again, but this time in England. In October 2001, Katherine Norfolk, nineteen, and her parents sued Hurstpierpoint College "for loss of earnings, damage to her career prospects, and personal distress" due to poor teaching by her Latin instructor. The first sentence about this case in *The Guardian* reflects considerable anxiety by the schools over this issue:

Head teachers of private schools urged parents yesterday not to resort to litigation if their children gained disappointing exam results, after it emerged that a Sussex school was being sued for £150,000 by the family of a star pupil who failed to get a top grade in A-level Latin.[1]

The worries are ill founded I believe, though they indicate considerable insecurity by school officials. As Holt noted, the courts wouldn't allow the schools to fail in this way for a number of reasons, and I think, in general, the public would side with the schools in a minute on the issue of teacher malpractice. Indeed, I first learned about the Norfolk case in a humor column featuring real news stories entitled "News of the Weird," which shows how seriously much of the public takes this claim. But Holt's point that even high-priced schools can't guarantee that they know best how to teach children is conveniently ignored by educationists, who insist that unqualified, uncertified, and unschooling parents haven't got a clue how to properly teach their own children. Perhaps they'd like to let us in on their secret? ☙

COURT STRATEGY IN GENERAL

As Justice Cardozo pointed out in his enormously valuable book *The Nature of the Judicial Process*, judges, in making their rulings, take into account a number of things—legal philosophy and principle, legal precedent, the will of the legislature as expressed in the statutes, and *the possible or probable social effects of their rulings*. Thus, as we have shown, parents who have sued the schools because their children did not learn anything there have so far been turned down by the courts, on the grounds that this would very quickly lead to a rush of lawsuits that would bankrupt the schools. We may take it as certain that the courts will not in any foreseeable future make rulings which they think will lead to the quick destruction of the public schools or the end of compulsory schooling. If we ask for such broad rulings, we will be turned down.

Beyond that, either in asking for narrow rulings, or speaking of any we may be able to win, we must be careful not to make large public boasts and outcries to the effect that "this means the downfall of compulsory schooling." In the first place, such boasts would be silly; even if the courts were by some miracle to strike down compulsory schooling, a furious majority of the people would quickly reestablish it, by constitutional amendment if they had to. In the second place, even making such boasts would greatly reduce our chances of getting even narrowly favorable rulings from the courts. In the third place, such boasts tend to terrify the schools, who are already far more terrified than they need be, and whom it is in our best interests to reassure.

◖◖ The importance of Holt's repeated advice to "think like a judge" when you consider going to court can't be underestimated. I've seen some homeschoolers decide to challenge compulsory school laws with a thin legal strategy, namely that somehow common sense will make the judges "see the light" and rule in favor of homeschooling and against compulsory schooling. Instead, as Holt indicates, judges prefer to rule in very narrow, case-specific decisions. When I hear about a court case of the "will be a major victory for homeschooling if we win it" sort I cringe; after twenty-two years in the field I've seen victories in our state legislatures for homeschooling, but also more losses and stalemates than clear victories in court cases. Judges tend to think of school and education as an important tool in their kit of remedies, and homeschoolers, no matter how persuasive their respective case, aren't going to wean judges from their reliance on and perception of schooling as a disciplinary tool.

As Holt puts it, "I see no point in confronting the authorities directly if you can dodge them." When dodging no longer is an option, then appealing to state legislators is often better than going to court. Holt's legislative statement and his description of the hearing, which follow, are models of how such action can work for homeschoolers. ◗◗

LEGISLATIVE STRATEGY

Early in 1980 I was invited by the Education Committee of the Minnesota House of Representatives to testify at hearings they were holding about home education and private schools. I said that I would be glad to, and sent them in advance a statement of my position. What I

said to them could, I believe, be equally and usefully said to any other
state or provincial legislatures giving homeschooling their attention.

The statement:

> Time being short, let us not waste any of it in arguments about whether
> the public schools are doing a good job. Such arguments cannot be set-
> tled here.

·   ·   ·

Let me sum up very briefly my position:

1. In terms of both the short-run and long-run interests of themselves and of the general public, the schools would be wise to view the
growing home education movement not as a threat but as an opportunity and a potential asset, and, rather than resist it, to support it to the
fullest extent.

2. The legislature itself would be wise, in any education laws it may
write, to affirm and support very strongly the right of parents to teach
their own children, and to make it as easy as possible for the schools to
assist them in this effort.

3. To try to do the opposite, i.e., to try to make it difficult or impossible for people to teach their own children, would be a most serious educational, legal, and political mistake.

What does the law have to say about all this? Here we must note that
"the law" is made up, not just of the laws or statutes, but of the ways in
which the courts have interpreted these laws.

According to repeated court decisions, there is here (as in many
places) some conflict between the constitutionally protected rights of
the parents and the equally protected rights of the states.

The courts have affirmed, in decisions too numerous to cite, that under the police powers delegated to them that several states have a right
to demand that all children be educated, and to that end, to write and
enforce compulsory school attendance laws.

But the U.S. Supreme Court has also held, first in *Pierce* v. *Society of
Sisters*, and later in *Farrington* v. *Tokushige*, that while the state may

demand that all children be educated, it may not demand that they be educated in the same way, and that, on the contrary, parents have a constitutionally protected right to get for their children an education which is in accord with their own principles and beliefs. The state, in other words, may not have a monopoly in education, either of schools or of methods. The parents have a right to choice, not just in minor details but in matters of significance.

Subsequent decisions in state courts, in Illinois, New Jersey, Massachusetts, and Iowa, among others, have held that this right of parents to control the education of their children includes the right to teach them themselves. In at least one state the courts have held that the burden of proof is not on such parents to show that they are capable of teaching their children, but on the state to show that they are not capable of doing so.

•   •   •

Some other legal points should be made here:

1. The courts, in upholding the right of the states to compel children to be educated, have upheld this on the sole ground that without such education children would be unfit for employment and would therefore become a burden on the state. It follows that when the states say that a given educational program, whether of parents or of a private school, is inadequate, it must be from this point of view and this one only. The courts have never said, for example, that compulsory schooling was necessary so that all children would have some kind of "social life." This is a fringe benefit—if indeed a benefit at all. Therefore the states cannot rule out an educational program on the grounds that it does not give students an adequate social life. In this area the states have no rights, and the rights of the parents are supreme.

2. A Massachusetts superior court held recently that the right of parents to teach their own children is located not just in the First and Fourteenth, but also the Ninth Amendment to the Constitution.

3. A Kentucky district court, in a ruling later upheld by the state supreme court, said that before the state could demand, for example, that all teachers be certified, it had to produce evidence to show that

certified teachers taught better than uncertified ones. In the court's words, the state was unable to produce "a scintilla" of such evidence. Nor, in all probability, could any other state. Indeed, it would be easy to show that the most exclusive and academically demanding and successful schools, to which the richest and most favored people send their children, have on their faculties few if any certified teachers, or graduates of schools of education.

4. When parents in San Francisco, in 1972, sued the schools because, after 13 years of school their son was reading only on a fifth-grade level, the California State Court of Appeals dismissed the suit saying, "Unlike the activity of the highway, or the marketplace, classroom methodology affords no readily acceptable standards of care, or cause, or injury. The science of pedagogy itself is fraught with different and conflicting theories of how or what a child should be taught . . . " and concluded that it was impossible for anyone to set guidelines for "proper" academic procedures which must be followed by all schools and all teachers. How can the schools, when charged with negligence, defend themselves as they did in this case by saying that no one really knows how children should be taught, and in the next breath say that they are the only ones who know?

The point is that if the legislature tries to prevent or even unduly circumscribe the right of parents to teach their own children, such laws will surely be challenged in the already overburdened courts, and will not stand up.

•　　　•　　　•

Though you may have been told the opposite, such laws are not necessary to "save" the public schools. The number of people who, even if it were easy to do so, would want to take their children out of school and teach them at home, is small. Not many people enjoy the company of their children that much, or would want to give that much attention to their interests and concerns, or take that much of the responsibility for their growth. In places where the schools have gone to court to prevent people from teaching their own children, they have told the courts that if they ruled in favor of the parents they would be "opening the floodgates," "setting a bad precedent," "starting a landslide." Nowhere have these dire predictions come true, even in communities in which, after much publicity, the parents won their case.

The best way for the public schools to save themselves, if they are in fact in any real danger, is to solve the problems they already have within the walls of their school buildings. In trying to find ways to solve these problems, they may in time be very much helped by what will be learned about effective teaching by people teaching their own children. They will be further helped by many of these children who will choose, as some are already choosing, to go to school part-time for those activities that interest then most. The example of these independent and self-motivated students will have a powerful effect on other students and on the schools in general.

Under present Minnesota law, local school boards have an unqualified legal right, if they wish, to allow parents to teach their children at home. In short, the law, *as it stands*, is sufficient to *permit* homeschooling. The law may allow local school districts and law enforcement authorities, if they so choose, to prosecute any family for trying to teach its children at home, but *it does not require* them to do so, for at least three reasons:

1. Under the law, school districts may define school attendance in any way they wish. School districts in many jurisdictions have instituted different kinds of off-campus study programs (like the Parkway Project in Philadelphia), or work-study or apprenticeship programs, or even programs which required students to travel to other cities or states. In like manner, schools have for generations been able to extend full academic credit to children of families living or traveling abroad, or traveling in this country in the course of business (i.e., families in the circus or theater) and studying from correspondence courses. No one has ever claimed or could sustain a claim that in doing this, the schools were somehow violating compulsory state attendance laws. Now do the schools, in such matters, have to defend their definitions of "attendance" to any other state authorities; in this matter they have absolute discretion.

2. Under the law, the school districts and/or the state may define private schools in any way they wish. There is—fortunately—no absolute

requirement that private school teachers be certified. All that is required is that the "common branches" be taught in the English language. As for hours of instruction, it is worth nothing that when children who ordinarily attend public schools are for reasons of sickness or injury unable to attend, public schools ordinarily send tutors to the homes of these children, so that they will not fall behind in their schoolwork. How much time these tutors spend with the children varies from district to district. My own limited investigation has shown that this varies from as little as an hour and a half a week to a maximum of four hours a week. It would be interesting for the legislature to check school practices on this throughout the state. Many families using materials from the long-accredited Calvert Institute or similar organizations have reported to me that their children are able to do what the correspondence school calls a week's worth of schoolwork in only a few hours.

3. The law as written gives the school board the right to excuse a child from attending school "if his bodily or mental condition is such as to prevent his attendance at school *or application to study* . . . " But it is undisputed that many children do badly in school, or fail, or drop out altogether, because they are bored, because the school will not permit them to study at their own level, or because the school has no programs that meet their special interests, capabilities, and needs, or because the competitive and/or threatening atmosphere of the school and classroom prevents them from working up to their capacity. In such cases, and others we might well imagine, it would be legally permissible and educationally wise for schools to grant parents of such children, if they asked for it, the right to educate their children in ways that, being in greater harmony with their interests, temperaments, and styles of learning, would produce more effective results. Nothing in the law as it stands denies school boards the right to do this, or makes them answerable to any higher authority for any exceptions they might grant.

In short, while the law could, and in my judgment should make more explicit the rights of parents to teach their own children, it does not have to be changed in order to permit this. It is only if the intent of the legislature is to make home teaching far more difficult or forbid it altogether that changes in the law are required.

If the legislature wishes to affirm the right of parents to teach their own children, while continuing to exercise its constitutional right to assure that all children are being taught, it could do so very well by passing resolutions which would, in effect, say more or less the following:

1. It is not the intent of the compulsory laws of this state to deny to parents the right to have for their children an education in reasonable harmony with their own deepest concerns and principles, including the right, if they wish, to teach their own children at home.

2. Nor is it the intent of this legislature to authorize any educational authorities to impose on students under their jurisdiction a uniform curriculum, or uniform methods of instruction and/or evaluation. There are and will remain large and legitimate differences of opinion, among experts and nonexperts alike, on the subjects that should be taught to children, on the order and ways in which these are to be taught, on the materials which are to be used, and on the ways in which this teaching and learning are to be evaluated. Only by allowing and supporting a wide range of education practices can we encourage the diversity of experience from which we can learn to educate our children more effectively, and it is the intent of this legislature to allow and encourage such variety.

3. Rather than draw up any set of detailed guidelines to regulate homeschooling, or set up some kind of special administrative machinery for this purpose, we would prefer to leave to the local school districts the responsibility for supervising and assisting home-teaching families according to their own best judgement, keeping always in mind the very general purposes noted above.

May I repeat once more, even if the legislature passes such resolutions or their equivalent, it will be a very long time before as many children are being taught at home as are right now truant every day from the schools of our larger cities.

The legislature, at least if it wishes to make homeschooling no more difficult than it is today, might be wise to write into law what at least one court, in Nebraska, has already affirmed in a ruling, namely, that the laws governing neglect were not intended to be considered as an integral part of the compulsory school attendance laws, and that the charge of neglect, and the probable consequence of removing children from the custody of their parents, is not to be understood as a natural and legitimate penalty for failing or refusing to send the children to an accredited school. Some considerations:

1. School personnel may say that a threat this severe is needed to guarantee compliance with compulsory school attendance laws. But this violates a very fundamental principle of the common law, perhaps nowhere made explicit but very thoroughly understood, that the penalty for an offense must be proportional to the offense. In the light of this principle, no local government would be able, for example, to punish parking violations with prison sentences, on the grounds that without such severe punishment they could not secure complete compliance with the law.

2. When legislators passed laws saying that the state could, for neglect, remove children from the custody of their parents, what they had in mind was children who were starved, or left naked, or were brutally beaten and tortured, or locked in closets, or chained to furniture. They did not have in mind the children of conscientious and devoted parents whose only crime was that they did not approve of the kind of education offered in the local schools. To lump such parents with gross abusers of children, as schools have quite often already done, is a most serious perversion of law and justice.

3. It should be added that even people convicted of the most serious crimes—assault, grand larceny, manslaughter, even murder—are not automatically deprived of the custody of their families. If and when such criminals finish their sentences, their families and children, at least if they choose to do so, are waiting for them. To say that violent criminals may be fit to raise their children but that people who want to teach them at home are not is again a serious perversion of justice.

It must be categorically said that if it were true (which I dispute) that the compulsory attendance laws could only be enforced by such severe and cruel penalties—for loving parents, the most severe of all penalties—there would be something inherently wrong with those laws. At any rate, this way of enforcing them, or of settling or rather foreclosing arguments about what kind of education is best for the children, ought in the name of justice and equity to be removed from the schools' hands.

What is true of the laws of Minnesota, i.e., that they permit (though they don't require) any school district to allow parents to teach their children at home, is equally true of the laws of all other states, for at least two and in many cases all three of the reasons given above. I know of no court cases in which the compulsory school attendance laws of a state have been used to restrict in any way the right of local school districts to establish any kinds of academic programs they wish, whether on-campus, off-campus, job-related, independent research, or whatever. As long as school districts have the support of the voters in their districts they can do what they want. The notion, apparently believed by quite a few superintendents, that one day a state attorney might prosecute a local school superintendent and/or school board for allowing some parents to teach their children at home is absurd.

In the same way, local school districts can, whenever they want and for whatever reasons they want, allow exceptions to the laws about attending school. State laws saying that parents must supply some kind of statement from a doctor put a burden on the parents, not the schools. In other words, they say that unless the parents produce a statement from a doctor, the schools do not even have to consider their request for an exception. They do not mean, and would not be construed to mean, that the schools are forbidden to consider exceptions unless these are supported by a doctor's report.

In my statement to the committee, I suggested that if the legislature wished to give additional encouragement and support to home teaching, they could do so by passing some rather simple and general resolutions. After the hearings, I said in a letter to the administrative assistant that I thought a resolution by the Education Committee itself, rather than the entire legislature, might do almost as well. If school districts merely wish to be reassured that they are not compelled by law to prosecute all home-teaching families, a statement to that effect by the committee would probably give all the reassurance they needed.

The hearings themselves were very interesting. In opening the hearings, the chairman of the committee pointed out that a number of school districts had asked the legislature to "clarify" the law. What this "clarify" meant was soon made clear. Two witnesses, one a district superintendent, the other a county attorney, told about the troubles they had had, trying to prosecute and send to jail and/or deprive of their children a few families that wanted to teach their children at home. They said to the committee, in effect, "Either rewrite these laws, saying in strict detail what is or is not a private school, so that we can easily and quickly prosecute and convict these people, or else do away with compulsory school attendance laws altogether." No doubt school people in many other states will be telling legislators that they must either allow no exceptions whatever to compulsory school attendance laws (except perhaps to rich people), or give up the whole idea.

In my testimony I did my best to persuade the committee that they were not faced with any such choice. To my written statements I added only these points: (1) In more and more jurisdictions, where families had prepared their case with enough care, i.e., made up a detailed educational plan, supported by quotes from educational authorities and many relevant court citations, the courts were increasingly ruling in their favor. (2) The movement for home teaching was part of a growing nationwide movement toward greater self-sufficiency and minimized dependence on large institutions, a movement that from many points of view could only be considered healthy and admirable and that in any case was certain to grow. (3) Trying to crack down on homeschooling families would increase, not lessen, the number and complexity of cases before their courts.

In this last connection the young county attorney had said indignantly at one point that one family was only using the Bible as a textbook. I asked him whether he thought he would have an easier time if he found himself arguing in court before a judge about how good a textbook the Bible was. I added that I thought it would not be hard to make a strong case that the Bible was a great deal better textbook than most of the ones used in schools. Did he really want to get involved in such arguments? The expression on his face as I said this suggested that he did not.

I went on to say that the committee had to understand that no matter how the legislature might change the laws, the people who for various reasons were now taking their children out of school and teaching them at home were going to go on doing so, no matter what. They will fight in the courts as long as they can, delay, stall, and appeal, for years if need be. If finally pinned to the wall, they will simply move to another district or out of the state altogether. The one thing they will not do is send their children back to the public schools. Is it really worth spending all this time, energy, and taxpayers' money to fight a battle that is lost before it is begun? The district superintendent, speaking of the bad publicity his district had received while prosecuting one family, had said at one point, "Even when we win, we lose." Did the schools, and the state, really want this kind of publicity?

One member of the committee asked me a question that, in one form or another, I hear at almost every meeting. It goes about like this, "What would you do about a family that didn't know anything, that didn't want their children to know anything, and that only took them out of school because they wanted to exploit their work, etc., etc." I replied by reminding them of an old legal maxim with which I was sure they were familiar—Hard Cases Make Bad Law. I said that if we write our laws—as we too often tend to—so as to take care of the worst possible hypothetical case that might arise, we are almost certain to have laws that are long, cumbersome, difficult or impossible to enforce, and far more likely to prevent good people from doing good work than bad people from doing bad. I went on to say that there might well be families like the one suggested, but that these people were the last ones in the world likely to be interested in teaching their children at home. On the contrary, they are only too eager to get them out of the house, and at the end of school vacations say, "Thank Heaven vacation is over, I can't wait to get these damn kids back in school." Committee members smiled; they obviously knew such people.

In closing, I said that there were limits to the power of governments, beyond which they could not go without losing their good faith and credit. A good case could have been made, and had once been made, that as a country we would be much better off if no one drank alcohol. But the Noble Experiment failed; people would not let the government stick its nose that far into their private affairs, and refused to obey the law. The only results were a great increase in corruption in government and general contempt for law.

As nearly as I could tell from their expressions and questions, the committee was interested in and responsive to what I had to say. Only one member seemed clearly angered and threatened by my words. The last question was asked by the chairman himself, "Do you mean that if we want to allow people to teach their children at home we don't need to make any changes in the law at all?" I assured him that was what I meant.

If any on the committee were not convinced by what I had said about how determined more and more people are to teach their children in accordance with their own beliefs, the next witness must have convinced them. She was a representative of some association for Christian education, and in her testimony she furiously denounced the public schools (as I had been careful not to). Compared to her I must have seemed a most mild and reasonable person. I like to think that at the end of the hearings some of the committee, at least, were thinking, "Maybe Holt is right, maybe we really don't want to spend the next ten years fighting these kinds of people, maybe we'd be smarter to leave them alone and concentrate on doing what we can to fix up our schools." For Minnesota or any other state, it would be the wiser course.

12

How to Get Started

🕮 "WHAT IS HOMESCHOOLING LIKE?"

There are as many ways to homeschool as there are families who do it. Indeed, many families discover that what helped one child learn to read or do math doesn't automatically help their other children learn, so it is difficult to say for certain, "Homeschooling is like this for everybody . . . " In general, many parents prefer to start teaching the way they were taught, using regularly scheduled classes and textbooks, and gradually adapting their programs to suit their children's interests and abilities. Shifting away from textbooks to primary source materials and real life experiences, they draw on other mentors or classes in the community. Some families prefer simply to do "school at home," duplicating school schedules and curricula but screening out objectionable content; there are correspondence and private schools in Appendices B and C that will sell you curricula and materials for this type of homeschooling. The way my wife and I prefer to homeschool is more the way Holt describes teaching and learning, which is often called "unschooling." Most families wind up adapting a position in between "school at home" and "unschooling;" in any case, the decision on what homeschooling will be like for you is yours to make, and it is not an unalterable one.

Certainly you can set up your home as a school, schedule it like school, and teach like in school. But the total "school-at-home" approach may become stifling to you or your kids, or, like many homeschoolers I know, you may prefer to move back and forth between imposed lessons and learning from the incidents of every day life on a relaxed, individualized schedule. It is also important to remember that homeschooling doesn't have to mean that your kids stay at home all day, with only their parents, using school materials. For instance, several times a week we schedule our children to be with other friends, typically, but not exclusively, homeschoolers; we reciprocate at other times during the week. My wife ran "The Detective Club," a popular meeting held every Wednesday night at our house for eight children—seven homeschoolers and a friend who attends public school. In return we make use of field trips, history clubs, drama clubs, and similar activities run by other homeschooling parents. Classes at museums, area library events, religious instruction, and the local gymnastics and dance academies our daughters attend, are among the resources we've found. Indeed, in some states you can probably arrange for your child to take classes in local public schools, as we've been able to do (it never hurts to ask no matter what state you live in). Some homeschooling support groups have listings of members who are willing to help tutor or converse with children who are interested in learning more about their areas of expertise.

Most important, homeschooling allows you to give your children time to explore and think about things on their own. Children who figure out things on their own, for their own purposes, literally *own* that knowledge and can build on it. So, for example, if your child wants to learn more about archaeology and you know nothing about the topic (and perhaps have no interest in it at all), then you can help them by locating books and materials they can read and use on their own; a friendly resource librarian at your local public library can be an invaluable ally in your homeschooling efforts for this reason alone. You can also consider calling local historical societies, museums, and college professors who might be willing to talk to your child, have them visit or volunteer, or simply allow the children to observe what various aspects of archaeology are actually like.

When we moved into our house, after years of apartment living in the city, our oldest daughter, Lauren, then six, liked to dig in our new backyard. She discovered an unusual round stone and showed it to my wife, Day. Day thought it might be a musket ball from colonial times, and this started a flurry of readings and conversations about colonial times, guns, and archaeology. Day soon found an archaeological dig being done on a colonial American site not far from our house, and she was able to arrange for Lauren to spend a day helping at the site. You needn't feel you must know everything to help your child; again, homeschooling doesn't have to be like regular school and you don't have to be like a typical school instructor. Instead, you can be a facilitator and guide for your children's explorations of areas in which you don't feel particularly well versed.

Madalene Axford Murphy of Pennsylvania writes about how she did this with her son:

> Early on, our son Christian began to reach the limits of his father's and my knowledge in science and math, and it became obvious that these would be major pursuits in his life. At first I cheerfully expanded my own knowledge, learning along with him, but finally I had neither the time nor the interest to keep up with him. We met this situation in a number of ways.
>
> . . . We discovered an astronomy group that met one evening a month, and he began to attend meetings. He discovered that one of the founders of the group was giving a twelve-session seminar on astronomy for adults at our local nature center. On the recommendation of the naturalist there (a friend of his), he was allowed to sign up, though he was only eleven. The first evening, he came home with about ten pages of small print that had to be read for the next class. This was not going to be a warm, fuzzy retelling of myths about constellations with a few facts thrown in here and there about planets and such, but rather a no-holds-barred immersion course in technical astronomy. I was concerned, but Christian wasn't. He plowed through the reading and was disappointed when the classes were over. Did he understand everything? No, nor did many of the adults in the class, but words like "parallax" and "gradient" had become part of his vocabulary and he knew a whole lot more about telescopes and the science of astronomy than he had before.
>
> Another group, the Audubon Society, helped open up several aspects of biology for him. . . . When they started planning their annual Christmas

Bird count, Christian and I decided to participate. . . . One of the Society's more active members was a biologist who worked at a nearby fish research lab, and I asked if we could tag along when he went on the bird count. The bird count itself was not a success: periods of freezing rain kept most of the birds out of sight and made me think they were definitely displaying intelligence superior to the humans on that particular occasion . . .

But the biggest success of the bird count was the friendship that developed between Christian and Bob, the biologist. Bob invited Christian on other bird counts and for the last two years has taken him along as a timekeeper/recorder on an intense five-hour government-sponsored survey of birds. Christian has become quite skilled at identifying birds and is even trying to improve his ability to recognize their calls.

The summer after the original bird count, Christian discovered he could volunteer at the fish research lab where Bob worked, and he ended up working two eight-hour days a week. . . . Christian learned a lot about lab techniques and about the amount of tedious work required to get accurate results for a study . . .

All of these biology activities took place during Christian's "high school" years, a time when homeschooling parents and sometimes children often begin to get a bit more nervous about whether they need to become more traditional, particularly if the children are planning on college. Christian did decide to use textbooks to fill in gaps in his knowledge of science, and activities like those I just described made the textbook knowledge real and useful.

Two other parents show the wide range of approaches that can be used in helping children learn math. Carla Stein of Massachusetts writes:

I took 51 pieces of typewriter paper and wrote the numbers 0 through 50 on them. We lay them out on the floor, Candy Land style, in all sorts of loops and turns around the furniture. . . . Then we took turns hopping along the trail, stepping only on numbers that were odd, or even, or divisible by 3, 4, 5, etc. . . . This made for silly fun, especially when the jumps got too long. Then they each got a small stuffed toy and tried to toss the toys onto the right numbers, with lots of misses and shrieking, of course.

Sue Smith-Heavenrich of New York writes:

Some time ago my children were doing "math before breakfast"—a sort of game where they ask each other questions while I get out the cereal and juice. Coulter (who's seven) asked, "What's 1 Toby plus 1 Toby?" Toby, four years old, answered, "Eight."

"No, no," responded Coulter. "What's 1 Toby plus 1 Toby?"

"Eight!" answered Toby, with more volume and conviction.

Suddenly it dawned on me that he was right. In terms of age, two Tobies is the same as 2 x 4, which is 8. So as I passed out the bowls, I asked if one Toby was equal to 4 years. "Yes," Toby replied. They then began to create equations using their friends' ages: "Does 1 J (9) – 1 K (7) + 1 I (6) = 1 T (4)?" and so on.

I wonder how often "wrong answers" are simply right answers to different interpretations of a question. If the purpose of math is to use symbols to phrase observations about the world, then we need to give our children time to grow up using the language of math, and exploring it. When they began to talk, we did not demand that they pronounce each word correctly or use proper grammar. So, too, I think mathematical thinking needs to grow naturally.

I grew up hating math. I remember my father sitting down with me each evening after dinner to go over flash cards. I feared getting the wrong answer. And so, as my reading and verbal abilities grew, my math skills remained stuck, as I made tortuous progress through workbook after workbook. I never, ever would have asked my sister at the breakfast table, "What's 1 Sue plus 1 Sue?" I simply avoided all math, believing (as my mom said) that I was "mathlexic."

Perhaps this is why I do not "teach" math to my children. We work out our problems, play games with numbers, and use math as a tool in our daily living. Today, we were sorting potatoes for market and weighing them. This led to all sorts of interesting math problems. The weight of the bowl we were using to hold the potatoes was 1/4 lb. Often we'd get a bowl full of potatoes that weighed something like 3 3/4 lbs. I haven't yet formally taught fractions, but Coulter figured out how much the potatoes weighed, and added different weights together for totals. His comments? "Gee, Mom, this is fun! When are you going to dig more?"

Stories in other homeschooling publications and in the growing number of books about homeschooling will give you a much fuller picture of how homeschooling works for different families, and how you can shape it to fit your own.

No state requires you to be a certified teacher in order to homeschool your kids. You should remember that you are not teaching a class of thirty children but just your own children, something you've been doing for years. The dynamics of classroom teaching and the tutorial approach you can use in homeschooling are completely different. Your children have large blocks of time with you so their questions can arise naturally and often throughout the course of the day. As any parent knows, young children will ask questions if they aren't conditioned to stop asking them. Just because lots of people put their children in school or, if younger, under professional day care, does not automatically mean that certified professionals are better at nurturing children's learning than uncertified parents.

For instance, a British study, described in the book *Young Children Learning*, compared tapes of the conversations of working-class parents with their four-year-old children to those of nursery school teachers with four-year-olds. It revealed that the children who stayed home asked all sorts of questions about a diverse number of topics, showing no fear of learning new words or concepts. The children under the care of professional teachers had much less range of thought and intensity, and they asked much fewer questions.

The Washington Homeschool Research Project's report, *The Relationship of Selected Input Variables to Academic Achievement among Washington's Homeschoolers*, by Jon Wartes, was able to examine this question in some detail. Wartes was able to study a group of homeschooled children whose parents were state-certified teachers and children of parents who were not certified. The results showed no difference in the learning outcomes of children in both groups, leading the researcher to note that this "suggests that contact with a certified teacher is not a necessary component of academic success. Policy decisions that would, as a general matter, require contact with a certified teacher as a condition to homeschool are not supported by this data."

Many private schools do not require their teachers to be state certified in education, but prefer instead to have teachers who have strong knowledge in the subject they plan to teach. The schools prefer a degree in the field of history for a history teacher, for example, rather than a certificate in education. Why do these schools not worry about certification? Because they know that enthusiasm for teaching, love of the subject matter, and a commitment to children aren't found only in certified teachers. The same is true in homeschooling.

Correspondence schools, such as the Calvert School and the Home Study Institute have been providing home study courses for American families abroad and at home for many decades. Alaska created a Centralized Correspondence Study program (CCS), which has been in existence for decades. The state mails a correspondence-study program to parents who then administer the materials to their children. There has been no evidence over all this time that homeschooled children using these programs do less well than their schooled peers in Alaska or elsewhere.

Homeschooling can allow learning to take place at more varying paces than the school schedule allows, giving you and your children lots of time to work on things in different ways than those taught in school, along with the time to obtain different results. Some parents find that being on a different schedule than that prescribed by school's developmental curriculum can be unnerving. However, my wife and I don't see ourselves as managing our children's development according to a strict schedule; we are simply nurturing our children, trying to be the best parents we can. In *The Disappearance of Childhood,* Neil Postman notes how the concept of school-managed child development came to be:

> . . . by writing sequenced textbooks and by organizing school classes according to calendar age, schoolmasters invented, as it were, the stages of childhood. Our notions of what a child can learn or ought to learn, and at what ages, were largely derived from the concept of sequenced curriculum; that is to say, from the concept of the prerequisite. . . .
>
> [T]he point is that the mastery of the alphabet and the mastery of all the skills and knowledge that were arranged to follow constituted not merely a curriculum but a definition of child development. By creating a concept of a hierarchy of knowledge and skills, adults invented the structure of child development.

Homeschoolers who do not use this structure of child development discover that children learn at widely varying rates; for instance, some homeschooled children do not learn to read until they are ten or eleven; others learn at much younger ages. Children in school must learn to read well enough by third grade in most schools or they will be unable to move apace with the increasingly book-oriented schooling at each grade; but when this administrative concern is ignored, it becomes a bit clearer that children can learn to read well at a wider range of ages than school allows. A study by Alan Thomas, *Educating Children at Home*, published in 1999, indicates that late reading among homeschooled children is common. Some children may not learn to read until they are ten or eleven years old, but "as far as could be ascertained, [there is] no adverse effect on intellectual development, self-worth, or even subsequent attainment in literacy." The "late" readers caught up with and soon surpassed the reading level of their schooled age-mates. Dr. Thomas also notes, in contrast to schoolchildren of the same ages,"in common with most other home educated children, [the late readers] went on to thoroughly enjoy reading."

FIRST STEPS

Broadly speaking, there are three steps you need to take in order to start homeschooling:

1. Know Your State's Laws and Regulations.

To find out what the laws or regulations are in your state contact someone who is currently homeschooling in your area. Local homeschooling groups are usually the best source of precise information about how to fulfill the requirements of the law in your area (see appendix D). Many state groups have information packets for new homeschoolers that include information about laws and regulations. See the listings for support groups in the appendix to find one in your area.

You can find the actual wording of your state's law under "compulsory education" or "school attendance" in a courthouse or law library, or you can write to your State Department of Education for a copy of the current regulations. In general, some states require you to submit an education plan to your local district, some require you to file simple documents with the your respecive state's department of education, and some allow you to register your home as a private school. Remember, you do not have to be a certified teacher to homeschool in any state.

In addition to being the best source of current information about laws and regulations, homeschooling support groups can help you meet a lot of people at once and can tell you about local activities. Support groups often have newsletters and meetings and sometimes organize field trips, sports teams, writing clubs, book discussion groups—whatever appeals to the families involved

2. Develop Your Curriculum.

I need to emphasize that you don't need a packaged curriculum in order to homeschool successfully. You can write your own curriculum based on your family's philosophy of education and change or adapt it as needed throughout the year and not run afoul with educational authorities. Many private schools have vastly different curricula from public schools. For instance, in schools using the educational philosophy of Rudolf Steiner, usually called Waldorf schools, children aren't taught to read until they've lost their eyeteeth, which is often later than when they would be taught in public school. Many alternative schools, such as the Albany Free School in New York State or the Sudbury Valley School in Massachusetts use no set curricula at all—you can, too. Think of the resources available in your community: libraries, museums, historical sites, courthouses, specialty shops, nature centers. Think of adults you know who can share a skill, answer a question, allow your children to observe or help them at work. Think of real-life activities: writing letters, handling money, measuring, observing the stars, talking to older people. These are some of the ways that homeschoolers learn writing, math, science, and history. Talking with other homeschoolers will give you further ideas.

Some families like to have an idea of what is expected of kids in school at various ages. You can ask a local schoolteacher, principal, or school board member for a copy of the curriculum outline for the grade your child would be in; some are happy to share this information, some are not. If you can get a copy of your school's curriculum, use it as a guide but don't make yourself follow it rigidly; one of the biggest advantages of homeschooling is that you don't have to operate exactly as school does or make your child follow the same timetable. Another useful document is the *Typical Course of Study, K–12* free pamphlet (see Appendix A, subsection Homeschooling).

For a more detailed, and unschooling-oriented curriculum guide, try Nancy Plent's *Living Is Learning Curriculum Guides*, available from FUN Books (see Appendix E, subsection Books, Games, Learning Materials). You can also use the *What Every First Grader Needs to Know* series edited by E. D. Hirsch to see what he thinks a "culturally literate" person needs to know at each grade level. Or ask your local Waldorf, Christian Independent, Montessori, Catholic, or other private school for their curriculum outlines to see what they think a "well-rounded individual" should know.

Some families prefer to start out using a packaged curriculum, and you can investigate which one best fits your family's need; I provide some suggestions in appendix B at the end of this book. You can also find ads for and reviews of curricula in many homeschooling magazines and examine and purchase them at homeschooling conferences. Generally, a correspondence school's assignments can be completed in a few hours a day, leaving time for other activities.

There is no need to spend lots of money on curricula, books, educational toys and videos, etc. You really need to spend no more than you would ordinarily spend on a child's interests and activities. Homeschoolers often use the library and other free or low-cost community resources. They share or barter materials and skills with one another or with other people in the community. Some families are able to barter for outside lessons and to volunteer in exchange for admission to arts events or museums. Older homeschoolers find that volunteering is a good way to learn from adults outside the family, and it is often less expensive than taking a class or buying equipment.

3. Enjoy Your Family.

Don't let your family get lost in your efforts to school your children. It's easy to replace teachers, but not parents. Some parents burn out from homeschooling by trying to be demanding, "professional" teachers for some parts of the day, then sympathetic parents for other parts, and the stress of switching between these two roles becomes too burdensome. Be a loving parent to your children all the time. Teaching and helping our children learn is an inherent part of parenting that we seem to forget we do once we send children to school. We don't need to—though, perhaps, there are situations where one would want to—imitate classroom teacher behavior and techniques in homeschooling. If you want to take a break and walk through the woods because it is a gorgeous day, you can; the curriculum can wait. Perhaps something you discover in the woods will become a piece of your studies; perhaps it will just be a nice walk. If your child wants to finish an exciting book she is reading instead of doing lessons one day, you can permit that. The lessons can be caught up with later. Homeschooling lets us set our own goals and our own schedules. Don't let curricula and schooling become the tail that wags the dog in your home; enjoy your time together as a family.

Also, try not to compare yourselves too much with other homeschooling families; each is different. Some families, particularly in rural areas, have a slower pace of life and fewer opportunities for museum trips, specialized classes, and so on. They are able to take advantage of their land, homes, and nature in ways urban homeschoolers cannot. Further, some urban homeschoolers may prefer a slower pace of life than their colleagues who lead very active lives; being a homeschooler does not mean you must be plugged into every activity you can find.

APPROACHES TO HOMESCHOOLING

Homeschooling changes and adapts to the needs of the learner, as well as to any special circumstances that may happen in the family (illness, a new baby, new job hours for a spouse, and so on). You do not, no matter what the law is in your state, need to plan out in precise detail what you will do for the entire year. However, you will probably want to have some sort of plan, or list of ideas, at the start.

It is useful for you and your spouse to clarify how you will homeschool, not only to answer skeptics' questions about what it is you're doing but also to keep yourselves from becoming rattled when things aren't going smoothly. It is also good to know where you stand philosophically so that you can present your home school in the best possible light to school officials who may question your approach. At the same time, it's crucial to remember that homeschooling is flexible. The word "homeschooling" doesn't refer to any one practice; it just refers to families learning outside of school. Choices you make at the start of the year are not irrevocable. You can—and you very likely will—adapt and change things as you go. You will also have many opportunities to learn from your mistakes, as we have found out in our own homeschooling. Live and learn!

All the books I mention in this chapter and in Appendix A will provide information, sometimes in great detail, as to the various methods of teaching and learning you may choose. For the sake of brevity, I will divide these approaches into two main philosophies:

1. *School at Home.* Families that choose this philosophy usually aren't worried about "why" their children must learn certain things at certain ages; they are far more concerned with how to help their children learn what they've decided their children should learn. Families with this philosophy of education have a large number of standardized textbooks and curricula to choose from, many of which they can purchase from school supply stores or textbook manufacturers. Often these materials can also be purchased in used book stores, at homeschooling "curriculum fairs," and through direct mail. The curriculum determines what and when subjects will be taught, the parent creates or purchases lesson plans to use on the specified days, and the children are regularly tested to see how much of the material they have learned.

A subset of this category is often called the "unit study," "thematic," or "project" approach. Parents following this approach design a series of projects, field trips, and readings that build on a particular theme and use it to address several subject areas at once. For instance, one can use Thanksgiving time to study the Pilgrim era for history, biology (what food Pilgrims grew), science (how Pilgrims took care of illnesses), math (calculating how big a plot each person could get at Plymouth Plantation), etc.

2. *Unschooling.* This is also known as interest-driven, child-led, natural, organic, eclectic, or self-directed learning. Lately, the term "unschooling" has come to be associated with the type of homeschooling that doesn't use a fixed curriculum. When pressed, I define unschooling as allowing children as much freedom to learn in the world as their parents can comfortably bear. The advantage of this method is that it doesn't

require you, the parent, to become someone else, i.e., a professional teacher pouring knowledge into child-vessels on a planned basis. Instead you live and learn together, pursuing questions and interests as they arise and using conventional schooling on an "on-demand" basis, if at all. This is the way we learn before going to school and the way we learn when we leave school and enter the world of work. So, for instance, a young child's interest in hot rods can lead him to a study of how the engine works (science), how and when the car was built (history and business), who built and designed the car (biography), etc. Certainly these interests can lead to reading texts, taking courses, or doing projects, but the important difference is that these activities were chosen and engaged in freely by the learner. They were not dictated to the learner through curricular mandate to be done at a specific time and place, though parents with a more hands-on approach to unschooling certainly can influence and guide their children's choices. Unschooling, for lack of a better term (until people start to accept "living" as part and parcel of learning), is the natural way to learn. However, this does not mean unschoolers do not take traditional classes or use curricular materials when the student, or parents and children together, decide that this is how they want to do it. Learning to read or do quadratic equations are not "natural" processes, but unschoolers nonetheless learn them when it makes sense to them to do so, not because they have reached a certain age or are compelled to do so by arbitrary authority. Therefore it isn't unusual to find unschoolers who are barely eight years old studying astronomy or who are ten years old and just learning to read.

It is unfair to think that either of the philosophies I present above are mutually exclusive of each other, though to some "school at homers" allowing children to determine what they will study is as distasteful as being forced to diagram sentences can be for some "unschoolers." Try not to let purists of either persuasion get to you. You must do what you are comfortable with; like your children, you, too, will learn and change as you get more experience with homeschooling. You can start out with a package of textbook and "teacher-proof curricula" (actually that's how some curriculum manufacturers refer to their materials) and if that isn't working you can switch to a unit study or unschooling approach. Indeed, you can do a little of each depending on your child's abilities and your ability to juggle different approaches. You may start out highly programmed and gradually loosen up and let your children have more say in what and how they study as you get comfortable with homeschooling. You may start out highly free-form and eventually find your child engaged in a very strict schedule of music or language lessons, Scout activities, and clubs.

You can also involve your children in creating their course of study for the year. Susan Jaffer of Pennsylvania writes:

> . . . Last year, at the beginning of the summer, I asked my daughters what I thought was a casual question: "What would you like to learn about this summer?" They began answering me right away, without so much as a pause, and this is what we ended up with: Suzanne, 8, wanted to learn about stories, poems, science, math, art, music, books, people, planting, animals, places, food, colors, rocks, babies, cars, eyes, and electricity. Gillian, 6, wanted to learn about seeds, bones, plants, books, evolution, dinosaurs, and experiments. I tend to think that the fact that I asked them in the summer freed them from the boundaries of school subjects. In any case, I was stunned by the fact that they had so many subjects in mind, and that their lists were right there waiting for me to ask the right question . . .

I like Susan's phrase about how her kids expressed such wide interests since they were "freed . . . from the boundaries of school subjects." It reminded me of a comment I heard author Grace Llewellyn make about helping homeschooled teenagers find ways to study subjects outside of school by not always limiting ourselves to school categories. Grace described a letter in *GWS* from a girl who asked her father what a person who studied whales was called. Her father told her such people were called "marine biologists" and she would have to go to college to become one and study whales. Grace pointed out that marine biology is but one way for children and adults to study and work with whales; the family could also encourage their daughter to study whales as an artist, musician, sailor, ecologist, naturalist, and so on. This point is very valuable to remember if you find your children getting frustrated in their studies and you need a new way to approach the material.

Oddly enough, parents who follow alternative education ideas sometimes find that their children desire and enjoy using conventional curricula. One fourteen-year-old girl strongly desired to use a packaged curriculum program to homeschool, which rattled her mom, an experienced unschooler, who had not used curricula with any of her other children. They agreed to try homeschooling with a packaged curriculum, and the girl flourished with it.

A mother from Kentucky, Cindy Gaddis, sums up this issue quite well. She writes:

> I declare myself an unschooler even though my daughter Abbey loves workbooks and my son Adam has to be taught most things in a highly structured manner. I say this because I am respecting their need to learn in the way that works best for them. I would declare an older homeschooler who decides to become much more structured in learning an unschooler because she is respecting her ability to know what she needs and wants at each stage of her life.

It is not unusual to feel overwhelmed by the amount of freedom learning at home allows, especially by those who were in school and are now being homeschooled. It often makes sense to let children get used to their newfound freedom gradually, allowing them more private time and space than they probably had before. But, as Susannah Sheffer writes in *GWS*:

> . . . at some point the need for that break diminishes and kids begin to feel ready for more activity and focus, [and] it can be difficult to know where to start.
>
> One thing I've found useful, when helping kids go through this process, is to make three lists. One list is for things that come easily, things that you would do anyway, whether or not you sat down and made a plan about them. The second list is for things that you want to work on but feel you need some help with—maybe suggestions of ways to pursue the activity, or maybe some sort of schedule or plan regarding it. The third list is for things you want to put aside for a while, things you don't want to work on right now.

The value of these lists, it seems to me, is that they show kids: (1) that they are already doing worthwhile things, and don't need outside intervention for everything; (2) at the same time, it's perfectly OK to want help in some areas, to have a list of things that you want to do but aren't sure what to do; and (3) that it's also OK to put some things aside for the time being. This might be especially important to kids who had bad experiences with particular subjects in school and who would benefit from realizing that they have much more control in their new situation. Fourteen-year-old Marianne was very emphatic, for example, about putting essay writing on list three, because she had had very unpleasant and discouraging experiences with essay writing in school, and for her, at that time, having control meant being able to say, "I choose not to work on that right now."

Marianne's list two was the longest, as I think it will be for many kids, and ultimately this list may be the most important, because it's the one from which ideas and plans can grow. As I said, it's very important to realize that much of what you're doing already has educational value (school doesn't usually give kids credit for the things they willingly and eagerly pursue on their own). But it's just as important for the new homeschooler (or the longtime homeschooler who is looking to make some changes) to realize that it's fine to need help and to ask for it. Suppose a teenager has a vague feeling that she wants to do something with animals, but isn't sure what. That could go on list two. Then, when the lists are made up and you sit down to give each item closer attention, you can begin to think: what kind of work with animals? what kind of help would you need in making that happen? and so on.

The same goes for more traditional academic work. Suppose the homeschooler says, "I want to keep up with the other kids who are doing algebra in school, but I'm just not sure I'm going to do that regularly on my own." Well, that's OK. What would help? Should we look into finding another adult to work with you? Would it be fun to meet regularly with another homeschooler who is working on algebra? Or would a schedule tacked up to the bulletin board help you remember that you wanted to work on this each week?

Sometime people emphasize the lack of scheduling and fixed appointments in homeschooling, because this open-endedness is one of the things that makes homeschooling feel so different to kids who have spent years in school—no bells ringing, no one telling you you have to do math at this time. And it's true that we often want to stress the way in which home-schooling lets kids take advantage of whatever arises . . . But in stressing these benefits and these ways in which homeschooling is different from school, we may sometimes forget that the most crucial benefit, and difference, is that in homeschooling you have control—which means that you can make schedules, and plans, and appointments, if you want to.

Most homeschooling books and magazines have stories by teens and elementary school-age children about the types of schedules and help they find useful. There are also many examples of how different families schedule their homeschooling in the firsthand accounts that are available in homeschooling periodicals and books.

Each family is different and each child is different, so don't assume that what worked for one child will work for all. The most important thing, besides love, that you can bring to your home school is the trust in yourself to help your children learn and the trust you have in your childen to learn in their own way.

You don't have to teach the way you were taught. In addition to materials and good texts that the students can use to learn on their own, many homeschooling families find tutors. These may be professional teachers, but are more likely to be people who are practitioners of what the child wishes to learn. This often puts parents in a different teaching role from that which occurs in schools; they are more facilitators, "askers," travel agents, general contractors, and counselors than instructors doling out lessons. Parents of homeschoolers learn to ferret out learning opportunities for their children, and they can become quite adept at networking through their local support groups, the Yellow Pages, local newspapers, and community bulletin boards. In short, parents do not have to be the sole instructors of their children.

Some homeschooling parents create clubs or learning cooperatives around certain interests their children may have, such as science, rocketry, or theater, and conduct weekly meetings at their homes or in local libraries. Some share their expertise in exchange for money, barter, or no payment at all: a single mother my wife and I know charges families a modest fee for tutoring children in math at her home; another mother

offers a free literature class in her home twice a week to ten homeschoolers; both mothers are former schoolteachers, by the way! A father we
know who makes his living as an illustrator is teaching an art course once
a week in the evening at his house, as a way to share his love of art with
his sons and their friends. Ordinary people, using their own resources,
can be highly effective teachers when they share their own interests with
children who wish to learn from them.

Some homeschoolers create resource centers to be used by large
numbers of homeschoolers, for free or for a fee. In London, England,
Leslie Barson created "The Otherwise Club" in her home as a place for
children to work together on projects of their own choosing. As her children got older and the club got bigger Barson wanted to reclaim her
home. She found a local community center that let her group meet two
days a week for two thousand pounds a year; Barson charges a membership fee of one hundred pounds per family, and has been able to gain
charitable status for the group. She writes:

> The Club provides the space for workshops and activities for families. We
> have three regular workshops—drama, pottery, and a science group for
> younger children—and we run a number of other activities. Past work-
> shops have included country dancing, visits from police dogs and their
> handlers, and talks by various experts in areas such as math, home educa-
> tion, and health. Recent workshops have included African drumming at
> several different levels and a workshop on *A Midsummer Night's Dream*
> and a trip to see the play. . . . The Otherwise Club has a small cafe which
> serves a vegetarian homemade lunch and cake as well as tea and coffee.
> This provides a small amount of funds and serves as a focal point for the
> community. We also keep a small lending library about alternative educa-
> tion and a large amount of information about activities and exhibitions in
> London . . .

Other homeschoolers find and publicize courses and offerings at local
museums, historic sites, community centers, and gymnasiums. In
Boston, Harvard University's Peabody Museum and the Boston Museum
of Science have advertised courses for homeschoolers. Technological advances now allow Internet courses for learning everything from jazz im-

provisation to secondary-school courses leading to diplomas; there are also video and audiotape lectures by experts in all kinds of fields that can be borrowed from libraries, or from homeschoolers who share the cost and the materials.

Most homeschooling, and certainly the formation and continuation of these clubs and groups, is performed by people not certified by the state as teachers. Participation is neither mandatory nor graded. The participants get what they put into each activity, and should they decide not to learn in these settings, no external failing grade or other penalty will be given. They can come back to these places and learn what they need when they are ready for it, or they can choose, or create, other situations in which they can learn what they wish to learn. These parents and children are not therefore recreating compulsory public school in their communities, nor are they creating alternative schools; they are creating alternatives to school for their children.

It's important to remember that some children need alternatives to home as well; clearly not every family is motivated to work with their children the way the homeschoolers I describe here are. However, the only place besides home for most children is school, a situation we have created with our compulsory education laws, and often school is not a good place for children either. When neither home nor school is a safe, productive environment for children and teens, the sorts of places that I describe above can be expanded to accommodate them. I doubt we can get people to change compulsory education laws in America, but there is wiggle room in these laws, as homeschooling and many out-of-school programs sanctioned by various school departments demonstrate. By expanding these exceptions to allow children and teenagers to observe real work or engage in it as apprentices, we will help them learn what is needed to do work well. Children also learn how to interact with others to get jobs done, and how to leave work they don't enjoy and find work they want to try; these are skills that are not only not taught in school but actually tend to atrophy in most schools. One typically works in silence in competition for grades and is penalized for sharing information, and one cannot change jobs when it is apparent that one does not have the capacity or interest to continue with a particular course in school and would like to try something different.

Not all activities are obviously educational, but that does not mean they are not important learning experiences for children. As many have pointed out, play is a child's work. Children typically use fantasy play, in particular, not to escape from the real world, but to get into it: When they pretend to be doctors, firefighters, police, and soldiers, they are using their imaginations to explore these roles. My own children often played school when they were younger! People benefit from periods of play throughout life, and some people are able to find or create adult work that often grows out of their childhood play. School is all too often opposed to the spontaneous play of children, a trend that is increasing as schools march to the drums of testing and standardization, and families bounce to the beat of professionalized after-school programs. Homeschoolers need not turn the screws tighter on children in order to make them learn; there is no need to duplicate school techniques in our homes.

RECORD KEEPING

There are two types of record keeping homeschoolers can do: that which is required by the state, and that which they want to do for themselves. Of course, there is some overlap, but on the whole these are very different types of records. States, and in some cases local school districts, vary in the amount and the kind of record keeping they require of homeschoolers. The first thing you want to do is find out what you have to do legally. Some states require testing (but not always every year); some allow parents to choose among testing, keeping a portfolio, or writing up reports; and some states don't require testing or much record keeping at all. No matter what your state's requirements, you can find a way to fulfill them without getting bogged down or worrying more than is necessary about how much your children are accomplishing. In any case, whether or not your state has record keeping requirements, you may find, as many parents do, that you want to keep some kind of record of your homeschooling, for your own peace of mind and for the fun of chronicling your child's growth—just as parents have always saved their children's drawings, stories, projects, and so on.

Katharine Houk, a longtime homeschooler from New York, wrote to *GWS* about several ways to keep records:

A topic that frequently comes up at homeschooling support-group meetings at the beginning of the homeschool year is record keeping. For those of us whose homeschooling approach is interest-initiated and far-ranging, it can be a challenge to write quarterly reports for submission to the school district, when learning is expected to be pigeonholed into subject areas.

When our family first started homeschooling, the New York State Home Instruction Regulation was not in effect. Homeschooling was permitted, but was handled differently by each school district, with guidelines from the State Education Department offering suggestions on how to handle homeschooling. Our district gave us a checklist to fill out periodically, and that was the extent of our reporting. But at that time, I kept daily logs of my children's activities, even though I didn't need them for reporting purposes. I was fascinated with their learning processes, and had great fun documenting all the wonderful things they did. Most of their learning was through play; they played intensely, happily, and for hours and days at a time. My challenge was in translating their activities and our conversations and experiences into a form that would fit in the subject area boxes in my log book.

When the need for reporting came along, with the passage of the current regulation, it was easy for us to make that transition; we had already been keeping records. Besides the requirement that as homeschoolers you must keep an attendance record (!), there is no specific requirement for record keeping in the regulation. But I knew that having a written record of our activities would be helpful to me in writing reports. Besides, I was already in the habit of doing it, and enjoyed creating a record of my children's learning.

I used a loose-leaf notebook for each child. In the front were pages that looked like a lesson plan book, with subject areas listed down the left side of the page, and the days of the week across the top of the page. I included Saturday and Sunday, because learning doesn't stop for weekends. In the notebook I also included a place to record field trips and keep photographs, pocket pages for papers, etc. It served us well, and the children enjoy looking back at them, laughing at the spelling in their early writings, and reminiscing about trips and other activities from years ago.

As the children grew older, I grew weary of sifting their learning into subject area categories. Their learning is all of a piece, and it became tedious to chop it up into artificial compartments on a daily basis. Therefore I changed the notebook to include lined paper, where each day I would write a few sentences about what was done that day. At the end of each month I would make a synopsis of the month by subject area. Then when it came time for a quarterly report I would have something to work from.

Now that the children are so much older (12 and 15), it is unnecessary for me alone to do all the record keeping. Also, my offspring are such independent learners and I am so busy that often I am not aware of their activities or of what books they are reading. I do jot things down from time to time that I am aware of and that I find especially noteworthy, but I ask each of them to keep their own notebook, and to write down the books they are reading and their activities, plus whatever else they care to put in their journals. This way I am not invading their privacy, and they have a record in their own writing of what they have done. At report time, they share with us the parts of their journals that they want in their reports. Privacy is an important issue, one that is sometimes not taken into account when school districts want to know everything that is happening with our children.

Some families I know use a spiral-bound notebook for record keeping, and store papers in a separate portfolio. Also there are commercially distributed record keeping systems you can purchase . . .

Whatever method of record keeping you choose, the results will help you in writing reports and complying with assessment requirements, and will be a wonderful chronicle of your children's growth and development.

If you want a more detailed presentation about record keeping and evaluations for homeschoolers, particularly for high school, I recommend Loretta Heuer's comprehensive book *The Homeschooler's Guide to Portfolios and Transcripts.* In about fourteen states, as of this writing, homeschoolers must formally write up their curriculum and submit it to their local education authorities. In other states, requirements are less extensive, so be sure to check the homeschooling laws or regulations in your state.

For those states that do require you to submit a curriculum or plan, here are some guidelines. If you purchase a curriculum, that is what you submit. You transfer the program's stated goals and objectives onto whatever forms or documents the local education authorities wish you to submit to them. If you follow your child's interests, as I'm suggesting throughout this book, then it is largely a matter of translating what one is going to do anyway into language the school officials can understand. Here is an example for you to consider, prefaced by Susannah Sheffer:

> . . . In states that require written proposals in the first place (and not all do), the actual wording of the law, the requirements or preferences of the particular school district, and the inclinations of the family itself will all influence what kind of proposal the family actually writes. Some people believe it's better to write a great deal so that the files are thick and the family appears thorough; others believe it's better to give only the minimum required by law and to let the school officials ask for more if they want more. Both approaches are valid. Some families see the fact that they must write a proposal as an opportunity to articulate their own philosophy and goals for the year for themselves as well as for the district; others view the proposal only as something they must do to satisfy legal requirements and would rather keep it as short as possible. Again, both approaches are valid . . . Here's a sample of an effective, shorter proposal [for first grade— PF] that Jane Dwinell (Vermont) wrote for her daughter Dana's first year of homeschooling (again, in the legal sense):

COURSE OF STUDY FOR DANA DWINELL-YARDLEY:

1. BASIC COMMUNICATION SKILLS

Language Arts.   Topics may include but shall not be limited to the following: Silent and oral reading; listening skills; telling stories; spelling; homonyms; synonyms and antonyms; writing letters, stories, and poems by hand, dictation, or typing; dictionary use for meaning and spelling; encyclopedia use; library skills; use of basic punctuation; use of table of contents and index; and computer skills.

Math. Topics may include but shall not be limited to the following: Count and write by 1s, 10s, 100s, 1000s; addition and subtraction with single and double digits; telling time and using the calendar; value of coins and making change; and meaning of inch, foot, yard.

2. CITIZENSHIP, HISTORY, AND GOVERNMENT IN VERMONT AND THE U.S.

Topics may include but shall not be limited to the following: Current events; town meeting; travel throughout New England and to Florida; national holidays; map reading: World—name and find oceans, continents, our country, our state; U.S.—name and find New England states; Vermont—find Irasburg, Montpelier, Burlington, Newport, Lake Memphremagog, Lake Champlain, Lake Willoughby, Lake Morey, Connecticut River, Black River, Barton River.

3. PHYSICAL EDUCATION AND COMPREHENSIVE HEALTH EDUCATION

Topics may include but shall not be limited to the following: Sports—cross country skiing, downhill skiing, sliding, biking, hiking, tree climbing, swimming, gymnastics, badminton, croquet, canoeing. Health Education—basic first aid for cuts, splinters, burns, sprains, and strains; treatment of common cold; care of teeth and regular dental visits; traffic safety; family meal planning and food preparation.

4. ENGLISH, AMERICAN, AND OTHER LITERATURE

Topics may include but shall not be limited to the following: Novels by nineteenth- and twentieth-century British and American authors; American poetry; Greek mythology.

5. THE NATURAL SCIENCES

Topics may include but shall not be limited to the following: Seeds, bulbs, plants, and flowers; common birds; sun, moon, stars, and basic constellations; seasons, weather, clouds; fire and temperature; farm animals—care from infancy to adulthood, slaughtering; maple sugaring.

6. THE FINE ARTS

Topics may include but shall not be limited to the following: Drawing; painting; computer graphics; making clothes and handkerchiefs for dolls and dress-up; attending concerts and plays; listening to music at home (live and taped); singing.

EVALUATIONS

John Holt writes about the value of feedback versus evaluation in the last chapter, and I won't labor the point here. However, in his book *What Do I Do Monday?* Holt provides some good context about evaluations outside of conventional schooling:

> In the kind of learning I have been talking about there is no place and no need for conventional testing and grading. In a class where children are doing things, and not getting ready to do them sometime in the distant future, what they do tells us what they have learned.
>
> . . . What sense does an average grade make in a course like English? Do we average a serious writer's best work against his worst? If I assigned a paper, and a student did badly on it, this only showed that this was the wrong paper for him, where he could not show the ability he had. The remedy was to try and give a wide enough variety of choices and opportunities for writing, reading, and talking so that everyone would have a fairly good chance of showing his best talents.
>
> It is not just in English that it makes no sense to figure students' grades by taking an average of all their daily or weekly work. It makes no sense in any subject . . .
>
> It is not grading alone that is stupid, but the whole idea of trying to have a class move along on a schedule, like a train. Children do not learn things at the same time, or equally easily and quickly.[1]

As you will see, portfolios and other descriptive measures of learning are well suited for homeschooling families who want to get away from grades and gold stars, particularly if they aren't following a conventional school curriculum. In states that require homeschoolers to provide a form of evaluation during, or at the end of, the school year homeschoolers can often choose from the following evaluation methods:

Standardized Testing.   This can be provided by the school, or, in some cases, you can negotiate to use a third party, such as a guidance counselor, teacher, or mutually agreed upon proctor, to administer the test in your home. If you feel the school's choice of test is biased against your homeschooling methods and philosophy, you can ask to administer a different test more to your liking. Before doing this, it is wise to consider how and what you will be teaching your children; if you are following a school curriculum and periodically giving your children tests, then they are probably ready to take these standardized tests. If you have created an individualized study plan for your child, and you do not use standardized testing during your homeschooling year, but your school is forcing standardized tests on you, then it is wise to do as they do in school: get a hold of previous editions of the test, spend some time teaching the subject matter that you see is on the test, and practice taking the test with your children.

Portfolio Assessments.   This, combined with a yearly progress report, is how my wife and I handle evaluations of our children for our local district. A portfolio is an extension of the refrigerator magnet: a place where you save and date your children's work. The difference is you want to save a lot of this stuff and sift through it later to find significant pieces of achievement or indications of development for school officials, such as the two-page report on "The Real Pocahontas" our daughter Lauren (then nine) did, or problem solving, such as a series of math problems, with her self-corrections, that Alison (then six) did. We also save workbook pages (our children sometimes ask for workbook pages just to see if they can do the same stuff their schooled friends do!), lists of books we buy or check out from the library to read to them or that they read themselves, and brief journal notes about significant events, such as a trip to

Plymouth Plantation when Lauren and a friend helped bake bread and make candles "the real way" by spending all day in one "Pilgrim's" house.

Progress Reports. These can take the form of written narratives of your children's learning over a quarter, a half-year, or a year; the periodicity of these reports will depend on your state laws or regulations. Consider that if you write at least one sentence a day, or at least five sentences at the end of each week, about each child, by the end of the year you will have many pages of detailed information about what your children actually did, rather than just a letter or number for a year's worth of work.

Performance Assessments. This term refers to the evaluation of the culmination of a body of work. These are becoming more in vogue with some current education reforms. For example, a child could successfully build a working volcano to demonstrate mastery of certain science principles, or actually perform in a play or concert to demonstrate ability and understanding. Many real-life activities demonstrate thought, responsibility, planning, and subject mastery. For example, a child might, for the ultimate purpose of setting up an aquarium, determine how much money he' has, budget it properly, and choose the right fish and equipment. Though it may sound like a homeschooling story, this particular example is taken from literature by the Wisconsin Department of Education about how it plans to evaluate students as part of its education reforms.

Assessments can also take the form of interviews with other types of educators (child psychologists, school counselors, etc.); written reports from people other than relatives and parents who work with your child; and videotapes, audio tapes, and newspaper clippings of activities your children do that prove they can use the skills and knowledge they have learned.

Many homeschoolers have been admitted to college or found work worth doing without college degrees. Researchers who study grown homeschoolers find them to be doing well individually and economically, and the list of selective colleges that admit homeschooled students continues to grow.

In general, homeschoolers apply to college just like anyone else, except they need to prepare their own transcripts or summarize what they have been doing to provide evidence that they can handle college-level courses, and be sure they have covered the subject matter that each college requires for entrance as first-year students. There are also several books, Web sites, and newsgroups just about college admissions for homeschoolers (see Appendices A and D).

Teenage homeschoolers can sometimes participate in "dual-enrollment" programs offered by their local high schools; this enables qualified teens to take community college courses instead of high school courses. However, if the school is not cooperative you can simply go directly to your local community college and see if your child can enroll in or audit classes. Our now sixteen-year-old daughter, Lauren, has taken biology and psychology classes at two area community colleges; the biology class, by the way, was offered just to high-school-age homeschoolers. Lauren will be able to prove that she can handle college-level work in more tangible ways than many of her peers will be able to with only high school diplomas.

Further, home-based education programs run by private schools, such as the Clonlara School and others (see Private Schools and Curriculum Providers in Appendices B and C), will provide high school degrees and transcripts for colleges. There are other types of homeschooling programs for teenagers as well. They are oriented toward internship and apprenticeship opportunities rather than conventional school work (see Learning Materials, Appendix E).

Besides questioning the conventional wisdom that all children must go to school, many homeschoolers also question if college is the best place for all teenagers to go in order to become successful adults. Many famous people who were homeschooled or who never graduated from or attended college have made important contributions to society, such as: Susan B. Anthony, Pearl S. Buck, Andrew Carnegie, Thomas Edison, Winston Churchill, Charles Dickens, Michael Faraday, Benjamin Franklin, Jane Goodall, Alex Haley, Patrick Henry, Eric Hoffer, Claude Monet, General George Patton, Bertram Russell, Harry S. Truman, Woodrow Wilson, Gloria Steinem, Mark Twain, and the Wright Brothers. Attending school, and college in particular, is not the only way for people to become valuable members of society and contributors to our culture.

In this chapter I've tried to show how homeschooling can be inherently different from traditional schooling. Once you start investigating resources (see Appendices), talking with your children about learning, and meeting other homeschoolers, you will find for yourself how one subject naturally leads to another and you will discover that you have, indeed, created your own "curriculum." The most important thing to do now is to do it! Enjoy your time with your children and the rest will follow. ☜

13

School Response

THE VALUE OF COOPERATION

HOW SHOULD THE SCHOOLS respond to parents who want to teach their children at home? Even in terms of their most immediate bread-and-butter interests—improving their public image, maintaining their budgets and salaries, keeping their jobs, etc.—the schools would be wise to try to help rather than hinder.

As we have seen, many school systems today still oppose home-schoolers by every possible means, some even trying to take their children away from them. They seem to fear that if they let one family teach their children at home, every family will want to, and they will be out of business. Given their present troubles and bad publicity, this worry is natural enough. But it is not realistic. Even with full school cooperation and support, it is unlikely that, in a generation, more than 10 percent of the families of school-age children would be teaching them at home. Most school-age children would still be in some school. There are simply not that many people who like or trust their children that much, or would want to have them around that much of the time, or would take that much time and effort to answer their questions and otherwise help them find out what they want to know.

It is not primarily compulsory attendance laws that keep most children in school so much as the fact that almost no one wants them anywhere else. Until recently, the state of Mississippi had no such laws. They are just now beginning to introduce them; so far they only cover children of ages seven to eight or so. Yet from all we know, about as many children go to school in Mississippi as anywhere else—probably more than in many of our major cities, where as much as half of the high school population is often truant.

Some school people say, "If we let people teach their children at home, the rich will all take their children out of school, and we will have only poor children to teach." One might ask, "Well, what's so bad about that? You will then at last be able to give these poor children your undivided attention." But the fact is, at least so far, that very few of the people who are teaching their children at home are rich. Homeschoolers, as far as I can tell from their letters, have average incomes or less. Perhaps a majority of them have gone to college, though many have not. Many of them have chosen, for different reasons, to live fairly simply in small towns or in the country. One reason why many of them are interested in homeschooling is that they can't afford private schools, even if there were any around that they liked. For a long time to come homeschooling will have little appeal to the rich, who will probably continue to hire other people to look after their children.

In short, there is no reason for school people to see homeschooling as any kind of serious threat to themselves. Such threats do most certainly exist. The rapidly declining birth rate is one. No one can predict the future, and perhaps in the next decade large numbers of people of child-bearing age will suddenly decide to have many more children. But from all we know about young people today in their teens or early twenties, it seems likely that even more of them than now will decide not to marry, or if they marry, not to have children, or if they have any, to have only one or two. They are terribly worried about their own economic futures, about the rapidly rising costs of rearing and educating children, and about the general uncertainty of the world. The best bet seems to be that our rapidly dropping birthrate will continue to drop for some time, so that within a generation the population of school-age children might well fall to half or less of what it is now.

⟪ The population of school-age children is still declining nationally and locally, despite the enrollment bubble caused by the "baby boomlet" toward the end of the last century. For instance, the *Boston Globe* recently reported that the population of school-age children living in Boston in 1970 was 127,405; in 2002 it was 82,405.[1] Some of this decline is the result of white flight from the city's neighborhoods and schools, but some of it is also the declining birthrate. Nationally, the number of elementary-school-age children is declining at the rate of about 1 percent a year now. The rate of secondary-school-age children is still climbing, at about 7 percent a year, but, according to the National Center for Education Statistics, around the year 2006 we will experience a slow, inevitable decline in secondary-school enrollments as well. ⟫

Beyond this, more and more parents, white and nonwhite, are determined, if they possibly can, to get their children into private schools. In large cities, more and more parochial school students are non-Catholic, nonwhite children. A mother in Chicago writes that her son is the only white child in such a school. Fundamentalist church schools are springing up in all parts of the country. Private school attendance, after declining for many years, has increased rapidly in recent years. There is no reason to believe this trend will stop.

⟪ Despite the considerable cost private schooling entails, enrollment in such schools has kept pace with the public school growth rate, particularly among minorities, in the past decade. According to the Council on American Private Education Web site: "Students at Catholic schools paid $2,178 on average and students at schools with other religious orientations paid $2,915 on average, compared with the average tuition of $6,631 for non-sectarian private schools . . . [From 1992–1999] the private school enrollment figure has risen 10.6 percent, about the same as the 10-percent public school growth rate for the same 10-year period." ⟫

Along with this there is the danger—from the public schools' point of view, at least—of voucher plans. Under these the various governments, instead of giving education money to schools, would give it directly to parents in the form of credits, which they could then use to send their children to whatever public or private school they liked best. Thus many more parents could afford to, and would, send their children to private schools, or start schools of their own. It now seems very likely that within a generation, and even a decade, voucher plans of one kind or another will be voted in by many or most states.

Voucher plans are more readily available today than when Holt wrote about them in 1981, and they continue to be fought by the schools. On June 27, 2002, the U.S. Supreme Court ruled that education vouchers are constitutional, and another of Holt's predictions has come true. But vouchers as a mechanism for school choice are overtaken in many instances by the charter school movement, which didn't exist at the time Holt wrote.

On one hand, I think that Holt would have approved of charter schools in concept, but not in practice in America because, all too often, government funding turns charter schools into just slight variations on the theme of state-approved compulsory schooling. In *Teach Your Own*, Holt suggests that parents start their own schools where possible, and he often talked about the Danish school system as a model of how this could work on a larger scale. The Danes not only allow small parent-run schools and have done so for years, but they also pay for them with public funds once certain criteria are met. Small, run by and for local families in conjunction with a few like-minded teachers, empowered by flexible curricula and public support, the many "little schools" of Denmark are much more difficult to create in America. The charter school movement, which is supposed to make it easier for the creation of alternatives to public schools, is meeting stiff resistance to the number of charters given out by the state. For instance, Massachusetts allowed the creation of charter schools in 1995, but only forty-two charter schools have been funded and operated since then. Now, with budget cuts looming, the public schools are demanding that no new charters be funded for the next two years. There is obvious interest and support for charter schools—Massachusetts has a state-wide waiting list of 11,000 students wanting to get into its charter schools, which currently enroll 15,000 children—but all sorts of forces are trying to keep charters from spreading quickly.

I've heard of a few charter schools that have been started and operated by parents in some states, but not many. Indeed, in their do-it-yourself fashion, some homeschoolers aren't waiting for the state to give them funds and permission to create the "cafeteria-style" schools they want: They're going ahead and doing it anyway. In an article titled "Home-schooled Away from Home,"[2] the *Washington Post* reported on this trend where "parents work together in learning cooperatives, sometimes in each other's homes and increasingly in empty wings of churches and community centers." This may be a new trend for people who follow a school-at-home approach, but as you've read here, Holt was writing about these clubs and cooperatives, and unschoolers have been creating and using them, for years. Fears school officials may have about home-schoolers taking their funding in order to start their own schools are simply overstated: Homeschoolers are determined to create what they need regardless of government funding. Schools would be wiser to seek accommodation with homeschoolers rather than continue to drive away these educators, especially now that there are so many free or for-profit options for learning outside of school.

Private companies are seeking charters and public funds, both as physical as well as virtual schools. Such actions should be worrying the public schools far more than parents seeking to create learning cooperatives for children in their local neighborhoods. Public schools will gain much-needed allies among the growing number of motivated parents seeking to homeschool if they would work with them rather than against them. As Holt notes, fighting homeschoolers should not be a big issue for public schools when there are so many more pressing dangers for them; cooperation will be far more fruitful for society, schools, and home-schoolers. ❧

The public schools have reason enough to worry about all these problems. But they have no good reason to worry about homeschooling. By opposing it they stand to gain little and to lose much of what is left of their good reputation and the confidence and trust of the public.

An example. A woman, a skilled performing classical musician, teacher, and conductor, moved to a small town in northern Minnesota. Her youngest daughter was herself training for a career as a professional violinist, and had played with professionals in small concerts. Since the school itself had no advanced music programs, and since in school subjects the girl was two or three years ahead of her class, the mother decided to take her out of school and teach her, in music and school subjects, at home. The schools called the mother's home education program inadequate and took her to court. She lost there, but was acquitted by a higher court.

This story from a small Minnesota town was printed in papers all over the country. Two *GWS* readers sent me long news stories about it, one from a paper in Louisville, Kentucky, and the other from a paper in southern New Jersey. Both stories were wholly sympathetic to the mother and the family.

In Providence, Rhode Island, Peter and Brigitta Van Daam, intelligent and well educated, wanted to take their daughter out of public school. They tried in repeated letters and visits to school officials to find out what kind of forms they needed to fill out and what procedures to follow to do this. The school people (perhaps in ignorance) repeatedly told them, *contrary to fact*, that there were no such forms or procedures. When at length the family, weary of this runaround, began teaching their child at home, the schools took legal action against them, and eventually had the entire family arrested and taken to jail. The Van Daams had worked hard to take their case to the public and the media. When the police came for them, all three major TV networks had cameras there. Soon after, on at least one nationwide TV show, millions of Americans could see these obviously intelligent, concerned, and capable parents, with their obviously intelligent small children, being taken to jail.

Such acts only make the schools look arrogant, greedy, cruel, and stupid. No need to cite other examples, of which there are many. In tough times like these the schools simply cannot stand any more of this kind of publicity. Public opinion on education is making a U-turn. Since they were founded, the public schools have enjoyed almost limitless public trust and confidence. People might criticize them in detail, but in principle almost everyone agreed that the public schools were a great thing. The idea of an effective government monopoly in education was accepted almost without question. Now, suddenly, more and more citizens do not believe any longer that the government should have such a monopoly, and many are beginning to ask whether the government should be in the school business at all.

Some claim that it is still only a minority who are turning against the schools, and then mostly for reasons that lie outside the schools themselves. To some extent this may be true. Today's antischool sentiment is clearly part of a larger reaction against all giant, remote, uncontrollable institutions—big corporations, big unions, big hospitals, above all big government itself. Part of it is the response of people to a shrinking economy, to worries about inflation, their homes, their jobs, gas for the car and oil for the furnace. But how much the schools may be responsible for this sudden turning against them makes little difference. The change of opinion is there and growing. In such a time the schools can't afford to do things that will make them still more enemies. Spending time and the public's money to make trouble for parents who want to teach their own children will surely do this.

But this is only the negative side of the picture. The real point I want to make here is that the schools have a great many things of real value to gain by cooperating fully with homeschooling families. Let me (in no particular order of importance) discuss some of them here.

RESEARCH

The schools have always needed places where people could do research in teaching. Here I don't mean research as the word is usually understood, with experimental groups, control groups, statistics, etc. I mean the kind of research I myself did in most of my years as a classroom teacher, in which I was continually trying out and improving new ways of teaching my students. This kind of research, done by teachers in their own classrooms, based on *experience* rather than experiments, is the only kind that will significantly improve teaching.

But it is almost impossible for schools, or teachers in schools, to do such research. One reason is that when schools or teachers use "tried-

and-true" methods that everyone is used to, i.e., rote-learning, drill, etc., and these methods don't work, as they usually don't, the public is willing to let the schools blame the students. But when a school or teacher uses a method that people consider new, and it doesn't work, the public blames *them*. So the rule is, to avoid trouble, stick to the old methods, *even* if they don't work.

Furthermore, whenever the schools do persuade the public to allow and the government to pay for some fairly fundamental research, they are always under heavy pressure to show quick results, i.e., higher test scores. The federally funded Follow Through programs were very rarely given even as much as three years to learn how to teach in a new way and to show that it worked; more often they had to produce their results in a year or two. So a really serious project, like finding out what would happen if children could decide for themselves when they wanted to read, with no teaching unless and until they asked for it, has no chance of being tested fairly or at all. A boy I know, by no means unique among children given such freedom and choice, did not learn to read at all until after he was eight, taught himself, and three years later, when tested by a school, scored at the twelfth-grade level in reading. In one of these short-term research projects, this boy would have simply gone down in the statistics as a nonreader, "proof" that the experiment of letting children decide when they would read did not work.

For all these reasons, it seems very likely that the one place where we can hope and expect to see some really fundamental and long-term research on learning, on the kinds and amounts of teaching that most help learning, and on the usefulness of different methods and materials, is in the homes of people teaching their own children. They can afford to be patient, to wait a long time for results; they are in complete control of their work, and can change their methods as they wish; they can observe closely; they are free from all the routine distractions of large schools; and they are interested only in results rather than excuses. From these people and their work, all serious schools and teachers, many of them now severely limited and handicapped by the conditions under which they have to work, stand to learn a great deal.

First, let it be clear what they will *not* learn. They will not learn that this or that is the *best* way to teach reading, or addition, or multiplication, etc.; or that certain books are the *best* books for children; or that such-and-such is the *best* curriculum for this or that grade; or that you should always teach this particular subject in this particular order. Homeschoolers will not teach the schools what they so yearn to know, the *one best way* to do anything. What they will teach is that there *is* no one best way, and that it is a waste of time and energy to look for it; that children (like adults) learn in a great many different ways; that each child learns best in the ways that most interest, excite, and satisfy her or him; and that the business of school should be to offer to learners the widest possible range of choices, both in what to learn and ways to learn it. If a number of parents report, as they regularly do in *GWS*, that their children love reading books about astronomy or architecture or anthropology or aircraft or atoms or rockets or space travel or microbes, or working with colored pencils or computers or puzzles or violins or typewriters or gardens or tape recorders or whatever, then that is a sign that these books and materials should be in the schools, not so that all children will have to use them, but so that any child who wants *can* use them.

Beyond this, homeschoolers may be able to teach the schools some very important general principles of teaching and learning. Right now, there are so few homeschoolers that the things they learn from their experience, about which I have written in *GWS* and in this book, can be and are dismissed by conventional educators as rare examples proving nothing. But as the numbers of homeschoolers increase, it will be harder for even their bitterest enemies to ignore or deny their findings. When we can show, as in time we surely will, tens of thousands of children who, having learned to read only when they wanted to, and with only as much instruction as they asked for, are a few years later reading two or three or more years beyond most children of their age in schools, it cannot fail to have a great impact on the schools themselves. The people in schools who want to move in these directions will be much encouraged, while the rest will find it harder and harder to oppose them.

FEEDBACK

People doing a task can only do it better when they can find out how well they are doing it. Experiments have shown this time and time again. If we are estimating the weight of objects, and if we never learn whether our guesses are too low or too high, we never get any better. But if we learn whether each guess was too low or too high, and by how much, we quickly improve. If you shoot at a target, but can't see where your shots hit, you have no way to improve them.

One of the reasons why schools and teachers usually find it so hard to do their work better is that they get so little good feedback from their students—candid information about how well they are teaching. A good friend of mine, while a brilliant, successful, and on the whole very happy student at a leading university, once told me that he and his friends never argued or disagreed with their professors, either in class discussions or in writing. He said, "The only way to be sure of an A on a paper or in a course is to say what you think the professor thinks, putting it of course in your own words so he won't think you are just imitating him." Since then, many other college students, in conversations, in letters, or in books about how to succeed at college, have said more or less the same thing. Professors who see themselves as telling truths to the ignorant may not care that students act this way. But others care a great deal. They chose to teach so that they might have lively talks with students about matters they all cared about, and are disappointed and hurt to find themselves dealing more and more with students who care only about getting a good (or at least passing) grade. They grow sick to death of hearing, "What do we have to do to get a good mark in this course? Are we going to be held responsible for this? Is this going to be on the exam?" Such questions drive many of them out of teaching altogether.

Teaching fifth grade, I finally learned that my hardest and most important task was to help my students become enough unafraid of me, and each other, to stop bluffing, faking, and playing testing games with me. Only when they were enough at ease in the class to be truly themselves could they begin to reveal their true interests and strengths, as well as their fears and weaknesses. Only then could I think about how to build on the strengths and overcome or avoid the weaknesses. All this took time and patience. Some of them would not for a long time tell me that they did not understand how to do a problem, or something I had told them or written on the board. A few never told me; their masks never came off.

If only to learn to do our work as teachers, we need students who are not afraid of us, and so not afraid to tell us what they think, or what they know and don't know. There may be a few such students in our schools right now, but not enough—we need many more. And we will have more as more and more children who are for the most part learning outside of school come to school for special classes and activities that they are interested in.

AUTHORITY AND LEADERSHIP

Because they don't understand natural authority, the schools are in an authority crisis. Their coercive authority breaks down more and more, but it is the only kind they know. They find it hard to imagine what it might be like to deal with children who were not in the least afraid of them and whom they had no reason to make afraid. Words alone won't change this. The schools will only learn about natural authority from those children for whom they *have* natural authority, that is, the children who come to school because they want to, to use it as a resource for purposes of their own. From them will come much of the kind of leadership that the schools so badly need.

While teaching fifth grade, I thought often about educational leadership. For a long time, I had no idea what it was. Slowly I began to see that the atmosphere and spirit of my classes were largely determined by the students themselves, above all by two or three who, whatever might be their schoolwork or behavior, were in fact the real leaders. Of the five fifth-grade classes I taught, all of which I liked, the last was much the best—the most interesting and active, the most fun for me, the most valuable for the children. But by all usual standards it should have been one of the worst; only three of the children were really good students, and more than half the class had serious academic and/or emotional problems. What made that class the best was the two children who (without knowing or trying) led it.

One, a black boy, was by far the most brilliant student I have ever taught, and not just school-smart but life-smart, smart in everything. The other, a girl, just as much a leader, was a very poor student, but exceptionally imaginative and artistic, and also smart in the real world. What made these children such a joy to be with, and such a powerful influence on the other children, was not just their obvious alertness, imagination, curiosity, good humor, high spirits, and interest in many things, but their energy, vitality, self-respect, courage and, above all, their true independence. They did not need to be bossed, told what to do. Nor were they interested in playing with me, or against me, the old school game of "You Can't Make Me Do It." No doubt they were helped by the fact that I, unlike so many adults, obviously enjoyed and valued those qualities in them that they most valued in themselves. But I did not create these qualities, they brought them to the class. What without these children might have been a miserable year turned out to be the most interesting and exciting year I ever spent in a schoolroom.

A few such children can make an enormous difference to a class or even an entire school. Far more than any principal or teacher, they set the tone of the place. If, on the other hand, the children with the most energy, imagination, and courage are constantly defying the school, and if the only ones who are "good" are obviously the ones who are too scared to be bad, most of the children will admire and envy the outlaws even if they don't dare imitate them. No one can maintain law and order, or authority, or discipline in such a place.

In my fifth-grade class the most admired children were not the outlaws. Not that the two leaders were docile teacher's pets, far from it. If they didn't like something I was doing, or wanted to do something else, or thought I was being unfair, they would tell me. But this had nothing to do with a struggle over who was boss. Our relationship was about something else altogether. They were in many ways interested in the world, and I knew more about the world than they did, so they were glad to find out and use much of what I knew. Meanwhile, we enjoyed each other's company. To be sure, the class had its cut-ups and You-Can't-Make-Me's. When they were really funny, as they sometimes were, the other kids might laugh at them, as I did myself. But they were not admired for being cut-ups. Their antics were often a distraction and a nuisance to kids who had better things to do. What was important and admired was being as alive, alert, active, curious, and committed as those leaders. The class discipline that grows out of that kind of feeling is as different as night from day from the discipline in a class where the children say to each other, "If you do that, I'll tell the teacher and you'll get in trouble." Not only is it a great deal more pleasant, it is a great deal more permanent.

The schools desperately need, if only as an example to the others, more of that kind of children, children whose dealings with them are not governed by fear. Such children will bring to the school not only a different attitude about the world (interesting and exciting), themselves (independent and competent), and the school (useful), but also interests that go far beyond last night's TV shows. Some of these interests, the other children will pick up. My black fifth-grader *taught* the other children in that class far more than I did; admiring him, they talked with him as much as they could (which I allowed), and from that talk they learned a great deal. In the same way, homeschooled children who come to school as part-time volunteers will bring with them many ideas, skills, activities, resources, for other children to share. Even if these children make up only a very small percentage of the student body, they will make the school a very different, and much nicer and more interesting place.

◖◗ All three of our homeschooled girls have been in and out of public and private schools, both as full-time and part-time students. I don't want to sound too much like a bragging father, but my girls have received complements from their schoolteachers and from other adults for bringing energy and leadership to their play, their classes, and their work with other children. I know many other homeschooling parents who can boast the same; so much for fears that homeschooling stunts social abilities! More often than not, school is considered an "all-or-nothing-at-all" proposition by its administrators, so the opportunities for all children to volunteer to attend school on a part-time basis are more limited by bureaucracy than the children's desire. But, as our experiences and many homeschoolers' experiences indicate, the smorgasbord approach to schooling works quite well, for all children and for all the people they learn with, and it doesn't take a lot of funding, rules, and regulations in order to make it happen. ☺*

MONEY, PUBLICITY, CLIENTS

One reason the schools worry about people teaching their children at home has to do with money. Most school districts receive financial aid from the state—so many dollars per pupil per day. This aid often makes up an important part of the school's income. So when a family talks about teaching their children at home, the schools think, "If they do, we will lose X hundred dollars a year, which we can't afford, so we'd better not let them." But clearly, if the schools cooperated with the parents, and the children came to school part-time for activities they liked, the school would be able to mark them present, and so would not lose their share of state aid.

In fact, there is no legal reason why a school district, having decided to cooperate with a homeschooling family, could not enroll their children and list them as attending the school, even if they seldom *came* to school. Nothing in any state education laws I have seen says that "attendance" can only mean physical presence in the school building, or would prevent any school district from doing what, for a while at least, the Philadelphia schools did in their Parkway Project, or the Toronto schools in their Metro Project. In these the students spent their days, not in school buildings, but in various institutions of the city itself. No one ever claimed, or could have sustained a claim, that in sending students around the city instead of shutting them up in school buildings these school systems were violating state attendance laws. Other public school systems have very wisely sent children out of the schools to work as apprentices in various local businesses, giving them school credit for the experience. No one ever claimed that this was a violation of the law.

Since the law gives school districts the right to define attendance in any way they and their constituents choose, there is no reason why a school district could not claim that children learning at home, with the school's support and supervision, were "attending" the school. Indeed, the school might claim that it was not only legally but morally justified in collecting state aid for such students, since in some ways they might be getting more individualized attention than the children in the school building. So there is no reason why schools have to see homeschooling as an immediate financial threat.

Cooperating with homeschooling families is not only a way to avoid bad publicity, but a way to get good publicity, which most school systems would very much like to have. During an appearance on a local TV talk show I happened to mention briefly that the schools in Barnstable, Massachusetts, were cooperating fully with a home-schooling family, whose children, whenever they wanted, could and did go to the school to take part in activities they liked. This very brief mention brought and is still bringing the school district a number of inquiring letters and phone calls, some even from outside the state, and all very favorable in tone. School folks, like everyone else, like to feel and have others feel that they are at the forefront of progress, blazing new trails, leading the way. Cooperating with homeschooling families is an easy and an authentic way for schools to put themselves in that position. Then why not do it? Why look bad when it is so easy to look good?

◖◐ Holt's question continues to resonate with me as I watch public schools shoot themselves in the foot time and again as they attempt to limit homeschooling. For years, local school districts in Massachusetts could count homeschooled students in their average daily attendance (ADA) formulas and receive funding for them. Massachusetts home-schoolers, by and large, had nothing to complain about as schools that took the funding often let homeschoolers take courses or use school resources without much difficulty. Indeed, one family in Boston received, via mail, a perfect-attendance award for their homeschooled son who had never set foot in his local public school, but whose name had appeared on the school's attendance rolls for funding purposes. The situation peaked a few years ago when the superintendent of Uxbridge, Massachusetts, offered to give a share of the ADA funds he received for homeschoolers to offset a portion of each homeschooling family's annual education expenses. This sort of arrangement is not unheard of; in recent years school districts in California and Washington have offered home-schoolers tax credits, financial incentives, and school resources in return for the schools being allowed to enroll homeschoolers in their Indepen-dent Study Programs or other types of full- or part-time school programs. But in 1996 the Massachusetts State Department of Education decided to push away homeschoolers; it passed a regulation that forbids counting homeschooled students in a school's ADA formula. Whatever funds the school would have received for these students now go to the general state fund. Though this move has hardened the "all-or-nothing-at-all" mentality among many Massachusetts's school administrators, nonethe-less a few superintendents continue to cooperate openly with home-schoolers and to show how easy it can be to look good and support learning for all the children in their districts. ☙

Because of the decline of the birthrate, no matter what else they do, schools are going to continue to lose more and more of their clients. To stay in business, they must find new ones. Many seem to think they can solve this problem by making compulsory education begin earlier and go on longer, if possible forever. Educators in many parts of the coun-try are trying to make kindergarten compulsory; some teachers' unions have even proposed that compulsory schooling should begin as early as age two or three. At the same time, educators talk a great deal about a rather sinister idea called Mandatory Continuing Education, which, if they can push it through, will mean that more and more people, having gone to school for years in order to get a job, will then have to keep go-ing to school in order to keep the job. A prominent educator, a very gifted promoter of education (and himself), used to say proudly that he considered himself a "womb-to-tomb" schooler. What he had in mind was, of course, that *other people* would have to spend their whole lives going to school. Not him; he would be running those schools.

This is the wrong approach. It might have sold in the days when everyone but a handful of cranks was behind the schools, or when people were sure that every extra year spent in school automatically meant so many extra dollars on your paycheck. But it won't sell now, in today's growing antischool climate, and our declining economy, where college and even graduate degrees are worth less and less every year. If the schools are to survive and thrive, as a few understand very well, it must be more and more as places that people go to *only be-cause they like to*, because they think of school as a place where you can find out about and do interesting things.

Very few people now feel that way. Even when most people still supported the schools in principle, hundreds of parents, many of whom had even been good students, were telling or writing me that most of their worst anxiety dreams were still school dreams, or that every time they went into their children's school, for whatever reason, they could feel their insides tighten up and their hands begin to sweat. Many kinds of places—concert halls, baseball parks, theaters, parks, beaches, to name a few—make most people feel good as soon as they step into them. They think that something pleasant, interest-ing, exciting, is about to happen. For their very survival, the schools *need* people who feel that way about them, for in the long run such people are the ones the schools will have to depend on for their sup-port, they are their only true friends.

Some school districts understand this very well. Here are some words from "Declining Enrollments," a pamphlet published by the Center for Community Education Development of the Santa Barbara County Schools.

When schools exist apart from the community, they stand as monu-ments to the School Board and their ability to get bond issues passed . . . as reminders to citizens of the unpleasant past of their own educa-tional experiences . . . as symbols of something to vote against in the fu-ture . . . they stand empty, unused, and economically unfeasible, they create a further segmented and fragmented society. On the other side of the coin is the school which is an integral part of the total resources of the community.

There is also what has become almost a classic story of making a building so indispensable that the School Board could not consider its closing. The principal of Fairlington Elementary School in Arlington, Virginia, saw her enrollment drop from 440 to 225. She first turned space over to a play school, then invited the recreation department to use the school for some of its programs, and then reserved space for use by a senior citizens group. A community theatre and several other local organizations soon joined in using the school's facilities. Before long, talk of closing the school ceased, and some began to wonder if perhaps it needed an addition.

TEACHER TRAINING

In time, the homeschooling movement could become very useful, at least to the more innovative schools of education, as a way of training teachers.

Professors of education have asked me many times over the years how we might improve teacher training. Until recently I have said that as long as we define teacher training as sending people to college to take education courses, nothing could make that process any less harmful than it already is. Young teachers so trained go into the classroom thinking that they know a great deal about children, learning, and teaching, when in fact they know next to nothing—which I would say even if I had taught all their classes. People so taught have nothing in their minds but words. They know no more about children and teaching than people who had lived all their lives in desert or jungle would know about snow-covered mountains just from hearing people talk about them. We cannot, by turning a complicated experience into words, *give* that experience to someone who has not had it. Hearing mountains or children described, even seeing photos or films of mountains or children, is no substitute at all for seeing and climbing actual mountains or working with actual children.

Since student teachers in their training hear and read only words, and have no experience in teaching or otherwise dealing with children to which they can relate and compare these words, they have no sound basis for saying that some ideas seem to make more sense or fit better with experience than others. What they are told about teaching, they tend to swallow whole. Such students, when they first enter classrooms as teachers, come in, so to speak, with a box of gummed labels: "underachiever," "overachiever," "learning disability," "brain damaged," "acting out," "emotionally disturbed," "culturally deprived," etc. Once in the class, instead of looking at what is before them, and slowly learning to describe and judge this experience in their own way, they look for children or events onto which they can stick one or more of the ready-made labels from their box. Thinking that a child labeled is a child understood, they quickly decide that Billy is an underachiever, and Susie is a typical this, and Tommy a typical that. This would be bad even if the labels themselves were good. Thus, even if the word "underachiever" described something real and important, instead of merely a discrepancy between the results of two different kinds of tests (neither worth much), there would be many different kinds of underachievers and ways of underachieving. But most teachers, satisfied with this kind of instant diagnosis, don't take time, or don't know how, to look further. And so these labels, wrong to start with and hastily slapped on, become a part of the official record of schoolchildren, and largely determine how the schools, and beyond that the world, will see them and deal with them.

None of these faults in teacher training are improved by having teachers, usually in their last year of ed school, do some "student teaching" or "practice teaching" in the classrooms of regular teachers in local public schools. What this "teaching" amounts to is mostly watching the regular teacher and helping out with minor chores. Only rarely, usually under the eye of the regular teacher, are the student teachers allowed to teach a "unit" or two of their own. To expect anyone to learn to teach by such methods is like expecting a child to learn to drive a car by sitting in his parents' laps and holding the wheel while they steer it.

When student teachers worked with me in my fifth-grade class, from time to time I used to turn the class over to them. When I did I would always leave the room, first telling the students that while I wasn't there Miss So-and-so was the boss and they had to do exactly what she said, etc. But they knew, and she knew, that I was the real boss; I gave out any serious punishments that had to be given out, and beyond that, the grades which were the true and ultimate reward and punishment. Their fate as fifth-graders lay in my hands, not Miss

So-and-so's. I, and not the student teacher, was still holding the wheel.

In any case, whether the regular "cooperating" teachers are in the room or not during this practice teaching, they will always demand a report on it, and will know if it went badly. Since student teachers need good reports from their cooperating teachers, they will not, as many have told me, run the risk of using in their practice teaching any methods that these teachers might not like. They will be thinking not about what will most help the students, but what will get the best report from the regular teacher. Beyond this, they get so few chances to teach, and these so brief, that they don't have time to make a serious trial of whatever teaching methods they want to use, far less find out how to improve them.

Student practice teaching is mostly a sham and a fraud. It gives the students a very brief look at the inside of a real schoolroom, and enables schools of education to say to future employers of their graduates that these graduates have had some "field experience." But that's all it does.

A more helpful way to train people for the work of teaching in classrooms would be to have them *begin* by teaching real classes in real schools, all the while giving them places and plenty of time to talk about their work with other new teachers in the same position, sometimes (but not always) in the company of a sympathetic and more experienced teacher. Along with these discussions, the new teachers could read and discuss a number of books about teaching, child psychology, etc., looking for ideas that might help them make sense of their experience, and so teach better. They would be encouraged to read these books critically, not passively. Perhaps, out of their experience, their discussions, and their reading, they might write some manuals or books of their own. We might then have many more textbooks about classroom teaching "methods" written by people who had actually and recently worked in classrooms.

But even if we could make these changes in the ways in which we hire and train teachers, teaching classes in compulsory schools would not tell them very much about learning. My own work as a teacher began exactly in the way described above. I started teaching without any formal training whatever. I read no books about education until after I had taught for a number of years. I had plenty of time and occasions to talk with other young teachers like myself about our mutual problems, and many of these talks, with my friend and colleague Bill Hull, were the seed of my first book. Yet in all my years in the classroom what I learned was not so much how children learn as how they defend themselves against learning, not so much how they explored and made sense of the world as how they worked out slippery strategies for dodging the dangers of school, the pain and shame of not knowing, being wrong, failing.

What I really learned about *learning*, in its best and deepest sense, I learned partly from my own adult experiences in learning languages, music, and sports, but mostly from watching and playing with babies and very young children in their parents' homes. Only as I began to understand how human beings learned when they learned *best* did I begin to understand what was wrong with the classroom and my own and others' teaching. Seeing human learning at its most powerful, i.e., the learning of infants, above all their amazing and always unique discovery and conquest of language, gave me a yardstick against which I could measure all other teaching and learning.

There is no better way to understand human learning than by closely watching babies and infants during those years in which they are learning (among many other things) to stand, walk, and talk, and no better place to do this than in the home, not as a teacher or coldly detached scientist but as *an attentive, concerned, and loving member of the family*. Such an experience, living like an older sister or brother in families with young children, would be invaluable to people who want to be teachers or helpers of learning of any kind. It is the only kind of training for teaching, other than teaching itself, which has any chance of being any use at all.

Looking into the future, I can see a day when at least a certain number of student teachers would have such an experience as part of their training. Of course, there would be problems to work out. Families would have to be paid, not just for the expense and trouble of housing and feeding students but in fair return for the important service they were doing them. Such an experience should not be compulsory; only those students who felt they could learn something important by living in another family with small children should be allowed to do it. Schools of education would have to give generous academic credits for such training. Nor should they demand from students too much in the way of papers and reports, since the whole point is to have the student in the family *not* as a reporter but as a family member. You can't play with little children and take notes at the same time. Any education professors who need piles of paper to prove that their students are learning anything would be better off left out of such a program. I would never have learned half as much from my own experience of living in families with children if I had been required to write papers about them. When I wrote, as I often did, it was only because, I realized later, I had seen something so interesting that I wanted to be sure to remember it, and perhaps to tell others about it.

Student and family would have to agree about how much the student, living as a family member, would be subject to the family's routines and disciplines. Many families would not want students in their homes doing things that they would not allow their own children to do. Families and students would also have to agree on how much of the family housework the students were expected to do, and how much free time they would have and when. There might well be other problems. But any education department that wanted to put such a program into effect could surely find a way to do so.

It will of course be essential to find the right kind of families. Students will not learn much about the learning of infants and children except in families which like, trust, and respect their children and enjoy watching their learning and helping it if and when they can. Here is where the homeschooling movement might be very useful to schools. People who are teaching children at home, or who would like to, or even think they might like to, are almost certain to be people who treat their children with loving courtesy, and allow and encourage them to explore the world in their own way.

This training might very well be valuable, not just to teachers but to future psychologists, psychiatrists, therapists, social workers, and others whose work might someday bring them into contact with children. Some young people might want to do it for a while just to get themselves more ready for having their own children. We hear much about the need for young people to take courses in "parenting." Six months living in a family with young children would be a great deal more valuable than any such course.

◖ Although I do know of situations where young adults lived with homeschooling families in exchange for help with tutoring and day care, and where anthropology and education researchers lived with homeschooling families, I know of no "teachers to be" who were encouraged by schools of education to spend time learning about young children in this way. Nevertheless, the Internet and the growing number of homeschooling resources at the local and state levels can be a great help to students interested in learning how children learn "in the field." ◗

CONCLUSION

Having said this much about why I think schools would be wise to give their full support to homeschooling families, I have to make two things clear. First, I do not claim that supporting homeschooling is going to be a quick solution to the school's problems. For these there are no quick solutions. It took the schools many years to get into their present bad position, and even after they come to understand how and why they got into it, it will take them many years to get out. Secondly, I am not proposing homeschooling *so that* the schools will change their ways and/or solve their problems. I would like to see both these things happen, and believe that homeschooling may in time help them to happen. But that is not why I am for homeschooling. It is an important and worthwhile idea in its own right.

To repeat once again the idea with which I began this book, it is a most serious mistake to think that learning is an activity separate from the rest of life, that people do best when they are not doing anything else and best of all in places where nothing else is done. It is an equally serious mistake to think that teaching, the assisting of learning and the sharing of knowledge and skill, is something that can be done only by a few specialists. When we lock learning and teaching in the school box, as we do, we do not get more effective teaching and learning in society, but much less.

What makes people smart, curious, alert, observant, competent, confident, resourceful, persistent—in the broadest and best sense, intelligent—is not having access to more and more *learning* places, resources, and specialists, but being able in their lives to do a wide variety of interesting things that matter, things that challenge their ingenuity, skill, and judgment, and that make an obvious difference in their lives and the lives of people around them. It is foolish to think that through "education" we can have a society in which, no matter how low may be the quality of work, the quality of learning and intelligence will remain high. People with dull and meaningless jobs are hardly likely to lead active, interesting, productive lives away from those jobs. They are much more likely to collapse in front of the TV set and take refuge from their own dreary daily life in a life of fantasy, by imagining for a while that they are one of those rich, beautiful, sexy, powerful, laughing, fast-moving, successful people on the screen.

I have used the words "homeschooling" to describe the process by which children grow and learn in the world without going, or going very much, to schools, because those words are familiar and quickly understood. But in one very important sense they are misleading. What is most important and valuable about the home as a base for children's growth into the world is not that it is a better school than the schools but *that it isn't a school at all*. It is not an artificial place, set up to make "learning" happen and in which nothing except "learning" ever happens. It is a natural, organic, central, fundamental human institution, one might easily and rightly say the foundation of all other institutions. We can imagine and indeed we have had human societies without schools, without factories, without libraries, museums, hospitals, roads, legislatures, courts, or any of the institutions which seem so indispensable and permanent a part of modern life. We might someday even choose, or be obliged, to live once again without some or all of these. But we cannot even imagine a society without homes, even if these should be no more than tents, or mud huts, or holes in the ground. What I am trying to say, in short, is that our chief educational problem is not to find a way to make homes *more* like schools. If anything, it is to make schools *less* like schools.

Whatever we may call the activity I have tried to describe in this book, it will go on more quickly, easily, painlessly, and productively if the schools will cooperate with it rather than trying to resist it. In these last chapters I have tried to say why I think they would be not simply generous but wise to do so, as some are already doing. (For a list of schools that are helping and supporting homeschooling families, see Appendix C.)

When John Merrow interviewed me for National Public Radio, I told him why I thought schools would be wise to support homeschooling. He said, "Aren't you being a bit naïve?" Well, I certainly would be if I thought that large numbers of school districts were going to do this in the next year or so. I don't at first expect many of them to take this path. But the path is there for those who are willing to take it. The list of supporting school districts is still very small. But, like the homeschooling movement itself, it is growing and will continue to grow, and for the same reason—because it makes sense, and because it works.

✎ In 1999 I was interviewed by John Merrow for National Public Radio; I was part of a panel of experts convened to discuss "The New Homeschoolers." We were "new" due to the greater number of support systems, recognition, and success stories—and a generation of homeschoolers has grown up and entered the world of work and college since 1981 when Merrow interviewed Holt. Furthermore, in 2002–2003, there are a lot more homeschoolers and cooperative school districts. Although the list we keep at Holt Associates never got larger than about twenty school districts that wished to be publicly listed as cooperative school districts in which to homeschool, there are many more districts that could be listed but chose not to for any number of reasons. For instance, my own local school district in Medford, Massachusetts, has been cooperative by letting our children take certain courses in elementary school, though they don't tell local real estate agents that Medford is a decent place to homeschool your children.

As I mentioned earlier, schools in the state of Washington actively recruit homeschooling families to join their independent study programs. Indeed, the situation in Washington is becoming one of too much cooperation from the schools; homeschooling is being co-opted by some of the schools into government-run "school-at-home" programs, where in exchange for your freedom to learn in your own ways, you get textbooks, computers, or other learning materials and services for learning the schools' way. There are justifiable and considerable controversies about homeschooling and schools being too cooperative, but there's no denying that this is a trend, particularly on the West Coast of the United States. Both schools and homeschoolers need to be alert as they move into this gray area where the family life of homeschoolers can become dominated by school and its demands, even when the children are not physically in a public school.

Holt wrote an article in 1983 for the educators' journal *Phi Delta Kappan* magazine, titled: "Schools and Homeschoolers: A Fruitful Partnership." Much of his thinking in this last chapter is reproduced in that essay that clearly shows there's much more to be gained by having public schools work with homeschoolers than by ignoring, co-opting, or fighting them. As Susannah Sheffer notes in her collection of Holt's letters, *A Life Worth Living*:

> During the last years of his life he was collecting material and making notes for a file marked "School Reform Book." Clearly he still believed he had something to say on the subject. Even though he had ostensibly given up the idea of reforming schools years before, even though he had made conscious resolutions to stop trying to change that which he could not change, he apparently never quite lost the hope that if shown the way more clearly we would do what needed to be done.[3]

Holt died in 1985, too soon to see homeschooling flourish to the point where it would be featured on the front pages of *Time*, *Newsweek*, the *New York Times*, and as a regular "back-to-school" topic on network television. I think John knew that the homeschooling movement would grow no matter what schools or politicians did to stop it, but I don't think he knew how quickly it would be accepted by the general population. For instance, a Gallup poll in 1985 asked whether homeschooling was a good or bad thing for the nation. Seventy-three percent of respondents disapproved. By September 1997, a poll showed that the disapproval rating had fallen to 59 percent.[4] When the pollsters asked if homeschoolers should be able to receive public school services, such as special-education services, driver's education, extracurricular activities, and teacher-development programs, support ranged from 72 percent to 92 percent. When asked if homeschoolers "should take all the state and national assessment tests that public school students are required to take" 92 percent of those surveyed agreed.

Homeschoolers need to take note of this public attitude and go into these situations with their eyes open: If homeschoolers wish to work with the schools, then they will be judged like the schools, which limits the possibilities for experimentation and exploration at home. As this issue becomes more openly discussed, and the significant shades of gray that color the issue become more distinct, I hope we'll see, as John wrote earlier, that homeschooling's strength lies in it being completely different from public school, and not that homeschooling is just public school done better. Homeschooling has grown successfully in the past twenty years without any open support from the education establishment; and, as this survey indicates, as homeschooling enters a new phase of growing public acceptance, it needs to be much more savvy about the costs and benefits of having schools work *on* them, not *with* them.

Furthermore, the pollsters framed their questions as if homeschooling is simply another form of public schooling, which causes considerable confusion. By not mentioning that home schools are regulated like private schools in many states, and are therefore exempt from state and national curricula and tests, the pollsters gloss over issues of great importance. For instance, it has been well documented that private and home schools nonetheless produce high achievement among their young regardless of the lack of national tests and the wide variety of curricula, methods, and philosophies being used. This is a vital point, and one that gets lost in all the talk about high standards, testing, and accountability. As Holt points out so well at the end of this book, schooling isn't everything. Spike Milligan, the late British comedian, puts it this way: "Education isn't everything. For a start, it isn't an elephant."

Our children suspect that school is not as relevant to their futures as officials claim, that other factors determine success far more than test scores, and so, as noted earlier in this book, a crisis of disillusionment has been brewing. Just as children in Japan are simply refusing to attend school, so are children in the United States, despite increasing social pressure to do well in school.

John Amos Comenius (1592–1679) is sometimes called "the father of modern education" for his work, four hundred years ago, at making school relevant and interesting to children (does this reform ever take hold?) and for his motto, "To teach everyone, everything, perfectly." This may have seemed reasonable in the seventeenth century, when few people read and the store of human knowledge seemed finite. This vision seems far-fetched now in a world where what we know and don't know increases exponentially every time the Internet adds a new Web page, a new book is published, a new species is discovered or an old one extinguished, or a new image is beamed back to our planet from our space probes. Yet our schools cling to Comenius's notion dearly.

Homeschoolers are creating a new ethos for education: "To learn everything one needs or wants to know when one needs or wants it." As John Holt and I have tried to demonstrate throughout this book, such an attitude does not preclude high standards, assessments, or adult involvement. What it does is put the individual learner in a new relationship to those elements, a relationship built by emphasizing personal commitment to learning, receiving useful feedback, and patience. As I noted at the beginning of this book, one *can* train football players and horses with invective and pain, but it is also equally possible to train them without resorting to these techniques, and the benefits of doing less physical and emotional harm during the learning process have a long-term value not just to an individual, but to society at large.

Teachers like John Holt, John Gagliardi, and Monty Roberts are considered to be "squishy" by our current political and school leaders, despite their significant achievements in their fields. Unlike these three leaders, our current educational leadership has a very limited amount of kindness and patience to dispense, preferring the stick to the carrot. But as Holt and many, many other teachers, parents, and researchers have noted, among the problems with this pedagogy is that it produces a highly superficial understanding and grasp of the curricula for most students. To paraphrase Holt, in this sort of pedagogy the only difference between a good student and a bad student is that a good student is careful not to forget what he or she studied until *after* the test. Holt also observed and detailed in his first and most popular book, *How Children Fail*, that fear impedes true learning—learning that lasts beyond test taking, and which is used and built upon by people throughout their lives. Nonetheless, we continue to raise the level of fear of failure in our schools as the best means for creating "good citizens," which is the ultimate legal reason that society compels children to attend school. However, homeschooling proves that good citizens can be nurtured outside of school and in a variety of ways that school is increasingly opposed to.

No matter what type of education one consumes, there is no guarantee that one has actually learned it, despite tests passed and degrees earned. Adults continually demand that children learn facts and information that they themselves do not use or know, which adds to the credibility gap we encounter between school learning and real life. For example, in an oft-repeated psychology experiment, the Bill of Rights is displayed on street corners but with no identifying headings, simply the body of the text. Passersby are asked to put their signatures on the document, but the vast majority of adults scoff at this document as something dangerous and they refuse to sign. A documentary film titled *A Private Universe* made a stir a few years ago; it shows an interviewer asking recent graduates from Harvard University if they could explain why the seasons change on earth; none could do so satisfactorily. A 1993 Gallup poll noted that one in seven adults couldn't identify the United States on an unmarked map; one in four couldn't find the Pacific Ocean. The *Christian Science Monitor* reported in 1996 that only 6 percent of Americans know the name of the chief justice of the United States; 46 percent didn't know the name of House Speaker Newt Gingrich. An editorial writer for the *Boston Globe* recently took the new statewide high school graduation exam, MCAS; he passed the verbal part but flunked the math part. He concluded that this proved the test was fair, because he has long known that he's poor in math. However, he didn't point out that he would not have been hired to write for the *Boston Globe* if he didn't have a high school diploma—which he wouldn't if he flunked MCAS—nor that his failure to remember and grasp high school mathematics has not prevented him from being an intellectual, an able writer, and a "good citizen." The assumption that people become good citizens, or well-rounded individuals, simply by passing a battery of tests in a school system is a false assumption.

While the state has made it a goal to ensure all its children are educated, the state is constitutionally prohibited from dictating any particular way of educating children, thus allowing for alternatives to school, ranging from private parochial schools to home schools. However, education is changing the definition of citizenship with very little debate. John Holt, in an unpublished talk to students in 1971, observed:

> Thomas Jefferson felt that education was needed to help become and be what he called citizens. By "citizens" he did not mean what most of us mean when we call ourselves "taxpayers" or "consumers." A citizen was not someone who worried about how to "fit into society." He was a maker and shaper of society. He held the highest office in the Republic; public servants were his *servants*, not his bosses and rulers.

Being a citizen seems to mean merely being an "employed consumer" today. It is popular among today's educational policy makers to refer to children as "resources" to be developed, rather than as individuals to be nurtured. It is hard to imagine how teachers and students are expected to become citizens who "make and shape society" when so much of their time together is spent trying to "make and shape" the kids to fit the demands of twelve to sixteen or more years of school.

Comenius, as Ivan Illich points out, was also an alchemist. His pursuit of the philosopher's stone, the secret that would change lead into gold, is now considered a futile pursuit, yet it persisted for centuries and tantalized thousands with its promise. Likewise with Comenius's dream "To teach everyone, everything, perfectly," which has seduced many of the best thinkers in politics and education. It is a dream to forge a national identity based on the shared experience of being forced to compete for grades to learn the same thing, at the same time, in the same way. This vision of schooling, as Holt points out in his books written before *Teach Your Own*, is not a good idea gone bad, but a crazy idea from the start. We learn at different rates, in different ways, and for different reasons. It is also rather inaccurate to claim that the experience of compulsory schooling in Beverly Hills, California, is the same as that of students experiencing compulsory schooling in Bronx, New York!

There are other shared experiences and projects we can emphasize and employ to create a national identity instead of our current unequal distribution of opportunity based on schooling. One can argue that television, the Internet, and other mass media have usurped the role of forging a national identity from our schools; but I take heart from the many families I've met who minimize the importance of mass media in their lives and who make other efforts to raise their children into good citizens. I know adults who share their political and charitable activism with children, inviting children and their parents to be with them as they engage in all sorts of valuable civic activities. I know of painters, potters, dramatists, writers, poets, musicians, and other artists who let children observe them create; some also tutor or involve children directly in creative actions. There are general contractors, electricians, lawyers, preachers, librarians, professors, and many other professionals who bring their children to work with them as an integral part of their education, and not just because it is the only way they could manage childcare for a certain day. All sorts of team and individual sports could be made more widely available to children, and they can be played throughout the school day, not just after school. Creating more opportunities for adults and children to share work and to talk about their lives together, creating more spaces and activities where children can explore and play in their own ways without adults directing or controlling all their interactions (but nearby to help when questions arise or disputes break out); these are but some of the ways that our lives can be shared outside of school.

Despite homeschooling's considerable growth and impact on the public's mind over the past twenty years, most school officials appear determined to fight it or ignore it. The National Education Association, the national Parent Teacher Association, and the National Association of Elementary School Principals continue to publicly oppose homeschooling, as they have for years. But they are not in step with public opinion, changing technologies, changing family and work schedules, nor the long and distinguished body of research that challenges the typical way we teach and learn in schools. Fortunately, you don't have to wait for these organizations or for the schools to change to help your own child learn now: You can teach your own. ♪

Appendix A
Selected Bibliography

EDUCATION AND SOCIETY

Appleton, Matthew. *A Free Range Childhood: Self-Regulation at Summerhill School.* Foundation for Educational Renewal, 2001.

Arons, Stephen. *Compelling Belief: The Culture of American Schooling.* University of Massachusetts Press, 1986.

Axline, Virginia. *Dibs in Search of Self.* Ballantine, 1990.

Berg, Ivar. *Education and Jobs: The Great Training Robbery.* Praeger, 1970.

Berry, Wendell. *Home Economics.* North Point Press, 1987.

_____. *Life Is a Miracle: An Essay Against Modern Superstition.* Counterpoint Press, 2001.

Betts, Roland. *Acting Out.* Little, Brown, 1978.

Brown, Jerry. *Dialogues.* Berkeley Hills, 1998.

Cardozo, Philip. *The Nature of the Judicial Process.* Yale University Press, 1921.

Cayley, David. *Ivan Illich: In Conversation.* House of Anansi, 1992.

Dennison, George. *The Lives of Children: The Story of the First Street School.* Heinemann/Boynton/Cook, 1999.

Elias, Stephen, and Susan Levinkind. *Legal Research: How to Find and Understand the Law.* Nolo Press, 2001.

Fader, Daniel. *The Naked Children*. Heinemann/Boynton/Cook, 1996.

Gatto, John Taylor. *A Different Kind of Teacher*. Berkeley Hills, 2000.

_____. *Dumbing Us Down: The Hidden Curriculum of Compulsory Schooling*. New Society Press, 2002.

_____. *The Exhausted School: Bending the Bars of Traditional Education*. Berkeley Hills Books, 2002.

_____. *The Underground History of American Education: A Schoolteacher's Intimate Investigation into the Problem of Modern Schooling*. Oxford Village Press, 2001.

Goodman, Paul. *Drawing the Line: The Political Essays of Paul Goodman*. Free Life Editions, 1977.

_____. *Growing Up Absurd*. Random House, 1960.

Greenberg, Daniel. *Free at Last: Sudbury Valley School*. Sudbury Valley School Press, 1987.

Herndon, James. *How to Survive In Your Native Land*. Simon & Schuster, 1971.

_____. *The Way It Spozed to Be*. Heinemann/Boynton/Cook, 1997.

Hirsch, E. D. *What Every First Grader Needs to Know*. Delta, 1991.

Holt, John Caldwell. *Escape from Childhood*. Holt Associates, 1981.

_____. *Freedom and Beyond*. Heinemann/Boynton/Cook, 1995

_____. *How Children Fail*. Perseus, 1995.

_____. *How Children Learn*. Perseus, 1995.

_____. *Instead of Education*. Sentient Publications, 2003.

_____. *Learning All the Time*. Perseus, 1990.

_____. *Never Too Late*. Perseus, 1991.

_____. *The Underachieving School*. Pittman, 1969.

_____. *What Do I Do Monday?* Heinemann/Boynton/Cook, 1995.

Illich, Ivan. *Deschooling Society*. Boyars, 1999.

_____. *In the Mirror of the Past: Lectures and Addresses, 1978–1990*. Boyars, 1992.

_____. *Shadow Work*. Boyars, 1981.

_____. *Tools for Conviviality*. Boyars, 2001.

Kohl, Herbert. *Growing with Your Children*. Little, Brown, 1978.

Lipson, Greta. *Everyday Law for Young Citizens*. Good Apple, 1988.

Mercogliano, Chris. *Making It Up as We Go Along: The Story of the Albany Free School*. Heinemann/Boynton/Cook, 1998.

Postman, Neil. *The Disappearance of Childhood*. Delacorte, 1982.

Rembar, Charles. *The End of Obscenity*. HarperTrade, 1986.

Salisbury, Harrison. *Travels Around America*. Walker & Co., 1976.

Sarason, Seymour. *Parental Involvement and the Political Principle: Why the Existing Governance Structure of Schools Should Be Abolished.* Jossey-Bass, 1995.

Sheffer, Susannah, ed. *A Life Worth Living: Selected Letters of John Holt.* The Ohio State University Press, 1990.

Silberman, Charles. *Crisis in the Classroom.* Random House, 1970.

Sizer, T., and N. Sizer. *The Children Are Watching.* Beacon Press, 1999.

Smith, Frank. *Essays into Literacy.* Heinemann, 1983.

_____. *Insult to Intelligence.* Arbor House, 1986.

_____. *Joining the Literacy Club: Further Essays into Education.* Heinemann, 1988.

_____. *Reading without Nonsense.* Teacher's College Press, 1997.

Spring, Joel. *Education and the Rise of the Corporate State.* Beacon Press, 1972.

HUMAN PSYCHOLOGY AND DEVELOPMENT

Armstrong, Thomas. *In Their Own Way: Discovering and Encouraging Your Child's Personal Learning Style.* Tarcher, 1988.

_____. *The Myth of the A.D.D. Child: 50 Ways to Improve Your Child's Behavior and Attention Span Without Drugs, Labels, or Coercion.* Houghton Mifflin, 1997.

Bateson, Gregory. *Steps to an Ecology of Mind.* University of Chicago Press, 2000.

Breggin, Peter. *Talking Back to Ritalin: What Doctors Aren't Telling You about Stimulants and ADHD.* Perseus, 2001.

Csikszentmihalyi, Mihaly. *Flow: The Psychology of Optimal Experience.* HarperCollins, 1991.

Goleman, Daniel. *Working with Emotional Intelligence.* Bantam, 1998.

Goodman, Paul. *Nature Heals: Psychological Essays.* Free Life Editions, 1977.

Greenspan, Stanley. *The Challenging Child: Understanding, Raising, and Enjoying the Five "Difficult" Types of Children.* Perseus, 1996.

_____. *The Four-thirds Solution: Solving the Childcare Crisis in America Today.* Perseus, 2000.

Hayes, Lenore. *Homeschooling the Child with ADD (or Other Special Needs).* Prima, 2002.

Healy, Jane. *Failure to Connect: How Computers Affect Our Children's Minds—for Better and Worse.* Simon & Schuster, 1998.

Kohn, Alfie. *No Contest: The Case Against Competition*. Mariner, 1992.

————. *Punished by Rewards: The Trouble with Gold Stars, Incentive Plans, A's, Praise, and Other Bribes*. Houghton Mifflin, 1993.

————. *The Schools Our Children Deserve*. Mariner, 2000.

Langer, Ellen. *Mindfulness*. Addison-Wesley, 1989.

————. *The Power of Mindful Learning*. Addison-Wesley, 1997.

Liedloff, Jean. *The Continuum Concept: Allowing Human Nature to Work Successfully*. Addison-Wesley, 1985.

Sacks, Peter. *Standardized Minds: The High Price of America's Testing Culture and What We Can Do to Change It*. Perseus, 1999.

Schrag, Peter, and Diane Divoky. *The Myth of the Hyperactive Child*. Pantheon, 1975.

Shinn, Millicent. *The Biography of a Baby*. Addison-Wesley, 1985.

Stallibrass, Alison. *The Self-Respecting Child: Development through Spontaneous Play*. Addison-Wesley, 1989.

Tizard, Barbara, and Martin Hughes. *Young Children Learning*. Harvard University Press, 1984.

Winnicott, D. W. *Winnicott on the Child*. Perseus, 2002.

HOMESCHOOLING

Albert, David. *And the Skylark Sings with Me: Adventures in Homeschooling and Community-based Education*. New Society Press/Holt Associates, 1999.

————. *Homeschooling and the Voyage of Self-Discovery*. Common Courage Press, 2003.

Blumenfeld, Samuel. *Homeschooling: A Parents Guide to Teaching Children*. Citadel, 1997.

Brown, Teri, and Elissa Wahl. *Christian Unschooling: Growing Your Children in the Freedom of Christ*. Champion Press, 2001.

Colfax, David, and Micki Colfax. *Hard Times in Paradise: An American Family's Struggle to Carve Out a Homestead in California's Redwood Mountains*. Warner, 1992.

————. *Homeschooling for Excellence*. Warner, 1988.

Dobson, Linda. *The Art of Education: Reclaiming Your Family, Community, and Self*. Holt Associates, 1997.

————. *Homeschoolers' Success Stories: 15 Adults and 12 Young People Share the Impact That Homeschooling Has Made on Their Lives*. Prima, 2000.

————. *The Homeschooling Book of Answers*. Prima, 2002.

Duffy, Cathy. *Christian Home Educators' Curriculum Manual.* Grove Publishing, 2000.

Gold, LauraMaery, and Joan Zielinski. *Homeschool Your Child for Free: More Than 1,200 Smart, Effective, and Practical Resources for Home Education on the Internet and Beyond.* Prima, 2000.

Griffith, Mary. *The Homeschooling Handbook.* Prima, 1999.

_____. *The Unschooling Handbook: How to Use the Whole World as Your Child's Classroom.* Prima, 1998.

Guterson, David. *Family Matters: Why Homeschooling Makes Sense.* Harcourt Brace Jovanovich, 1992.

Hayes, Lenore. *Homeschooling the Child with ADD (or Other Special Needs).* Prima, 2002.

Hern, Matt, ed. *Deschooling Our Lives.* New Society Publishers, 1996.

Holt, John, ed. *Growing without Schooling: A Record of a Grassroots Movement.* Holt Associates, 1999.

Hood, Mary. *The Relaxed Home School.* Ambleside Educational Press, 1994.

Hunt, Jan. *The Natural Child: Parenting from the Heart.* New Society Publishers, 2001.

Kaseman, Larry, and Susan Kaseman. *Taking Charge through Homeschooling.* Koshkonong Press, 1990.

Leistico, Agnes. *I Learn Better by Teaching Myself* and *Still Teaching Ourselves.* Holt Associates, 1997.

Leppert, Mary, and Mike Leppert. *The Homeschooling Almanac.* Prima, 2001.

Llewellyn, Grace, ed. *Freedom Challenge: African American Homeschoolers.* Lowry House, 1996.

_____, and Amy Silver. *Guerrilla Learning: How to Give Your Kids a Real Education with or without School.* John Wiley & Sons, 2001.

Macaulay, Susan Schaeffer. *For the Children's Sake: Foundations of Education for Home and School.* Crossway, 1984.

McKee, Alison. *Homeschooling Our Children, Unschooling Ourselves.* Bittersweet House, 2002.

Meighan, Roland. *Learning Unlimited: The Home-based Education Files.* Educational Heretics Press, 2001.

_____. *The Next Learning System and Why Homeschoolers Are Trailblazers.* Educational Heretics Press, 1997.

Moore, Raymond, and Dorothy Moore. *Better Late Than Early: A New Approach to Your Child's Education.* Reader's Digest Press, 1989.

_____. *School Can Wait.* Brigham Young University Press, 1989.

_____. *The Successful Homeschool Family Handbook: A Creative and Stress-Free Approach to Homeschooling.* Thomas Nelson, 1994.

Orr, Tamra. *A Parent's Guide to Home Schooling.* Parent's Guide Press, 2002.

Pride, Mary. *The Big Book of Home Learning.* Alpha Omega, 1999.

Priesnitz, Wendy. *Challenging Assumptions in Education: From Institutionalized Education to a Learning Society.* The Alternate Press, 2000.

Ransom, Marsha. *The Complete Idiot's Guide to Homeschooling.* Alpha Books, 2001.

Reed, Donn. *The Home School Source Book.* Brook Farm Books, 2001.

Sheffer, Susannah. *Writing Because We Love To: Homeschoolers at Work.* Heinemann/Boynton/Cook, 1992.

Wade, Ted. *The Homeschool Manual.* Gazelle, 2000.

Wallace, Nancy. *Better Than School.* Larson, 1983.

_____. *Child's Work: Taking Children's Choices Seriously.* Holt Associates, 1991.

Wise, Jessie, and Susan Wise Bauer. *The Well-Trained Mind: A Guide to Classical Education at Home.* Norton, 1999.

Worldbook International. *Typical Course of Study, K–12.* 4788 Highway 3775, Fort Worth, TX, 76116, 1–800–967–5325.

HOMESCHOOLED TEENAGERS AND COLLEGE ADMISSIONS

Bear, John. *Bear's Guide to Non-Traditional College Degrees: How to Get the Degree You Want.* Rev. ed. Ten Speed Press, 1997.

Cohen, Cafi. *And What about College? How Homeschooling Leads to Admissions to the Best Colleges and Universities.* Holt Associates, 2000.

_____. *Homeschoolers' College Admissions Handbook: Preparing 12- to 18-Year-Olds for Success in the College of Their Choice.* Prima, 2000.

_____. *Homeschooling the Teen Years: Your Complete Guide to Successfully Homeschooling the 13- to 18-Year-Old.* Prima, 2000.

Heuer, Loretta. *The Homeschooler's Guide to Portfolios and Transcripts.* Arco, 2000.

Llewellyn, Grace. *Real Lives: Eleven Teenagers Who Don't Go to School.* Lowry House, 1993.

_____. *The Teenage Liberation Handbook: How to Quit School and Get a Real Life and Education.* Lowry House, 1998.

Sheffer, Susannah. *A Sense of Self: Listening to Homeschooled Adolescent Girls.* Heinemann/Boynton/Cook, 1995.

Wood, Danielle. *The Uncollege Alternative: Your Guide to Incredible Careers and Amazing Adventures Outside College*. ReganBooks, 2000.

LEARNING COOPERATIVES AND COMMUNITIES

Ellis, William, et al. *A Guidebook for Creating Learning Communities*. Coalition for Self Learning, 2002.

Houk, Katherine. *Creating a Cooperative Learning Center: An Idea-Book for Homeschooling Families*. Longview, 2000.

Miller, Ron, ed. *Creating Learning Communities: Models, Resources, and New Ways of Thinking about Teaching and Learning*. Foundation for Educational Renewal, 2001.

Pearse, Innes, and Lucy Crocker. *The Peckham Experiment: A Study of the Living Structure of Society*. George Allen & Unwin, 1947.

Stallibrass, Alison. *Being Me and Also Us: Lessons from the Peckham Experiment*. Scottish Academic Press, 1989.

SIMPLE LIVING AND HOMESCHOOLING

Allee, Judith, and Melissa Morgan. *Educational Travel on a Shoestring*. Harold Shaw, 2002.

_____. *Homeschooling on a Shoe String*. Harold Shaw, 1999.

Dominguez, Joe, and Vicki Robin. *Your Money or Your Life: Transforming Your Relationship with Money and Achieving Financial Independence*. Viking, 1992.

Fogler, Michael. *Un-Jobbing: The Adult Liberation Handbook*. Free Choice Press, 1997.

SCHOLARLY BOOKS ABOUT HOMESCHOOLING

Mayberry, Knowles, et al. *Home Schooling: Parents as Educators*. Corwin Press, 1995.

Ray, Brian. *Worldwide Guide to Homeschooling: Facts and Stats on the Benefits of Home School*. Broadman & Holman, 2002.

Stephens, Mitchell. *Kingdom of Children: Culture and Controversy in the Homeschooling Movement*. Princeton University Press, 2001.

Thomas, Alan. *Educating Children at Home*. Continuum, 1999.

Van Galen, Jane, and Mary Anne Pitman, eds. *Home Schooling: Political, Historical, and Pedagogical Perspectives*. Ablex, 1991.

PERIODICALS

Compleat Mother, 5703 Hillcrest, Richmond, IL, 60071. 815–678–0880, *www.compleatmother.com.*

Education Now, 113 Arundel Drive, Bramcote Hills, Nottingham, UK, NG9 3FQ.

The Education Revolution, 417 Roslyn Road, Roslyn Heights, NY, 11577, *www.educationrevolution.org.*

Empathic Parenting: Journal of the Canadian Society for the Prevention of Cruelty to Children, 356 1st Street, P.O. Box 700, Midland, Ontario, Canada, L4R 4P4, *www.empathicparenting.org.*

FAIRTEST, 342 Broadway, Cambridge, MA, 02139, 617–864–4810, Fax 617–497–2224, *www.fairtest.org.*

Home Education Magazine, P.O. Box 1083, Tonasket, WA, 98855, 800–236–3278, *www.home-ed-magazine.com.*

Home Educator's Family Times, P.O. Box 708, Gray, ME, 04039, 207–657–2800, *www.HomeEducator.com/FamilyTimes.*

Home School Researcher newsletter, National Home Education Research Institute (NHERI), P.O. Box 13939, Salem, OR, 97309–1939, *www.nheri.org.*

Homeschooling Today, P.O. Box 1608, Fort Collins, CO, 80522–1608, 970–493–2716, *www.homeschooltoday.com.*

Life Learning: The International Magazine of Self-Directed Learning, P.O. Box 112, Niagra Falls, NY, 14304–0112, 800–215–9574, *www.lifelearningmagazine.com.*

The LINK News, 587 North Ventu Park Road, Suite F–911, Newbury Park, CA, 91320, *www.homeschoolnewslink.com.*

Moore Report International, Box 1, Camas, WA, 98607, 360–835–5500, *www.moorefoundation.com.*

Mothering, P.O. Box 1690, Santa Fe, NM, 87504, *www.mothering.com.*

The Old Schoolhouse, P.O. Box 185, Cool, CA, 95614, *www.thehomeschoolmagazine.com.*

Paths of Learning, P.O. Box 328, Brandon, VT, 05733–0328, 800–639–4122, *www.pathsoflearning.net.*

Practical Homeschooling, P.O. Box 1190, Fenton, MO, 63026–1190, *www.Home-school.com.*

The Teaching Home, P.O. Box 20219, Portland, OR, 97220–0219, *www.teachinghome.com.*

Appendix B

Correspondence Schools and Curriculum Suppliers

A Beka Book, P.O. Box 19100, Pensacola, FL, 32523–9160, 1–800–874–BEKA, *www.ABEKA.com*.

Alpha Omega Publications, 300 North McKerney Avenue, Chandler, AZ, 85226, 800–622–3070, *www.home-schooling.com*.

American School, 2200 East 170th Street, Lansing, IL, 60438–9909, 800–531–9268 (high school only).

Brigham Young University–Department of Independent Study, P.O. Box 21514, 206 Harman Continuing Education Building, Provo, UT, 84602, 800–914–8931, *indstudy@byu.edu*, *www.ce.byu.edu*.

Calvert School, 10713 Gilroy Road, Suite B, Hunt Valley, MD, 21031, 410–785–3400, 888–487–4652, *www.calvertschool.org*.

Christian Liberty Academy, 502 West Euclid Avenue, Arlington Heights, IL, 60004, *www.homeschools.org*.

Clonlara Distance Learning Program, 1289 Jewett Street, Ann Arbor, MI, 48104, 734–769–4511, *www.clonlara.org*.

Core Curriculum, 14503 South Tamiani Trail, North Port, FL, 34287, *www.core-curriculum.com*.

Educators Publishing Service, 31 Smith Place, Cambridge, MA, 02138, 617–547–6706, 800–435–7728, *www.epsbooks.com*.

Hewitt Homeschooling Resources, P.O. Box 9, Washougal, WA, 98671, 360–835–8708, *www.hewitthomeschooling.com*.

Kolbe Academy, 1600 F Street, Napa, CA, 94559, 707–256–4306, 702–255–6499, *dayinfo@kolbe.org, www.kolbe.org.*

Laurel Spring School, 1002 East Ojai Avenue, Ojai, CA, 93024–1440, *www.laurelsprings.com.*

Living Heritage Academy, P.O. Box 299000, Lewisville, TX, 75029, *livingheritageacademy@schooloftomorrow.com.*

McGuffey Academy, P.O. Box 109, Lakemont, GA, 30552, 706–782–7709, *McGuffey2@juno.com.*

The Moore Foundation, Box 1, Camas, WA, 98607, 360–835–5500, *www.moorefoundation.com.*

National Book Company, P.O. Box 8795, 333 SW Park Avenue, Portland, OR, 97207–8795, 503–228–6345, *www.halcyon.org.*

Oak Meadow School, P.O. Box 740, Putney, VT, 05346, 802–387–2021, *www.oakweadow.com.*

Our Lady of Victory School, 103 East 10th Avenue, Post Falls, ID, 83854, 208–773–7265, *www.olvs.org.*

Phoenix Special Programs, 1717 West Northern Avenue, Suite 104, Phoenix, AZ, 85021, 800–426–4952, 602–674–5555, *www.phoenixacademies.org* (high school).

Rod & Staff Publishers, P.O. Box 3, Highway 172, Crockett, KY, 41413, 606–522–4348, *www.anabaptists.org/ras/.*

Seton School Home Study, 1350 Progress Avenue, Front Royal, VA, 22630, 540–636–9990, *www.setonhome.org.*

Appendix C

Helpful Private Schools

*Private schools enrolling or helping homeschoolers
in various ways (curricula, legal help, support)*

Abbott Loop Christian Center, 2626 Abbott Raod, Anchorage, AK, 99507.

Bay Shore School, P.O. Box 13038, Long Beach, CA, 90803, 310–434–3940, *www.bayshoreeducational.com*, *bayshoredu@aol.com*.

Cascade Canyon School, 2626 Sir Francis Drake Boulevard, Fairfax, CA, 94930, 415–459–3464, *cascade@marin.k12.ca.us*.

Clonlara Distance Learning Program, 1289 Jewett Street, Ann Arbor, MI, 48104, 734–769–4511, *www.clonlara.org*.

Cooperative Learning Center, 60 Peik Hall, University of Minnesota, Minneapolis, MN, 55455, 612–624–7031, *www.clcrc.com*.

Dayspring Christian Academy, P.O. Drawer 909, Blacksburg, VA, 24063–0909, 540–552–7777, *www.dayspringchristianacad.org*.

Family Academy, 146 SW 153rd Street, #290, Seattle, WA, 98166.

Grassroots Free School, 2458 Grassroots Way, Tallahassee, FL, 32301, 904–656–3629.

HCL Boston School, P.O. Box 2920, Big Bear City, CA, 92314, 909–585–7188.

Headwaters School, 139 Madison 3605, Pettigrew, AR, 72752, *www.headwaters-school.org* (homeschooler-run community school).

The Learning Community, Inc., Great Falls, VA, 22066, 703–759–2010.

The Learning Community Network, 9085 Flamepool Way, Columbia, MD, 21045–2901, *www.tlcn.org*.

Mount Vernon Language Academy, 184 Vine Street, Murray, UT, 84107, 801–266–5521.

Newbridge School, 1512 Pearl Street, Santa Monica, CA, 90405, 310–452–8111, *www.newbridgeschool.org, biederman@hotmail.com.*

Puget Sound Community School, 1310 North 45th, P.O. Box 31014, Seattle, WA, 98103, 206–524–0916, *www.pscs.org.*

The Santa Fe Community School, P.O. Box 289 (L), Torreon, NM, 87061, 866–703–9375.

Sidney Ledson School, 220 Duncan Mill Road, Suite 7, North York, Ontario, Canada, M3B 3J5, 416–447–5355.

Upattinas School, 429 Greenridge Road, Glenmoore, PA, 19343, *upattinas.school@upattinas.org, www.upattinas.org.*

The Venice Community School, 31191 Road 180, Exeter, CA, 93292, 559–592–4999.

Appendix D

Homeschooling Organizations

NATIONAL HOMESCHOOL GROUPS

American Homeschool Association (AHA), P.O. Box 218, Tonasket, WA, 98855, *www.home-ed-magazine.com/AHA/aha.html.*
Home School Legal Defense Association (HSLDA), 1 Patrick Henry Circle, Purcellville, VA, 20132, 540–338–5600, *www.hslda.org.*
National Home Education Network (NHEN), P.O. Box 41067, Long Beach, CA, 90853, *www.nhen.org.*

STATE OR LOCAL GROUPS

Lists of organizations are usually out of date the minute they're made because lists don't move but people do. Further, there are so many state and local homeschooling support groups that a Web search, or book or periodical research will inevitably turn up new listings. So don't use this list as your sole resource, use it as a networking tool. Begin with one contact until you locate the needed information or people you trust.

Statewide groups are likely to have information about state laws or regulations, and about conferences, along with literature for new homeschoolers. Other groups are local support groups that are likely to have meetings and activities. Both state and local groups may have newsletters. Try getting in touch with a state group even if it's far away from your home area, as many state groups can refer you to families, or smaller support groups, in your immediate vicinity.

Alabama

Dayspring Academy, 1293 County Road, 524 Verbena, 36091, 205–755–8112.

East Lake UMC Academy, 6206 Whipoorwill Drive, Pinson, 205–680–6881, *www.teachus.com.*

Home Educators of Alabama Round Table (HEART), P.O. Box 1091, Huntsville, 35807, 205–933–2571.

Alaska

Alaska Parent and Home Educators Association (APHEA), P.O. Box 141764, Anchorage, 99514, *www.aphea.org.*

Homeschoolers of Cordova, P.O. Box 782, Cordova, 99574, 907–424–3943.

Sitka Home Education Association, 506 Verstovia Street, Sitka, 99835, 907–747–1483.

Arizona

Arizona Families for Home Education, P.O. Box 2035, Chandler, 85244–2035, 800–929–3927.

SPICE, 10414 West Mulberry Drive, Avondale, 85323, 602–877–3642.

TELAO Home Educators, 6941 North Polaris Place, Tucson, 85741, 502–531–1047.

Arkansas

The Education Alliance, 414 South Pulaski, Suite 2, Little Rock, 72201, 501–375–7000, *www.familycouncil.org.*

Home Educators of Arkansas (HEAR), P.O. Box 192455, Little Rock, 72219, 501–513–2618, *coalarkparents@yahoo.com, www.geocities.com/heartland/garden/4555/hear.html.*

California

California Homeschool Network, P.O. Box 55485, Hayward, 94545, 800–327–5339, *www.cahomeschoolnet.org.*

Home School Association of California, P.O. Box 868, Davis, 95617, 888–HSC–4440, *www.hsc.org.*

Homeschooling Cooperative of Sacramento, P.O. Box 217, Rio Linda, 95673.

Humboldt Homeschoolers, 477 Crosby Road, Ferndale, 95536, 707–786–4157.

Mindful Education, P.O. Box 4606, Davis, 95617, 530–759–1106.

Riverside Area Home Learners, c/o Leslie Shores, 3356 Freeport Drive, Corona, 92881, 909–272–6132.

Sonoma County Homeschoolers Association, 1260 Slater Street, Sebastopol, 95404, 707–571–0086.

SPICE, P.O. Box 282, Wilton, 95693, 916–687–7053.

Tri-City Homeschoolers, 36551 Mulberry Street, Newark, 94560, 510–790–3871.

Yosemite Area Homeschoolers, P.O. Box 74, Midpines, 95345, 209–742–6802.

Colorado

Christian Home Educators of Colorado (CHEC), 10431 South Parker Road, Parker, 80134, 720–842–4852, *www.chec.org.*

Secular Homeschool Support Group, 21135 Warriors Path Drive, Peyton, 80831, 719–749–0200.

West River Unschoolers, 779 Jasmine Court, Grand Junction, 81506.

Connecticut

Connecticut Home Educators Association, P.O. Box 242, New Hartford, 06057, 203–781–8569, *www.cthomeschoolers.com.*

Unschoolers' Unlimited, 22 Wildrose Avenue, Guilford, 06437, 203–458–7402, *www.borntoexplore.org/unschool.*

Delaware

Delaware Home Education Association, P.O. Box 268, Hartly, 19953, *www.dheadonline.org.*

Tri-State Homeschoolers Association, P.O. Box 7193, Newark, 19714, 302–368–4217.

District of Columbia

Bolling Area Home Educators, P.O. Box 8401, Washington, 20336.

Florida

Florida Parent-Educators Association, P.O. Box 50685, Jacksonville Beach, 32240, 877–275–3732, *www.fpea.com.*

Teaching Our Own in Palm Beach County, P.O. Box 426, Boynton Beach, 33425, 561–547–5531.

Georgia

Atlanta Alternative Education Network, 1586 Rainier Falls Drive, Atlanta, 30329, 404–636–6348.

Georgians for Freedom in Education, 209 Cobb Street, Palmetto, 30268–1235, 404–463–3719.

Harvest Home Educators, P.O. Box 1551, Clarksville, 30523, 770–455–0449, *www.harvesthomeeducators.com.*

Home Education Information Resources, P.O. Box 2111, Rosewell, 30077, 404–681–HEIR, *www.heir.org.*

Hawaii

Christian Homeschoolers of Hawaii, 91–824 Oama Street, Ewa Beach, 96706, 808–689–6398.

Hawaii Homeschool Association, P.O. Box 893513, Mililani, 96789, 808–944–3339, *www.hawaiihomeschoolassociation.org.*

Idaho

Family Unschoolers Network, 1809 North 7th Street, Boise, 83702, 208–345–2703.

Home Educators of Idaho, 3618 Pine Hill Drive, Coeur d'Alene, 83815, 208–667–2778.

Illinois

HOUSE, c/o Teresa Sneade, 2508 East 22nd Place, Sauk Village, 60411, 708–758–7374, *www.illinoishouse.org.*

Illinois Christian Home Educators, P.O. Box 775, Harvard, IL, 60033, 815–943–7883, *www.iche.org.*

Jewish Homeschool Association of Greater Chicago, 773–764–5137, *www.bnoshenya.org.*

Indiana

Families Learning Together, c/o Jill Whelan, 1714 East 51st Street, Indianapolis, 46205, 317–255–9298.

Hamilton County Homeschoolers, 317–776–0965, *www.expage.com/ hchomeschoolers.*

Indiana Association of Home Educators, 8106 Madison Avenue, Indianapolis, 46227, 317–859–1202, *www.inhomeeducators.org.*

Iowa

Iowans Dedicated to Educational Alternatives (IDEA), c/o Katy Diltz, 3296 Linn-Buchanan Road, Coggon, 52218, 319–224–3675, *home.plutonium.net/ ~pdiltz/idea/.*

Network of Iowa Christian Home Educators (NICHE), Box 158, Dexter, 50070, 515–830–1614.

Kansas

Christian Home Educators Confederation of Kansas, P.O. Box 3968, Wichita, 67201, 316–945–0810.

Konza Homeschooler Association, c/o Martha Hackney, 7675 Jenkins Road, Saint George, 66535, 785–494–2884.

Teaching Parents Association, P.O. Box 3968, Wichita, 67201, 316–945–0810.

Kentucky

Bluegrass Home Educators, 600 Shake Rag Road, Waynesburg, 40489, 606–365–8568, *www.ky-on-line.com/bhe.*

Kentucky Home Education Association, P.O. Box 81, Winchester, 40392–0081, *www.khea.8k.com.*

Louisiana

Westbank Homeschool Organization, P.O. Box 569, Marrero, 70073, *www.angelfire.com/home/whoedu.*

Wild Azalea Unschoolers, 6055 General Meyer Avenue, New Orleans, 70131, 504–392–5647, *wildazaleas@hotmail.com.*

Maine

Central Maine Self-Learners, 36 Country Acres, Monmouth, 04259, 207–933–5055.

Maine Home Education Association, 19 Willowdale Drive, Gorham, 04038, *www.geocities.com/mainehomeed.*

Peninsula Area Homeschooling Association, P.O. Box 235, Deer Isle, 04084, 207–642–4368.

Sebago Lake Homeschoolers Support Group, 5 School Street, Sebago Lake, 04075, 207–642–4368.

Southern Maine Home Education Support Network, 42 Hammond Road, Parsonsfield, 04047, 207–793–8670.

Maryland

Educating Our Own, 3816 Wine Road, Westminster, 21158, 410–848–3390.

Glen Burnie Home School Support Group, c/o Whetzel, 6514 Dolphin Court, Glen Burnie, 21061.

Maryland Home Education Association, 9085 Flamepool Way, Columbia, 21045, 410–730–0073, *www.MHEA.com.*

North County Home Educators, 1688 Belhaven Woods Court, Pasadena, 21122–3727, 410–437–5109, *www.IQCweb.com/NCHE.*

Prince George's Home Learning Network, 3730 Marlborough Way, College Park, 20740.

Massachusetts

Family Resource Center, 19 Cedarview Street, Salem, 01970, 978–741–7449, www.homestead.com/prosites-bigbear001/index.html.

Homeschoolers of Massachusetts Education Club (Boston area), c/o Phoebe Wells, 17 Florence Street, Cambridge, 02139, 617–876–7273.

Homeschooling Together (Arlington/Belmont area), c/o Sophia Sayigh, 24 Avon Place, Arlington, 02474, 781–641–0566, www.homeschoolingtogether.org.

Massachusetts Home Learning Association, P.O. Box 1558, Marstons Mills, 02648, www.mhla.org.

Massachusetts Homeschool Organization of Parent Educators (Mass HOPE), 5 Atwood Road, Cherry Valley, 01611, www.masshope.org.

Merrimack Valley Homelearners Group, 13 Ashdale Road, North Billerica, 01862, Alysa Dudley, 978–663–2755.

New Grant Homeschoolers (Sharon area), c/o Wendy Hirshman, 781–784–1310, newgrant@homeschoolmedia.com.

Newburyport Area Homeschool Network, c/o Faith Dudley Nguyen, 978–388–6448, happyfiddlers@aol.com.

North Star: Self-directed Learning for Teens, 104 Russell Street, Route 9, Hadley, 01035, 413–582–0193, www.northstarteens.org.

North Suburban Homelearners, 89 Webb Street, Salem, 01970, 978–744–4796, KathrynJB@aol.com.

Michigan

Families Learning and Schooling at Home (FLASH), 21671 B Drive North, Marshall, 49068, 616–781–1069.

Information Network for Christian Homes (INCH), 4934 Cannonsburg Road, Belmont, 49306, 616–874–5656, www.inch.org.

Open Homeschoolers' Group, c/o Dianne Linn, 9120 Dwight Drive, Detroit, 48214, 313–331–8406, www.OHG.cjb.net.

Minnesota

Fargo-Moorehead Homeschool Association, 1909 8th Street South, Moorehead, 56560.

Minnesota Homeschoolers Alliance, P.O. Box 23072, Richfield, 55423, 888–346–7622, www.homeschoolers.org.

Mississippi

Home Educators of Central Mississippi, 1500 Beverly Drive, Clinton, 39056–3507.

Mississippi Home Educators Assocation, P.O. Box 855, Batesville, 38606, www.mhea.net.

Missouri

Families for Home Education, P.O. Box 800, Platte City, 64079–0800, *www.fhe-mo.org*.

Ozark Lore Society (Ozark area), c/o Eisenmann, HC 73 Box 160, Drury, 65638, 417–679–3391.

Montana

Mid-Mountain Home Education Network, 34 Mergenthaler Road, Montana City, 59634, 406–443–3376.

Montana Coalition of Home Educators, P.O. Box 43, Gallatin Gateway, 59730, 406–587–6163.

Nebraska

LEARN, 7741 East Avon Lane, Lincoln, 68505, 402–488–7741.

Nevada

Home Schools United/Vegas Valley, P.O. Box 93564, Las Vegas, 89193, 702–870–9566, *www.homeschool8.tripod.com*.

New Hampshire

New Hampshire Alliance for Home Education, 17 Preserve Drive, Nashua, 03060, 603–880–8629.

New Hampshire Home School Coalition, P.O. Box 2224, Concord, 03302, 603–664–9673, *www.nhhomeschooling.org*.

New Jersey

Homeschoolers of Central New Jersey, 1 Long Way, Hopewell, 08525, 609–333–1119.

New Jersey Homeschool Association, P.O. Box 1386, Medford, 08055.

Unschoolers Network, 2 Smith Street, Farmingdale, 07727, 908–938–2473.

New Mexico

Home Educators of Santa Fe, 21 Frasco Road, Santa Fe, 87505, 505–466–4462.

Homeschooling PACT, c/o Barbara Senn, Box 961, Portales, 88130, 505–359–1618.

New Mexico Family Educators, P.O. Box 92276, Albuquerque, 87199, 505–275–7053.

New Mexico Homeschooling, c/o Sandra Dodd, 2905 Tahiti Court Northeast, Albuquerque, 87112, 505–299–2476.

New York

Families for Home Education, 3219 Coulter Road, Cazenovia, 13035, 315–655–2574.

Homeschoolers and Unschoolers of Staten Island, c/o Elsa Haas, 140 Sparkill Avenue, Dongan Hills, Staten Island, 10304–3141.

New York City Home Educators Alliance, 367 East 10th Street, #13, New York, 10009.

New York Home Educators' Network, P.O. Box 24, Sylvan Beach, 13157, 313–762–5166, *www.nyhen.org.*

Oneonta Area Sharing in Schooling (OASIS), P.O. Box 177, Otego, 13825, 607–783–2413.

Rochester Area Homeschoolers Association, 275 Yarmouth Road, Rochester, 14610, 716–234–0298.

Tri-County Homeschoolers, c/o Lynda & Alex Elie, 37 Birch Drive, Hopewell Junction, 12533, 845–896–5847.

Woodstock Home Educators Network, 12 Cantines Island, Saugerties, NY, 12477, 845–247–0319, *msklaroff@ulster.net.*

North Carolina

Families Learning Together, 1670 North Carolina 33 West, Chocowinity, 27817, *www.fltnc.cjb.net.*

North Carolinians for Home Education, 419 North Boylan Avenue, Raleigh, 27603, 919–834–NCHE, *www.nche.com.*

North Dakota

North Dakota Home School Association, P.O. Box 7400, Bismarck, 58507, 701–223–4080, *www.ndhsa.org.*

Ohio

Growing Together, c/o Nancy McKibben, 1676 Trendril Court, Columbus, 43229.

Home School Network of Greater Cincinnati, c/o Donna Brott, P.O. Box 31088, Mount Healthy, 45231, 513–941–0568.

Learning in Family Environments Support Group (LIFE), P.O. Box 2512, Columbus, 43216, 614–241–6957, *hometown.aol.com/~lifehmsl/life.htm.*

Ohio Home Educators Network, P.O. Box 38132, Olmsted Falls, 44138, *www.ohiohomeeducators.net.*

Oklahoma

Home Educators Resource Organization, 302 North Coolidge, Enid, 73703, 580–446–5679, *www.OklahomaHomeschooling.org.*

Oklahoma Home Educators Network, P.O. Box 1420, Blanchard, 73010, *www.att.net/~ok-he/*.

Oregon

Greater Portland Homeschoolers, P.O. Box 82265, Portland, 97282, 503–241–5350, *www.gphomeschool.org*.

Oregon Home Education Network, P.O. Box 218, Beaverton, 97075–0218, 503–321–5166, *www.teleport.com/~ohen*.

Pennsylvania

Pennsylvania Home Education Network, 285 Allegheny Street, Meadville, 16335, 412–561–5288.

Pennsylvania Homeschoolers, RD 2 Box 117, Kittanning, 16201, 412–783–6512, *www.pahomeschoolers.com*.

People Always Learning Something (PALS), 1751 Hollywood Road, Pittsburgh, 15227, 412–884–1469.

Valley Unschoolers Network (Lehigh Valley area), 565 Forgedale Road, Barto, 19504, 610–845–8941.

Rhode Island

Parent Educators of Rhode Island, P.O. Box 782, Glendale, 02826.

Rhode Island Guild of Home Teachers (RIGHT), Box 11, Hope, 02831, 401–821–7700.

South Carolina

Christian Home Educators of Laurens County, c/o Roxanne Mann, 205 Dixon Street, Clinton, 29325, 864–833–4502, *www.geocities.com/wehomeeducate/chelc.htm*.

South Carolina Association of Independent Home Schools, 930 Knox Abbott Drive, Cayce, 29033, 803–454–0427, *www.scaihs.org*.

Spartanburg Homeschoolers, 365 Wadsworth Road, Spartanburg, 29031, *www.sptbghomeschoolers.org*.

South Dakota

South Dakota Christian Home Educators, P.O. Box 9571, Rapid City, 57709, 605–348–2001, *www.sdche.org*.

South Dakota Home School Association, P.O. Box 882, Sioux Falls, 57101, 605–338–9689.

Tennessee

Tennessee Home Education Association, P.O. Box 68152, Franklin, 37068, 858–623–7899, *www.tnhea.org*.

Tennessee Home Education Information Site, *www.tnhomeed.com*.

Unschoolers of Memphis, c/o Margaret Meyer, 901–757–9859, *www.geocities.com/unschoolersofmemphis.*

Texas

Austin Area Homeschoolers, 510 Park Boulevard, Austin, 78751.

Houston Unschoolers Group, c/o Holly Furgason, 9625 Exeter Road, Houston 77093, 713–695–4888, *mhfurgason@hotmail.com.*

North Texas Self-Educators, c/o Sarah Jordan, 150 Forest Lane, Double Oak/Lewisville, 75067, 817–430–4835.

Texas Homeschool Coalition, P.O. Box 6747, Lubbock, 79493, 806–797–4927, *www.thsc.org.*

Utah

Latter-day Saint Home Educators' Association, 2475 South 1150 West, Syracuse, 84075, 801–776–3555, *www.ldshea.org.*

Utah Home Education Association, P.O. Box 1492, Riverton, 84065, 888–887–UHEA.

Vermont

Vermont Association of Home Educators, RR 1 Box 847, Bethel, 05032, 802–234–6804, *www.vermonthomeschool.org.*

Virginia

Delmarva Homeschoolers, c/o Deborah Blair, 4288 Sunrise Drive Circle, Chincoteague Island, 23336, 757–336–0667.

Home Educators Are Restoring Their Heritage (HEARTH), P.O. Box 1506, Front Royal, 22630, 877–570–1544, *www.hearth.org.*

Virginia Home Education Association, P.O. Box 5131, Charlottesville, 22905, *www.vhea.org.*

Washington

Family Learning Organization, c/o Kathleen McCurdy, P.O. Box 7247, Spokane, 99207, 509–467–2552, *www.familylearning.org.*

Homeschoolers' Support Association, P.O. Box 413, Maple Valley, 98038.

Teaching Parents Association, P.O. Box 1934, Woodinville, 98072–1934, 206–654–5658, *www.washtpa.org.*

Washington Homeschool Organization (WHO), 6632 South 191 Place, Suite E100, Kent, 98032–2117, 425–251–0439, *www.washhomeschool.org.*

West Virginia

West Virginia Home Educators Association, P.O. Box 3707, Charleston, 25337, 800–736–9843, *www.wvheahome.homestead.com.*

Wisconsin

HOME, c/o Alison McKee, 5745 Bittersweet Place, Madison, 53705, 608–238–3302.

Wisconsin Parents Association (WPA), P.O. Box 2502, Madison, 53701, *www.homeschooling-WPA.org.*

Wyoming

Homeschoolers of Wyoming (HOW), c/o Cindy Munger, P.O. Box 3151, Jackson, 83001, *www.freewebs.com/basedintheword/how/.*

Unschoolers of Wyoming, 429 Highway 230 #20, Laramie, 82010.

HOMESCHOOL GROUPS OUTSIDE OF THE UNITED STATES

Australia

Accelerated Christian Education, P.O. Box 10, Strathpine, Queensland, 07–205–7503.

Alternative Education Resource Group, P.O. Box 461, Daylesford, Victoria 3460, *www.home-ed.vic.edu.au.*

Brisbane Natural Learners, P.O. Box 2157, Tingalpa, Queensland, 4173.

Canberra Home Education Network, 23 Bardolph Street, Bonython, Australian Capital Territory 2905.

Home Education Association Inc., 4 Bruce Street, Stanmore, New South Wales, 2048, *www.hea.asn.au.*

Homeschoolers Australia Party Ltd, P.O. Box 420, Kellyville, 2153, New South Wales.

New South Wales Central Coast Homeschool Group, RMB 6346, MacDonalds Road, Lisarow, New South Wales, 2250.

Canada

Canadian Alliance of Home Schoolers, Box 340, Saint George, Ontario, N0E 1N0, contact: Wendy Priesnitz, 519–442–1404, *www.life.ca/hs.*

The Canadian Homeschool Resource Page, *www.flora.org/homeschool-ca.*

Co-operative: Home Options in Childhood Education, (C:HOICE), London, Ontario, 519–680–7590, *c-hoice@rogers.com, www.members.rogers.com/c-hoice.*

Home Learners New Brunswick, Canada, *www.homeschoolingnb.com.*

Ontario Federation of Teaching Parents, 145 Taylor Road West, Gananoque, Ontario, K7G 2V3, 613–382–4947, *www.flora.org/oftp.*

Yukon Home Educators Society, P.O. Box 4993, Whitehorse, Yukon, Y1A 4S2.

China

Homeschooling International Group of Hong Kong, General P.O. 12114, Central Hong Kong, *www.geocities.com/homeschoolinghk.*

England

Education Otherwise, P.O. Box 7420, London, N9 9SG, 0870 7300074, *www.education-otherwise.org.* (Has local contacts throughout England and the United Kingdom.)

Home Education Advisory Service, P.O. Box 98, Welwyn Garden City, Herts AL8 6AN, *www.heas.org.uk.*

Taking Children Seriously, Ref WE, TCS, 2 Cedar Close, Teignmouth, Devon TQ14 8UZ, England, UK, *www.eeng.dcu.ie/~tcs.*

France

Homeschooling Bulletin, c/o Sophie Haesen, 7 rue de la Montagne, F–68480, Vieux Ferrette.

L'Ecole a la Maison, c/o Nadine Stewart, 6 Grande Rue, F–38660, Le Touvet.

Les Enfants D'Abord, c/o Elyane Delmares, Le Croix Saint Fiacre, 03110, Vendat, *dls@cs3i.fr*, *www.multimania.com/possible/art21ab.html.*

Ireland

Home Education Network, *oscar.gen.tcd.ie/hen/.*

Japan

Otherwise Japan, P.O. Box Kugayama, Suginami-ku, Tokyo, *owj@eomax.net.*

The Netherlands

Netherlands Homeschoolers, Raadhuislaan 31, 2131, Hoofddoorp.

New Zealand

Home Educator's Network of Aotearoa, P.O. Box 11–645, Ellerslie 1131, Auckland.

Homeschooling Federation of New Zealand, P.O. Box 41–226, Saint Lukes, Auckland.

The New Zealand Home Schooling Association, 5 Thanet Avenue, Mount Albert, Auckland.

South Africa

National Coalition of Home Schoolers, P.O. Box 14, Dundee, 3000, Phone: 0341 23712, *durham@liadun.dundee.lia.net.*

Spain

Crecer Sin Escuela, Rocio Ramos, Apdo. De Coreeeos 27, 26250—Santo Domingo De La Calzada (La Rioja).

Taiwan

Resource Center of Self-Directed Learning, 8F, #68, San-Chung 1st Road, Chu-Dung, Hsin-Chu, 310, *rcsdl@yahoo.com*.

SPECIAL INTEREST HOMESCHOOLING GROUPS

At Our Own Pace, c/o Jean Kulczyk, 102 Willow Drive, Waukegan, IL, 60087, 847–662–5432 (newsletter for homeschooling families with special needs).

Home School Association for Christian Science Families, 445 Airport Road, Tioga, TX, 76271.

Jewish Home Educator's Network, c/o Kander, 2122 Houser, Holly, MI, 48442, *jhen@snj.com*.

Muslim Home School Network and Resource, P.O. Box 803, Attleboro, MA, 02730, *www.muslimhomeschool.com*.

National Association of Catholic Home Educators, 6102 Saints Hill Lane, Broad Run, VA, 22014, 540–349–4314, *www.nache.org*.

National Association of Mormon Home Educators, 2770 South 1000 West, Perry, UT, 84302.

National Challenged Homeschoolers Association (NATHHAN), P.O. Box 39, Porthill, ID, 83853, 208–267–6246, *www.nathhan.com*.

New England Jewish Homeschoolers, 11 Gannett Terrace, Sharon, MA, 02067, *newengl_jhs@yahoo.com*.

Unitarian Universalist Homeschoolers, *www.uuhomeschool.org*.

Single Parent Homeschooling, *www.groups.yahoo.com/group/singleparenthsing*.

OTHER ORGANIZATIONS

These educational, child-raising, or self-reliance organizations and their publications are good sources of help, and are also homeschooling allies.

Alliance for Parental Involvement in Education, P.O. Box 59, East Chatham, NY, 12060, 518–392–6900, *www.croton.com/Allpie* (deals with public, private, and home schools).

Alternative Education Resource Organization, 417 Roslyn Road, Roslyn Heights, NY, 11577, 516–621–2195, *www.educationrevolution.org*.

Association of Waldorf Schools of North America, 3911 Bannister Road, Fair Oaks, CA, 95628, 916–961–0927, *www.waldorfeducation.org.*

The Aware Parenting Institute, P.O. Box 206, Goleta, CA, 93116, 805–968–1868, *info@awareparenting.com, www.awareparenting.com.*

Coalition for Self-Learning, P.O. Box 567, Rangeley, ME, 04970–0567, *www.CreatingLearningCommunities.org.*

EPOCH (End Physical Punishment of Children), 155 Main Street, Suite 1603, Columbus, OH, 43215, *www.stophitting.com.*

ERIC (Educational Resources Information Center), 2277 Research Boulevard MS4M, Rockville, MD, 20850, 800–538–3742, *www.accesseric.org.*

Family Policy Compliance Office, U.S. Department of Education, 400 Maryland Avenue SW, Washington, DC, 20202–4605, Phone: 202–260–3887, 800–437–0833, Fax: 202–401–0689, *www.ed.gov.* Access to school records.

Great Ideas in Education/Holistic Education Press, P.O. Box 328, Brandon, VT, 05733, 800–639–4122, *www.great-ideas.org.*

La Leche League International, 1400 North Meacham Road, P.O. Box 4079, Schaumberg, IL, 60168–4079, 1–800–LA LECHE.

Liedloff Continuum Network, P.O. Box 1634, Sausalito, CA, 94966, 415–332–1570, *www.continuum-concept.org.*

Montessori World Educational Institute (Australia), 150 Antigua Street, Christchurch, 8002, Phone: 365–2148, Fax: 365–2147, *www.montessori.org.nz.*

Mothers at Home, 9493-C Silverking Court, Fairfax, VA, 22031, 703–352–1072, *www.mah.org.*

National Association for the Legal Support of Alternative Schools, P.O. Box 2823, Santa Fe, NM, 87501, 505–471–6928.

National Center for Fair and Open Testing (FairTest), 342 Broadway, Cambridge, MA, 02139, 617–864–4810, *www.fairtest.org.*

National Coalition Of Alternative Community Schools, c/o Alan Benard, 1266 Rosewood Unit 1, Ann Arbor, MI, 48104–6205, 888–771–9171, *www.ncacs.org.*

Open Connections: Feedom to Learn and Create, 1616 Delchester Road, Newtown Square, PA, 19073, 610–459–3366, *www.openconnections.org.*

The Self-Education Foundation, P.O. Box 30790, Philadelphia, PA, 19104–0790, *www.selfeducation.org.*

Appendix E
Learning Materials

This list is just a sampling to help jump-start your thinking and to learn what materials are available for home use with your children. Many of the books and magazines mentioned throughout this book contain further resources. Following each listing, I give brief descriptions of what the companies provide.

ARTS, CRAFTS, VIDEOS

Grown Without Schooling, P.O. Box 772, Mentor, OH, 44061, 740–589–5242, *www.grownwithoutschooling.com*. Video documentary about adults who were homeschooled.

How to Homeschool, 108 Monaco Road, West Melbourne, FL, 32904, 321–951–2612, *www.howtohomeschool.com*. Videotapes for parents of children between ages two and nine.

KidsArt News, P.O. Box 274, Mount Shasta, CA, 96067, 530–926–5076, *www.kidsart.com*. Series of art-teaching booklets. Children's art-supplies catalog.

NASCO Arts & Crafts, 901 Janesville Avenue, Fort Atkinson, WI, 53538, 920–563–2446. Free catalog.

Sculpture House, 100 Camp Meeting Avenue, Skillman, NJ, 08558, 609–466–2986. Clay, supplies.

Standard Deviants, Cerebellum Corporation, 2890 Emma Lee Street, Falls Church, VA, 22042, 800–238–9669, *www.standarddeviants.com*. Educational videos and DVDs.

BOOKS, GAMES, LEARNING MATERIALS

American Audio Prose Library, P.O. Box 842, Columbia, MO, 65205, 1–800–447–2275, *www.americanaudioprose.com*. Authors on tape.

American Printing House for the Blind, 1839 Frankfort Avenue, Louisville, KY, 40206, 502–895–2405. Books and materials, such as the Cranmer Abacus.

Ball-Stick-Bird Reading System, P.O. Box 13, Colebrook, CT, 06021, 860–738–8871. Phonics using science-fiction adventures.

Booklist, American Library Association, 50 East Huron Street, Chicago, IL, 60611, 312–944–6780. "Purchasing an Encyclopedia: 12 points to consider" ($4.95).

Center for Innovation in Education, P.O. Box 2070, Saratoga, CA, 95070–0070, 800–395–6088. *www.center.edu*. Math, reading.

Chinaberry Book Service, 2780 Via Orange Way, Suite B, Spring Valley, CA, 91978, 800–776–2242. Catalog of books.

Creative Kids, HC03, Box 9550-S, Palmer, AK, 99645, 907–746–3073. School supplies for homeschooling families.

Cricket, P.O. Box 9304, La Salle, IL, 61301, 800–827–0227, *www.cricketmag.com*. Children's literary magazine.

EDC Publishing, 10302 East 55th Place, Tulsa, OK, 74146, *www.edcpub.com*. Usborne activity and beginning-to-read books for elementary years.

Educators Publishing Service, 31 Smith Place, Cambridge, MA, 02138–1089, 800–225–5750, *www.epsbooks.com*. School workbooks for all ages and subjects.

Family Pastimes, RR 4, Perth, Ontario, Canada, K7H 3C6, 613–267–4819. Cooperative board games.

Follett Educational Service, 1433 International Parkway, Woodridge, IL, 60517, 800–621–4272, or –1474. Used textbooks.

Frank Schaffer Publications, McGrawHill Children's Publishing, 3195 Wilson Drive NW, Grand Rapids, MI, 49544. Phone: 800–253–5469, Fax: 800–837–7260, *www.frankschaffer.com*. Educational materials for ages 3–14.

Front Row Experience, 540 Discovery Bay Boulevard, Discovery Bay, CA, 94514–9454, 800–524–9091. Materials about movement education, perceptual-motor development, coordination activities for preschool through sixth-grade age group.

FUN Books, Department W, 1688 Belhaven Woods Court, Pasadena, MD, 21122–3727, 888–386–7020, *www.Fun-Books.com, FUN@FUN-Books.com.* John Holt books and *GWS* back issues, as well as many other homeschooling materials.

A Gentle Wind, P.O. Box 3103, Albany, NY, 12203, 888–386–7664, *www.gentlewind.com.* Stories and songs on cassette.

Gifted Education Press, 10201 Yuma Court, Manassas, VA, 20109, 703–369–5017, *www.giftededpress.com.* Free newsletter.

Hearthsong, P.O. Box 1050, Madison, VA, 22727–1050, Phone: 800–533–4397, Fax: 309–689–3857. Toy/craft catalog for families.

The Horn Book, Inc., 57 Roland Street, Suite 200, Boston, MA, 02129, 800–325–1170, *www.hbook.com.* Magazine for children's book recommendations.

I Can Read Books, HarperCollins Children's Books, 10 East 53rd Street, New York, NY, 10022, 800–242–7737, *www.harperchildrens.com.* Free catalog of beginning-to-read books.

Johnny's Selected Seeds, 184 Foss Hill Road, Albion, ME, 04910, 207–437–4301. Child-sized tools.

Key Curriculum Press, 1150 65th Street, Emeryville, CA, 94608, Phone: 800–541–2442, Fax: 510–595–7040, *www.keypress.com.* Miquon math workbooks, math books, and software.

Lauri Early Learning Puzzles, P.O. Box F (Avon Valley Road), Phillips-Avon, ME, 04966, 207–639–2000. Rubber puzzles and educational toys.

Learning Horizons, 1 American Road, Cleveland, OH, 44144–2398, 800–321–3040. Supplemental workbooks for all elementary ages and subjects.

Math Products Plus, P.O. Box 64, San Carlos, CA, 94070, Phone: 650–593–2839, Fax: 650–595–0802. Math books, T-shirts, calendars, novelties.

McGuffey's Readers, Mott Media, 112 East Ellen, Fenton, MI, 48430, 248–685–8773. Beginning readers.

Michael Olaf Company, Montessori Store, 65 Ericson Court, Arcata, CA, 95521, 707–826–1557. Tools, playthings, math manipulatives; catalog is available ($5.00).

Montessori Services, 11 West Barham Avenue, Santa Rosa, CA, 95407, 707–579–3003. Free supply catalog.

National Storytelling Network (formerly known as National Association for Preservation and Perpetuation of Storytelling), 101 Court House Square, Jonesborough, TN, 37659, 800–525–4514. Books, tapes.

Parents' Choice, 210 West Padonia Road, Suite 303, Timonium, MD, 21093, 410–308–3858, *www.parents-choice.org*. Review of children's media.

Recorded Books, Inc., 270 Skipjack Road, Prince Frederick, MD, 20678, 800–638–1304. Novels, classics, history, science, on tape.

Resource Games, P.O. Box 151, Redmond, WA, 98052, 425–883–3143, *www.resourcegames.com*. Geography game, without quizzes.

Saxon Publishers, 2600 John Saxon Boulevard, Norman, OK, 73071, 800–284–7019, *www.saxonpublishers.com*. Mathematics and phonics programs.

Scholastic Book Clubs, P.O. Box 7503, Jefferson City, MO, 65102, 573–636–5271. Inexpensive paperbacks.

South Carolina Educational TV, P.O. Box 11000, 1101 George Rogers Boulevard, Columbia, SC, 29201, 800–277–0829. Free booklet *Guide to Learning*.

The Teaching Company, 4151 Lafayette Center Drive, Suite 100, Chantilly, VA, 20151, 800–TEACH12, *www.teachco.com*. High school and college lectures on videotape.

Trumpet Book Club, P.O. Box 6003, Columbia, MO, 65205–9888, 800–826–0110, *www.trumpetclub.com*. Children's books.

FOREIGN LANGUAGES

Bolchazy-Carducci Publishers, 1000 Brown Street, Unit 101, Wauconda, IL, 60084, 847–526–2867, *www.bolchazy.com*. Audiocassettes and texts for learning Latin.

Calliope, Route 3, Box 3395, Saylorsburg, PA, 18353, 610–381–2587. Foreign-language materials and imported books for infants to adults.

Editions Champlain, 468 Queen Street East, Toronto, Ontario, M5A 1T7. Phone: 416–364–4345, Fax: 416–364–8843. French-language books.

French for Tots, OptimaLearning Language Land, Barzak Educational Institute, 885 Olive Avenue, Suite A, Novato, CA, 94945, 800–672–1717, *www.optimalearning.com*.

The Learnables, International Linguistics, 12220 Blue Ridge Boulevard., Suite G, Kansas City, MO, 64030–1175, 816–765–8855, *www.learnables.com*, *learn@accessus.net*. Foreign-language tapes.

Lectorum Publications, 205 Chubb Avenue, Lyndhurst, NJ, 07071, 800–345–5946. Catalog of Spanish-language children's books and magazines.

Mangajin, 1025 Moreland Avenue SE, Atlanta, GA, 30316, Phone: 404–622–4902, Fax: 404–622–5322, *www.mangajin.com.* Magazine of cartoons in both Japanese and English.

Schoenhofs, 76A Mount Auburn Street, Cambridge, MA, 02138, 617–547–8855, *www.schoenhofs.com.* Source of foreign books.

Sky Oaks Productions, P.O. Box 1102, Los Gatos, CA, 95031, 408–395–7600. Total Physical Response approach to teaching and learning languages.

MUSIC

Drumbeat Indian Arts, 4143 North 16th Street, Phoenix, AZ, 85016, 602–266–4823. Native-American music, books.

Homespun Music Tapes, P.O. Box 340, Woodstock, NY, 12498, Phone: 845–246–2550, Fax: 845–246–5282, *www.homespuntapes.com.* Audio- and videotaped lessons for folk instruments.

The Langstaff Video Project, 683 Santa Barbara Road, Berkeley, CA, 94707, Phone: 510–841–6628, Fax: 510–841–6471. *Making Music with John Langstaff* videos and workshops.

Lark in the Morning, Box 799, Fort Bragg, CA, 95437, 707–964–5569. Folk music and instruments for purchase.

Suzuki Association of the Americas, P.O. Box 17310, Boulder, CO, 80308, Phone: 303–444–0948, Fax: 303–444–0984, *www.suzukiassociation.org.* Suzuki music method parent/teacher information packet ($2.00).

SCIENCE AND NATURE

Abrams Planetarium, Michigan State University, East Lansing, MI, 48824, 517–355–4672. Sky calendar.

American Science & Surplus, 3605 Howard, Skokie, IL, 60076, 847–982–0870, *www.sciplus.com.* Catalog of industrial and scientific materials, reduced from normal list prices ($1.00).

Anatomical Chart Company, 8221 Kimball Avenue, Skokie, IL, 60076, 800–621–7500, *www.anatomical.com.*

Around Alone Student Ocean Challenge, P.O. Box 268, Newport, RI, 02840, 401–847–7612, *www.bwsailing.com/soc.html.*

Astronomical Society of the Pacific, 390 Ashton Avenue, San Francisco, CA, 94112, 415–337–1100. Free catalog of slides, videos, books, posters, software, sky-observing aids.

Carolina Biological Supply Company, 2700 York Road, Burlington, NC, 27215, 336–584–0381, 800–334–5551, *www.carolina.com*. Catalog for science teachers.

Celestial Products, P.O. Box 801, Middleburg, VA, 20118, Phone: 800–235–3783, Fax: 540–338–4042, *www.celestialproducts.com*. Sky charts, posters, maps, and books.

Exploratorium Store, 3601 Lyon Street, San Francisco, CA, 94123, 415–561–0372, *www.exploratorium.edu*. Hands-on science with educator resources, free downloadable activities, and newsletter.

Hawkhill Associates, 125 East Gilman Street, Madison, WI, 53703, 608–251–3934. Science videos.

NASA CORE, Lorain County JVS, 15181 Route 58 South, Oberlin, OH, 44074, 440–986–6601. Catalog of materials about space and space exploration.

Ranger Rick's Nature Magazine, National Wildlife Federation, 11100 Wildlife Center Drive, Reston, VA, 20190. Membership: P.O. Box 2038, Harlan, IA, 51593, *www.nwf.org*.

Sanctuary Magazine, Massachusetts Audubon Society, South Great Road, Lincoln, MA, 01773, 781–259–9500. April 1990 issue on kids working to help the environment ($1.00, plus 65¢ postage).

Skeptical Inquirer, Box 703, Amherst, NY, 14226, 800–634–1610, 716–636–1425, *www.csicop.org*. Looks into claims concerning paranormal phenomena ($19.95/yr).

TOPS Learning Systems, 10970 South Mulino Road, Canby, OR, 97013, 503–263–2040. Science lessons.

Ursa Major, P.O. Box 639, Macomb, IL, 61455, 1–800–999–3433, *www. ontimecolor.com*. Large stencils of world maps and of the night sky, plus free teacher guide for using stencils.

Your Big Backyard, National Wildlife Federation, 11100 Wildlife Center Drive, Reston, VA, 20190, *www.nwf.org*. Magazine for 3–5-year-olds.

ZooBooks, Wildlife Education Ltd., 12233 Thatcher Court, Poway, CA, 92064, 619–574–7866.

SOCIAL STUDIES

Amazon Vinegar & Pickling Works Dry Goods, 411 Brady Street, Davenport, IA, 52801, 800–798–7979. Catalogs of historical clothing, footwear, and window treatments. Call for catalog prices.

Asia for Kids, 4480 Lake Forest Drive, Suite 302, Cincinnati, OH, 45242, 513–563–3100. Books, cassettes, software related to Asian cultures.

Calliope, 30 Grove Street, Suite C, Peterborough, NH, 03458, 603–924–7209. Children's magazine on world history.

Cobblestone, 30 Grove Street, Suite C, Peterborough, NH, 03458, 800–821–0115. U.S. history magazine for children.

Faces, 30 Grove Street, Suite C, Peterborough, NH, 03458. World cultures magazine for children.

Hubbard Scientific, Scott Resources, P.O. Box 2121, Fort Collins, CO, 80522, 800–289–9299, *www.AMEP.com*. Raised relief maps, models to use in learning about human body, zoology.

League of Women Voters, 1730 M Street NW, Suite 1000, Washington, DC, 20036, 202–429–1965, *www.lwv.org*. Pamphlets: government, current events.

National Geographic Society, 1145 17th Street NW, Washington, DC, 20036, 202–857–7000, *www.nationalgeographic.com*. Magazines, including *World* for children, books, maps.

National Geography Bee (same as National Geographic Society above).

National Women's History Project, 3343 Industrial Drive, Suite 4, Santa Rosa, CA, 95403, 707–636–2888, *www.nwhp.org*. Materials about women in history; multicultural.

Replogle Globes, Inc., 2801 South 25th Avenue, Broadview, IL, 60153, 708–343–0900.

Resource Center of the Americas, 3019 Minnehaha Avenue South, Minneapolis, MN, 55406, 612–276–0788, *www.americas.org/rcta/*. K–12 curriculum about the Americas.

Smithsonian Magazine, 7509 9th Street NW, Suite 7100, Washington, DC, 20560, 202–275–2000.

Wide World Books & Maps, 4411 A Wallingford Avenue North, Seattle, WA, 98103, 206–634–3453, *www.travelbooksandmaps.com*.

Young Biz, A KidsWay Company, P.O. Box 7987, Atlanta, GA, 30357–9911, 1–888–543–7929, *www.kidsway.com*. News magazine, curriculum, books.

SPECIAL NEEDS

See "Special Interest Homeschooling Groups," Appendix D, for more listings.

Deaf Homeschool Network, c/o Marilyn Agenbroad, 116 Jerome, Silverton, OR, 97381, 503–873–8451, *agie@ncn.com*.

National Association for the Deaf, 814 Thayer Avenue, Suite 250, Silver Spring, MD, 20910, 301–587–1788. Sign language videos, books.

T. J. Publishers, Inc., 817 Silver Spring Avenue, Silver Spring, MD, 20910, Phone: 301–585–4440, Fax: 301–585–5930. Materials and books about American Sign Language and deafness.

WRITING

Child's Play Touring Theatre, 2518 West Armitage, Chicago, IL, 60647, 773–235–8911, 800–353–3402, *www.cptt.org*. Play development from stories and poems written by kids.

Heinemann Educational Books, 361 Hanover Street, Portsmouth, NH, 03801, 800–541–2086. Videos, books on writing.

Stone Soup, P.O. Box 83, Santa Cruz, CA, 95063, 800–447–4569. Children's literary magazine.

Teachers & Writers Collaborative, 5 Union Square West, 7th floor, New York, NY, 10013, 212–691–6590, *www.twc.org*. Catalog of books about writing.

Appendix F

Opportunities and Activities

AFS International Exchange Program, 71 West 23rd Street, 17th Floor, New York, NY, 10010, Phone: 212–807–8686, 800–AFS–INFO, Fax: 503–241–1653, *www.afs.org*, *info@afs.org*.

Center for Interim Programs, P.O. Box 2347, Cambridge, MA, 02238, Phone: 617–547–0980, Fax: 617–661–2864, *www.interimprograms.com*. Apprenticeship placement service.

Chesapeake Bay Foundation, 6 Herndon Avenue, Annapolis, MD, 21403, 800–445–5572, *www.cbf.org*.

Crow Canyon Archaeological Center, 23390 County Road K, Cortez, CO, 81321, 970–565–8975, 800–422–8975, *www.crowcanyon.org*.

Encompass Learning Center, 11011 Tyler Foot Road, Nevada City, CA, 95959, 530–282–1000, *www.encompass-nlr.org*. Whole family and teen program with focus on outdoor education and adventure courses.

Experiment in International Living, Kipling Road, P.O. Box 676, Brattleboro, VT, 05302–0676, 800–257–7751, *www.worldlearning.org*, *info@worldlearning.org*. Summer exchange program immerses high school students in another culture in one of more than twenty countries.

Farm Sanctuary, P.O. Box 150, Watkins Glen, NY, 14891, Phone: 607–583–2225. Fax: 607–583–2041, *www.farmsanctuary.org*. H. McNulty, administrative director. Apprenticeships in veterinary science.

Great Smoky Mountains Institute at Tremont, 9275 Tremont Road, Townsend, TN, 37882, 865–448–6709, *www.gsmit.org*. Naturalist Workshops, programs for teenagers.

Hulbert Outdoor Center, 2968 Lake Morey Road, Fairless, VT, 05045, Phone: 888–333–3405, Fax: 802–333–3404. Camp for ages 9–17 (vegetarian food can be provided).

Kids for Saving Earth Clubs, P.O. Box 421118, Plymouth, MN, 55442, 763–559–1234, *www.kidsforsavingearth.org.*

Living Routes: Ecovillage Education, 85 Baker Road, Shutesbury, MA, 01072–9703, Phone: 888–515–7333, Fax: 413–259–1256, *www.Living Routes.org.* College-level programs based in sustainable communities called "ecovillages" around the world.

National Wildlife Federation Wildlife Camp, 800–822–9919, *www.nfw.org.*

Not Back to School Camp, P.O. Box 1014, Eugene, OR, 97440, 541–686–2315. Grace Llewellyn's camp for ages 13–18. Only vegetarian/vegan food provided.

SERVAS, 11 John Street, Room 505, New York, NY, 10038, 212–267–0252. Visit or host a foreign family.

TIA Architects, 592 Main Street, Amherst, MA, 01002, 413–256–8025, *www.nacul.com.* Architectural internships.

Tree People, 12601 Mulholland Drive, Beverly Hills, CA, 90210, 818–753–4600. Environmental leadership program.

Notes

PREFACE

1. Ross Atkin, "Unorthodox Coach Gets Results." *The Christian Science Monitor*, September 23, 1994, p. 13.
2. Monty Roberts, *The Man Who Listens to Horses* (New York: Random House, 1997), pp. 87–88.
3. Susannah Sheffer, ed. *A Life Worth Living: Selected Letters of John Holt.* (Columbus: The Ohio State University Press, 1990), p. 55.

CHAPTER 1: WHY TAKE THEM OUT?

1. S. Bielick, K. Chandler, and S.P. Broughman. *Homeschooling in the United States: 1999* (NCES 2001–033). (U.S. Department of Education, Washington, D.C: National Center for Education Statistics, 2001), p. 1.
2. Leon Lynn, "Language-Rich Home and School Environments Are Key to Reading Success: Children learn some of their most important reading lessons at the dinner table, according to a groundbreaking study." *Harvard Education Letter*, July/August 1997.
3. Barbara Meltz, "Family Mealtime Can Nourish Your Children's Minds." *Boston Globe*, September 21, 2000, p. H3.
4. Susannah Sheffer, *A Sense of Self: Listening to Homeschooled Adolescent Girls* (Portsmouth, NH: Heinemann/Boynton/Cook, 1995), p. 64.
5. "Corporal Punishment in Schools," *American Academy of Pediatrics* vol. 106, no. 2, August 2000, p. 343.
6. News stories collected from World Corporal Punishment Research, www.corpun.com. "Paddling in US schools," February 2002, Corpun Archive.
7. "Life Is Too Hard, Say Children Aged Four." *The London Times*, June 16, 1999, p. 12.

8. home.kyodo.co.jp, August 10, 2001.
9. *Boston Globe*, November 24, 2001, Editorial page.
10. *The Shell Poll* vol. 1, issue 4, Summer 1999, p. 1.
11. *The Wakefield Observer*, August 3, 2001, p. 1.
12. Greg Toppo, "NEA Offers Homicide Insurance." Associated Press, January 11, 2002.

CHAPTER 3: POLITICS OF UNSCHOOLING

1. Currently the percentage of children being taught at home is near 2 percent and growing. This can indicate that there are probably more and more adults who share this belief in children's ability to learn without coercion.
2. U.S. Department of Justice, Office of Juvenile Justice and Delinquency Prevention, Juvenile Justice Bulletin, September 2001 p. 2.
3. *GWS* 97, January/February 1994, p. 30–31.
4. *Boston Globe*, January 7, 2002, p. B12.
5. Northeastern University Center of Labor Market Studies, reported in *Boston Globe*, December 20, 2001, p. 1.

CHAPTER 11: HOMESCHOOLING IN AMERICA

1. Rebecca Smithers, "Poor A-Levels Leads Family to Sue." *The Guardian*, October 2, 2001, www.guardian.co.uk/Archive.

CHAPTER 12: HOW TO GET STARTED

1. John Holt, *What Do I Do Monday?* (Portsmouth, NH: Heinemann, 1995), pp. 223–224.

CHAPTER 13: SCHOOL RESPONSE

1. *Boston Globe*, editorial correction to a letter titled "Boston's Changing Demographics." February 16, 2002, p. A15.
2. Rosalind S. Helderma, "Home-Schooled Away from Home: Parents Form Academies to Support One Another. *Washington Post*, March 26, 2002, p. B01.
3. Susannah Sheffer, *A Life Worth Living: Selected Letters of John Holt* (Columbus: The Ohio State University Press, 1990), pp. 10–11.
4. "The 31st Annual Phi Delta Kappa/Gallup Poll of the Public's Attitudes toward the Public Schools." *Phi Delta Kappan* 81, 1, September 1999, pp. 41–56.

Index